A Music Transcription Method

A Music Transcription Method: Notating Recorded Music by Ear teaches how to leverage music dictation in the modern music industry. The book's four parts cover aspects of preparation, process, interpretation, and industry resources related to notating recorded music by ear.

Taking a modular approach, the book guides readers from an initial subject overview to leveraging the craft for their own projects and careers. Each chapter includes an industry interview featuring diverse practitioner perspectives from Broadway, LA's film scoring scene, contemporary Jazz and Pop, orchestral and marching band styles, music educators, and music entrepreneurs. Transcribed sheet music examples, provided by members of GroundUP Music and several independent creators illustrate the transcription process, while field-relevant scholarly, educational, and professional references further illuminate the state of inquiry in music transcription. Learning outcomes, exploratory chapter activities, visual chapter maps, and further instructional visuals are included to support the learning styles of diverse readers.

Supported by online resources offering a growing repository of reference materials, including sample materials and instructional videos with a focus on technology literacy, this is essential reading for undergraduates on music transcription, arranging, and orchestration courses for a variety of musical contexts and genres, as well as for musicians perfecting their music notation skills.

Dr. Andreas Häberlin is Adjunct Instructor at Nova Southeastern University, USA, alongside his work as a music transcriptionist. In this capacity, he has worked for industry figures including David Foster, Michael Bearden, and members of Snarky Puppy. Past transcription work includes projects for the Mark Twain Prize, Michael League, Michael Bublé, Barbra Streisand, Asher Monroe, *Boop! The Musical*, and Music Will Benefit.

"Dr. Andreas Häberlin's *A Music Transcription Method: Notating Recorded Music by Ear* is an invaluable resource for musicians, educators, and industry professionals. It masterfully combines theoretical insights with practical frameworks, making the complex art of music transcription accessible and engaging. The book's structured approach, paired with real-world applications and cutting-edge tools, ensures that readers not only develop technical skills but also gain a deeper appreciation for the nuances of recorded music. A must-read for anyone serious about honing their transcription craft!"
—**Dr. Camille Colatosti**, Provost, Interlochen Center for the Arts

"Dr. Andreas Häberlin's first book is a groundbreaking resource that redefines how we approach the art of music transcription. By blending analytical listening, structured processes, and practical application, this book enables readers to decode recorded music with precision and creativity. What sets this work apart is Häberlin's ability to demystify complex methodologies while fostering a holistic understanding of musical structure, orchestration, and interpretation. It's not just a guide—it's an invitation to experience music in a profoundly deeper way. Perfect for anyone looking to elevate their transcription skills or uncover new dimensions in music analysis."
—**Gael Hedding**, Grammy- and Latin Grammy-winning Music Producer and Engineer; Director, Berklee Abu Dhabi

"In film scoring and media composition, the development of a fine-tuned ear is a necessity. Many scores are born from abstractions and musical improvisation, and with constantly tight deadlines, a composer's greatest strength is the ability to accurately transcribe on the fly. While active listening and devoted practice can help sharpen this skill, the craft itself can often feel nebulous and difficult to navigate. Dr. Andreas Häberlin has astutely found a way to isolate this intricate process, offering detailed, practical tools and an intuitive creative perspective. Through his new book, *A Music Transcription Method: Notating Recorded Music by Ear*, we can begin to appreciate not only the granularity and detail of his transcription methods, but find ways to broaden our technical scope and analyze musical intent through a holistic lens."
—**Stephanie Economou**, Grammy-winning Film and Video Game Composer, *My Big Fat Greek Wedding 3*; *Assassin's Creed Valhalla: Dawn Of Ragnarok*

A Music Transcription Method
Notating Recorded Music by Ear

Andreas Häberlin

Cover image: junce / Getty Images

First published 2026
by Routledge
605 Third Avenue, New York, NY 10158

and by Routledge
4 Park Square, Milton Park, Abingdon, Oxon, OX14 4RN

Routledge is an imprint of the Taylor & Francis Group, an informa business

© 2026 Andreas Häberlin

The right of Andreas Häberlin to be identified as author of this work has been asserted in accordance with sections 77 and 78 of the Copyright, Designs and Patents Act 1988.

All rights reserved. No part of this book may be reprinted or reproduced or utilised in any form or by any electronic, mechanical, or other means, now known or hereafter invented, including photocopying and recording, or in any information storage or retrieval system, without permission in writing from the publishers.

Trademark notice: Product or corporate names may be trademarks or registered trademarks, and are used only for identification and explanation without intent to infringe.

ISBN: 978-1-032-84258-5 (hbk)
ISBN: 978-1-032-84254-7 (pbk)
ISBN: 978-1-003-51194-6 (ebk)

DOI: 10.4324/9781003511946

Typeset in Sabon
by Apex CoVantage, LLC

Access the Support Material: www.routledge.com/9781032842585
Additional Resources Available at: www.haberlinmusic.com

To my parents Marlies Häberlin and Walter R. Häberlin, whom I owe everything. Throughout a journey into the unknown, you have selflessly supported my every step.

Contents

Preface   x
About the Author   xii
Acknowledgments   xiii
Glossary   xiv

PART I
Preparation   1

1   Field Introduction   3
Introductory Definition 4
Methodological Inquiry 5
Music Industry Applications 8

2   Analytical Listening   12
Listening Approaches 13
Listening Dimensions 14
Auditory Analysis 17

3   Transcription Setup   22
Playback 23
Listening and Referencing 25
Music Notation 28

PART II
Process   33

4   Outline   35
Setting the Scope 36
Sheet Music Formats 38
Global Music Information Layers 43

5   Foundational Layers   50
Individual Layers 51

Music Note Series 53
Transcription Roadmap 56

6 **Dependent Layers**   61
Note and Pattern Perspective 62
Phrase and Section Perspective 65
Transcription Roadmap 68

7 **Process Variants**   72
Procedures in Context 73
Transcribing Multi-File Sources 74
Compact Target Formats 78

PART III
Interpretation   85

8 **Music Notation**   87
A Prescriptive Approach 88
Level of Notation Detail 91
Decision-Frame 93

9 **Macrostructure**   98
Form 99
Time Signatures 101
Tempo 104

10 **Microstructure**   111
Pattern Repetition 112
Harmonic Qualities 114
Nuance in Phrasing 116

11 **Orchestration**   121
Individual Sound Sources 122
Stacked Composite Sounds 126
Dynamics and Timbre 128

PART IV
Resources   133

12 **Opportunities**   135
Common Career Profiles 136
Music Transcription Services 137
Self-Marketing 140

13 **Project Management** 144
    General Guidelines 145
    Planning 148
    Executing 150

14 **Workflow Concepts** 153
    Procedural Preparation 154
    Systematic Approach 155
    Digital Literacy 157

    Index *161*

Preface

This book (my first one) has been 15 years in the making. To sum up a full-circle journey: I would consider myself one of those students who, equally curious and unaware of my teachers' dismay, would keep asking complex questions in the classroom. It was the type of inquiry that teachers would respond to with "There is no easy answer to your question." Driven by the idea that there had to be answers to my questions, I ventured beyond the classroom and immersed myself in all parts of the music industry. The inspiration to write this book stems in significant parts from my motivation to address those questions left unanswered by others.

In retrospect, I would differentiate between factual and analytical questions. Factual questions have definite answers, while analytical questions are perhaps better answered by applying frameworks and following processes. The answers to analytical questions depend more on the context. For as long as I can remember, I have always had an intrinsic preference for analyses over factual knowledge. It might have been this preference that earned me the title of *nerd* early on in elementary school. To cut a long story short: Music transcription relies on constant analysis – and this book offers several frameworks to help you streamline this process. It is my hope that you will find these frameworks helpful on your own musical journey.

Each of the book's 14 modular chapters covers a specific aspect of the craft. The chapters are grouped into four thematic parts to guide the reader through the *preparation*, *process* foundations, aspects of *interpretation*, and industry *resources* related to music transcription. All in-text citations are either from scholarly, industry, or educational publications. To familiarize with terminology and constructs, first-time readers are encouraged to progress through the book sequentially, part by part and chapter by chapter. Thereafter, readers are encouraged to reference specific parts of the book as relevant to their journey and craft.

This book includes several pedagogical features to support readers on their journeys. At the book's core are three hierarchical types of learning outcomes: Book outcomes (BO), part outcomes (PO), and chapter outcomes (CO). Each type summarizes what the reader will learn by working through the book, a specific part, or chapter respectively. At the chapter level, outcomes can be assessed through section and chapter activities. Also take note of the content maps at the beginning of each part and chapter. These maps summarize visually what content will be covered in that section, along with recommendations on how to assess learning outcomes. The remaining instructional visuals help illustrate the chapter contents. Finally, several excerpts of industry interviews help illuminate the field perspectives of active music transcriptionists.

One more pedagogical feature, the use of italics in the main text, requires an advance explanation: Traditionally, italicized phrases draw the reader's attention to a selection of

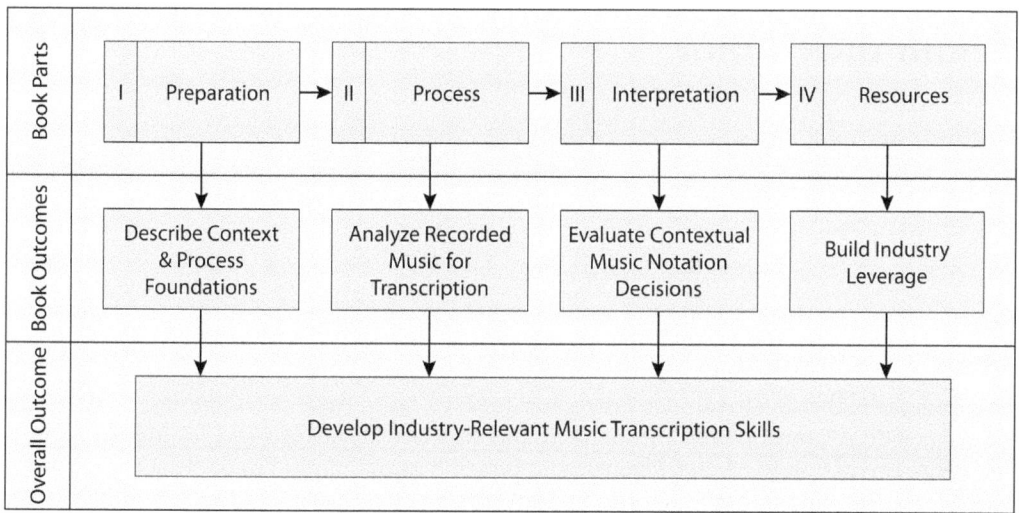

Figure 0.0 Book map.

key terms essential to the subject matter. This book takes a more learner-centered approach. Within the main text, italicized phrases summarize key concepts of their respective paragraphs. If read successively, these phrases offer a narrative shorthand of what is discussed. Readers may alternate freely between reading paragraphs and shorthand. The intended purpose of this feature is twofold: 1) To support reading speed and comprehension, and 2) to facilitate content reviews. As an avid learning designer, I invite you to test and leverage this feature to personalize your reading experience.

Further to the book's embedded features, the Routledge Resource Centre and the author's website offer a growing repository of companion materials. The audio examples referenced in the book's section activities are available at www.routledge.com/9781032842585. The website further offers dedicated instructor resources, including an instructor manual on how to incorporate the book into different course types. In contrast, the author's website (www.haberlinmusic.com) hosts instructional videos that demonstrate the music transcription process both step-by-step and in context. The author's website further offers a curated selection of online multimedia resources to help learners contextualize music transcription.

About the Author

Dr. Andreas Häberlin is Adjunct Instructor at Nova Southeastern University, USA, alongside his work as a music transcriptionist. In this capacity, he has worked for industry figures including David Foster, Michael Bearden, and members of Snarky Puppy. Past transcription work includes projects for the Mark Twain Prize, Michael League, Michael Bublé, Barbra Streisand, Asher Monroe, *Boop! The Musical*, and Music Will Benefit.

Acknowledgments

My sincere appreciation goes out to the many pairs of helping hands who have enabled the production of this book:

- My editorial team at Routledge, spearheaded by Hannah Rowe, Zoe Thomson-Kemp, and Neha Peri . . ., and the copy-editing team, spearheaded by Katharine Atherton. Thank you for your generous support, trust, and for believing in this book.
- Several industry experts who have generously shared their perspectives: Dr. Emily Williams Burch, Boh Cooper, Claire Cowan, Vanessa Garde, Yaron Gershovksy, Gregory Jamrok, Oriol López Calle, Zane Mark, Chris McQueen, Dylan Parrilla-Koester, Gregory Pliska, Erin J. Reifler, Martin Romberg, and Tracie Turnbull.
- Those generous creators and editors who have permitted the use of their sheet music in this book: Zach Brock (Secret Fort Publishing), Robert J. Lanzetti, Michael T. Maher, Molenaar Edition, Justin Stanton, Elizabeth Allen Turner, and Michelle Willis.
- The music software companies who have permitted the visual coverage of their software applications: Lunacy Inc., Seventh String Software, and Steinberg Media Technologies GmbH.

Furthermore, as a first-generation college student, every step toward success takes extra effort. Unlike those peers growing up in families with college graduates, first-generation college students navigate without the competitive advantage of an insider roadmap. Therefore, every achievement in academia and beyond is truly a personal first. To celebrate this book exclusively as my own success would be unjust. In the following paragraph, I want to express my gratitude to several individuals who have supported my growth journey, knowingly or unknowingly.

Juandalynn R. Abernathy; William J. Adams, D.M.A.; Oscar Albin (lic. phil. I); Sarah E. Baker; Olivier Bassil; Felix Baumann; Michael Bearden; André Bellmont; Tom Brooks; Camille Colatosti, Ph.D.; André Desponds; Kaspar Ewald; David Foster; Brigitte and Heinz Friedrich; Vanessa Garde; Lucio Godoy; Ruedi and Astrid Keller; Joe and Ines Koster; Colette Linton-Meyer; Colin J.B. Morton; John D. Rudnick, Jr., Ed.D.; Jürg Rutishauser; Walter Schmid; Judith Slapak-Barski, Ed.D.; members of Snarky Puppy; members of the SCL NY; Martha Snyder, Ph.D.; Timothy M. Stafford, Ph.D.; Clydia Allen Turner, Esq.; Elizabeth Allen Turner, Ed.D.; Paul Walker; Rafael Wespi, Ph.D.; Carlos de Yarza; and Annetta Zehnder.

Glossary

Aftertouch a MIDI message type changing a played note's sound over time.
Arranger a practitioner customizing a musical work for a specific context and purpose.
Audiation analyzing heard music in one's mind.
Beatmapping loosely defined synonym for metering, typically in a DAW environment.
Continuous Controllers a MIDI message type changing a played note's sound over time.
Demo a recording of an unfinished musical work.
Dependent Layers music information building on foundational layers: Articulations, ornamentation, lyrics, dynamics, chord symbols.
Descriptive Notation music notation focusing on analysis rather than performance instructions.
Digital Audio Workstation (DAW) computer software for producing music digitally.
Digital Literacy the proficient and responsible use of digital technology.
Doubling two instruments playing the same note(s) concurrently.
Foundational Layers music information building on global layers: Timing, length, and pitch of played music notes.
Global Layers sheet music parameters applying to all instruments: Meter, time signatures, tempo, and key signatures.
Lead Sheet a single-staff sheet music format.
Lyric Sheet a textual sheet music format, often limited to lyrics and chord symbols.
Master Rhythm Chart multi-stave part addressing rhythm section players collectively.
Metering determining a conducive way to count main beat and sub-beat patterns.
Music Copyist a practitioner responsible for sheet music preparation.
Music Information notation data and metadata related to music recordings.
Music Information Retrieval the primarily computer-based science of extracting music information from recordings.
Music With Broad Appeal easy-listening music that appeals to a general audience.
Musical Instrument Digital Interface (MIDI) a digital communication protocol frequently used in music production and performance.
Note Events a MIDI message type defining each note's timing, duration, pitch, and velocity.
Orchestrator a practitioner customizing a musical work for a specific instrumentation.
Particell a sheet music format condensing instrumental parts on fewer staves.
Passage a time-based selection of the recording, made by the transcriptionist.
Peripherals hardware devices to control computer software.
Pitch Bend a MIDI message type, use to change a played note's pitch over time.
Prescriptive Notation music notation focusing on performance instructions rather than analysis.

Reduction a sheet music format with a smaller instrumentation than the recording's instrumentation.
Rhythm Section collective term for those instruments establishing the groove in groove-based music: Drums, band percussion, bass, keyboards, and guitars.
Sampler a musical instrument capable of playing back recorded sounds.
Score Study familiarizing in-depth with a work's sheet music.
Section a specific form part of a musical work.
Segment a smaller part within a passage, played by one or several instruments.
Sheet Music Preparation preparing sheet music for publication or a performance.
Solfège pedagogical tool to associate pitches with syllables.
Sound Source any musical instrument audible on a recording, including the human voice, synthesizers, and samplers.
Source Format the audio and/or MIDI file(s) available for transcription.
Stacked Composite Sounds two or more instruments playing the same part concurrently.
Stem Session several vertically stacked audio and/or MIDI files that collectively represent a recorded musical work.
Synthesizer a musical instrument generating sound electronically.
Takedown a loosely defined synonym for music transcription.
Target Format a transcription's final sheet music format.
Timbre a description of a sound's tone color or characteristics.
Velocity a MIDI message type describing a played note's attack strength.
Virtual Instrument a software-based musical instrument.
Voicing Structure the presence and vertical sequence of notes in a chord.

Part I

Preparation

Part Overview

Chapters 1, 2, and 3 cover a high-level overview of music transcription, the listening skills, and setup for transcribing music. Chapter 1 covers an introductory definition, emerging methodological inquiries, and five industry applications of music transcription. Chapter 2 covers several listening foundations and music learning theory for notating recorded music by ear. Chapter 3 covers setup considerations with a focus on playback, listening and referencing, and music notation. In summary, Part I prepares readers for the music transcription process.

Learning Outcomes

After reading Part I, the learner will be able to:

BO 1: Describe the context and process foundations of music transcription.

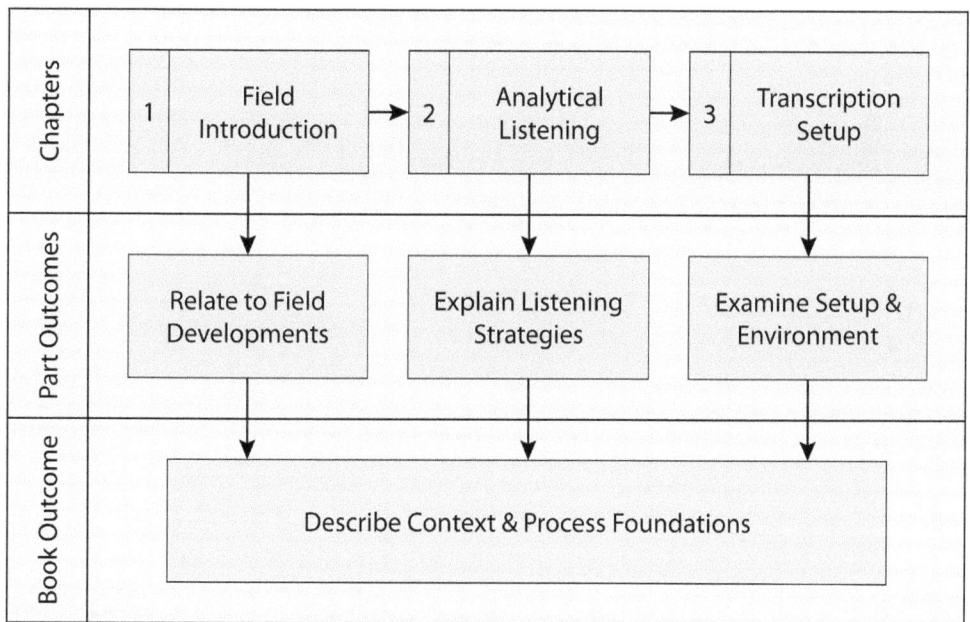

Figure 0.1 Part I map.

DOI: 10.4324/9781003511946-1

1 Field Introduction

Chapter Overview

This chapter covers a high-level overview of the music transcription process, related research fields, and common applications in the music industry. The first section provides an introductory definition of music transcription that sets the stage for the remaining book. The second section then summarizes emerging methodological inquiries of researchers, practitioners, and educators. Finally, the third section explores common application areas of music transcription in the music industry. The section activities help learners explore the application of music transcription in the music industry. In summary, this chapter illuminates a field that has received diverse and enduring inquiry, but scattered across time, disciplines, and context.

Learning Outcomes

After reading this chapter, the learner will be able to:

CO 1: Relate to research inquiry in the field of music transcription.
CO 2: Relate to the role of music transcription in the music industry.

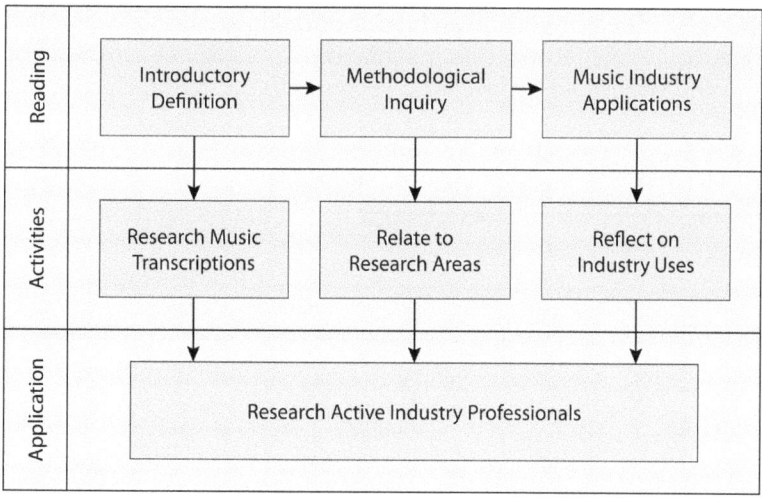

Figure 1.1 Chapter 1 map.

4 A Music Transcription Method

Introductory Definition

Two broader definitions exist for *music transcription*. First, in the classical music genre, music transcription refers to *adapting* an existing, *notated work* for a different instrumentation. For example, Italian composer and pianist Ferruccio Busoni transcribed several of J. S. Bach's keyboard works for piano (Kogan & Belsky, 2010). Another example is French composer and pianist Maurice Ravel, who transcribed Mussorgsky's piano work *Pictures at an Exhibition* for orchestra (Del Mar, 2023). The adaptation of existing musical works has been a popular practice in the past and continues to be popular in present times.

This book focuses on the second definition of *music transcription*. The second definition describes the process of *notating recorded music* as sheet music (Bhattarai & Lee, 2023). In this context, music transcription describes the transformation of recorded music to symbolic notation. This definition is common in contemporary music genres with a broad appeal, including jazz, pop, further groove-based genres, film scores, and video game scores. A notable commercial example is Hal Leonard's jazz transcription series, which features solos from iconic jazz artists. Countless further transcription examples exist, including an online trove of unofficial sheet music transcriptions spanning genres with a broad appeal.

Transcription Skills

Music transcription, or notating recorded music, is a skill at the intersection of ear training, general musicianship, and music notation. Ear training enables musicians to *analyze* heard music. For example, ear training includes determining a note's pitch and timing. General musicianship then helps *contextualize* the analyzed music. Contextualization helps transcriptionists make notation decisions when doubts arise about the analytical findings. Finally, music notation serves as an outlet to *capture* the findings. In analogy to general literacy, music notation knowledge is a requirement to read and notate music.

Ear training, general musicianship, and music notation knowledge are embedded in Gordon's (2012) music learning theory about audiation. To transcribe music, the transcriptionist must go *beyond general music listening*. The procedural steps include:

1. Listening to a specific passage of a recorded musical work.
2. Analyzing the heard music cognitively and internally.
3. Translating the heard music into sheet music.

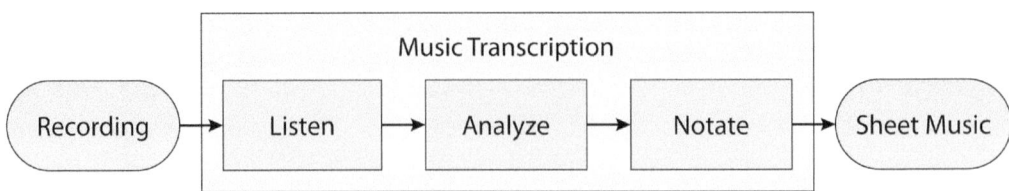

Figure 1.2 Notating recorded music.

Each step builds on the transcriptionist's *experience* with that specific activity. As transcriptionists gain mileage, their abilities to listen to, analyze, and *translate* recorded music into sheet music become more directed and intentional.

Transcription Equipment

Adding to the primary transcription skills, Gorow's (2002) method for hearing and writing music asserts the importance of *technology* in the transcription process. Like any digital process, music-related or not, music transcription requires selecting *suitable* equipment and operating it with *fluency*. Today's essential music transcription equipment includes the following tools:

- A playback device that allows for seamless navigation and repeat play.
- Headphones that evenly represent the frequencies within the human hearing range.
- Reference tools to analyze the heard music.
- Notation software to notate the analyzed music.
- Keyboard, mouse, and MIDI device to increase notation speed.

Some transcriptionists prefer to notate music with pen and paper instead of notation software. With proper training, handwritten transcriptions can reach engraving quality comparable to digital transcriptions. However, handwritten engraving tends to take more time and be less flexible with editing and formatting compared with digital engraving (Nicholl & Grudzinski, 2007). This book follows the industry standard of *digital music transcription*. Overall, a conducive setup helps transcriptionists hear and analyze music with *increased granularity*, then translate their findings into sheet music. In summary, ear training, musicianship, music notation understanding, and technology literacy all influence the transcription *pace and quality*.

Section Activities

1. Conduct a Google search for sheet music transcriptions. What names do you recognize from the search results?
2. Next, search for sheet music transcriptions of a contemporary artist of choice. How well is this artist represented through transcriptions, and who created them?

Methodological Inquiry

The preceding definition is just the tip of a larger field of inquiry. Diverse professionals from both the music industry and related fields have published about music transcription. Besides actual music transcriptions, publications cover the larger methodological scope, ranging from *scholarly* field contributions to *practical* how-to guides. Textual resources cover common formats, including textbooks, scholarly articles, and blogs. The field has also seen a rapidly growing number of *educational* YouTube tutorials covering work analyses and practical foundations of the craft. In summary, the publication scope reveals interest from researchers, practitioners, and educators alike. Overall, three larger inquiry categories intersect with music transcription: Music education, music production, and related music research areas.

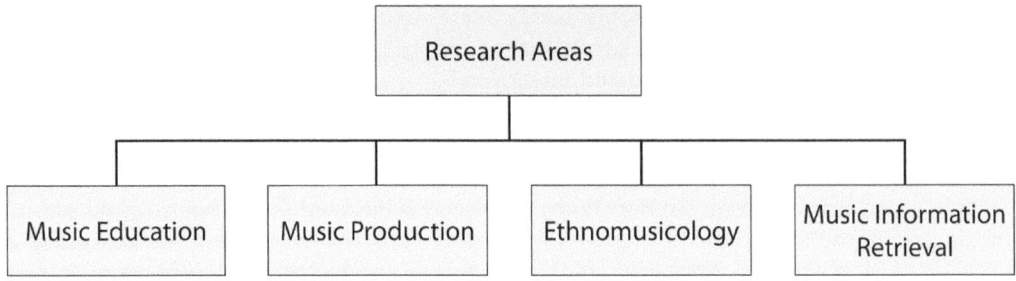

Figure 1.3 Methodological inquiry.

Music Education

Music transcription plays an integral part in formal music education, and particularly in the context of ear training. In formal education, music transcription is often referred to as *music dictation*, or the classroom equivalent of music transcription (Cleland & Dobrea-Grindahl, 2020; McCarthy & Turek, 2020; Radley, 2016). In classroom settings, the instructor plays a musical sequence for students to *notate by ear*. As a slight exception to transcribing recorded music, instructors sometimes perform music dictation exercises live on a musical instrument. Music dictation is widely used to cultivate and assess students' development of *aural skills*.

Both seasoned and aspiring music professionals spend ample time *studying* their music of interest independently. While official sheet music exists for some musical works, it does not always cover a musician's needs. For example, a lead sheet will provide limited, if any, information about a recorded, *improvised solo*. Similarly, a specific sheet music arrangement of a work will provide limited information about a *different arrangement* of the same work. For these and similar reasons, music transcription is central to *studying* contemporary music with a broad appeal (Doky, 2018; Sikora, 2022). These musicians transcribe music to analyze, learn, internalize, and eventually perform or write music based on the absorbed elements. The practice extends to most non-classical genres with a broader appeal. In this context, transcriptions inform the work of both music performers and creators.

Industry Voice: Connecting Creativity and Practice

Andreas: How do you approach teaching music transcription at the collegiate level?

Emily: It is hands down one of the hardest courses I teach mentally as we must be insanely focused and learn (for most) a few new skills. If you consider introductory music theory the course where everyone's getting on the same page so you can talk about music theory in a way that anyone would understand, while also mastering the fundamental concepts that apply to your creative area. Students then take the music composition course, which is what I call music theory on steroids. Every day, we apply a concept from music theory to their compositional creations, as if daily they're getting a new tool in their creator's toolbox. Once they get to the arranging and transcription course, the third class in our music composition minor sequence, the concepts go complete internal. Everything is now happening in your ears and in your brain. You're learning how to translate everything you learned in music theory and composition through your ears and then recreate in a variety of styles and mediums. It's all about how we approach each course and their objectives, skills, and applications. The arranging and transcription course is designed to not just build students' aural skills, but also help them become better composers. Every single class starts with some type of rhythmic and melodic dictation practice, followed by a short activity where students must rearrange, transcribe, or recreate a sound, song, or concept. And then we dive into new tools or resources for that class. It's super fun. We have benchmarks. Students get to find and develop their own process for transcribing. They also explore their own method model or process for arranging. The final course outcome, in addition to what they're creating, is to discover how they could use these resources to create music and generate income as a composer or musician.

Emily Williams Burch, D.M.A. – Music Educator, Savannah, GA
Professor of Music at Savannah College of Art and Design

Music Production

Beyond educational settings, music transcription finds broad use in applied industry contexts. For example, *film scoring* professionals use music transcription to create sheet music from demo recordings (Rona, 2022; Sapiro, 2016). Like most industries, film scoring has experienced a major digital shift since the millennium turn. Today's expectation is that film composers deliver a demo recording of each music cue to the director for approval. Once a cue is approved, and provided there is a budget and intent to record, the music department will *create session sheet music* and record the cue with session musicians.

The same practice has become an industry standard across the larger recording industry. Composers, songwriters, and recording artists all tend to create an initial *demo recording*, followed by sheet music transcriptions that eventually facilitate the official recording. Similar to the film scoring industry, music transcription plays a crucial role in *translating* demo recordings *into sheet music* for the purpose of creating release recordings.

One more music transcription application concerns *live performances* of already recorded music. Although more performance-oriented, this application still relates closely to music production. For example, an artist may need band sheet music to perform a previously recorded song with local musicians (Green, 2002). As another example, a musical theater composer may need piano vocal scores from demo recordings to rehearse and perform a show. In both scenarios, rehearsal time with all musicians present is often limited. Creating effective sheet music helps musicians *perform together effectively* with minimal rehearsal time.

Related Research Areas

Ethnomusicologists use music transcription to notate and analyze music from diverse cultures (Nettl, 1964, 2015). The larger field distinguishes between *prescriptive* and *descriptive*

8 A Music Transcription Method

notation (Kanno, 2007; Seeger, 1958). Prescriptive notation frames music information as performance instructions, while descriptive notation focuses on presenting musical parameters in rich detail. As part of an ongoing debate, ethnomusicologists have been discussing the effectiveness and limitations of both music notation approaches. Owing to the widely acknowledged limitations of Western music notation, ethnomusicological transcriptionists will sometimes expand or adapt existing music notation systems to *capture music information*.

Finally, technological innovation is the focus of *music information retrieval* (MIR) research (Lerch, 2022; Müller, 2015). This field is concerned with the computer-based extraction of music information from recordings. A key objective in this field is the *automation* of the MIR process with high-quality results and minimal human intervention. MIR finds application in sheet music transcription, music metadata extraction, and the broader field of audio editing. Overall, the field of music information retrieval has received increasing scholarly attention over the last decade. MIR shows potential for automating parts of the *music transcription process* at some point in the future.

Section Activities

1. Looking back on your music journey up to this point, which research areas of music transcription capture your interest?
2. Which research areas of music transcription might be relevant to your future journey in music?

Music Industry Applications

The previous section highlights the diverse field inquiry and enduring practice that music transcription has received. Music educators, practitioners, and researchers of related fields all describe, for their own purposes, a process of notating recording music. However, the question arises of how *music transcription* is applied in the music industry. In other words, how do musicians *leverage* music transcription for their *industry activities*? Applied music transcription remains a scarcely illuminated field for both seasoned and emerging music professionals. The following subsections describe several impactful uses for music practitioners and educators.

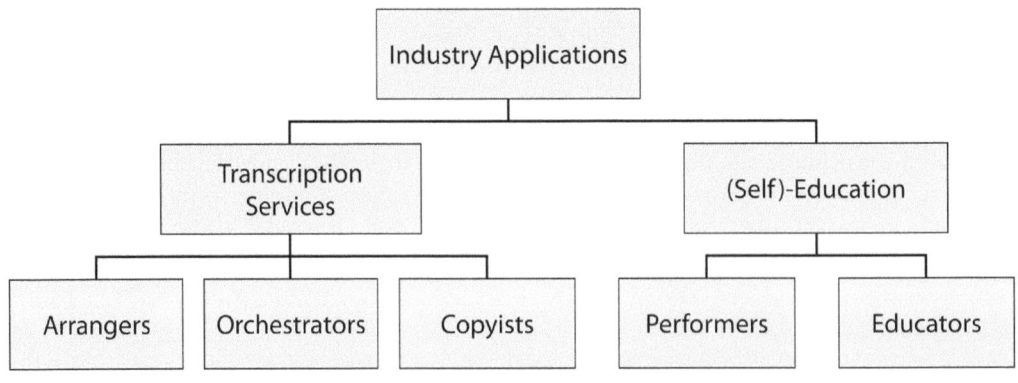

Figure 1.4 Music industry applications.

Arrangers, Orchestrators, and Copyists

Much of today's music transcription work is for recording or performance projects. For example, music creators write a new work and record a first demo of it in their home studio. The music creators plan to have their work *commercially recorded* and eventually performed by other musicians. With these objectives in mind, creating custom-tailored sheet music for the target instrumentation helps navigate time and available resources. Creating the sheet music is typically the responsibility of an arranger or orchestrator. However, before the sheet music can be arranged or orchestrated, an *initial draft* must be *transcribed* from the demo recording (Sapiro, 2016). This frequently overlooked step is critical to the project's outcome quality and turnaround time.

Music transcription is also immediately relevant to music copyists. This little-known job profile includes any combination of *sheet music preparation* responsibilities. Music copyists may proofread, format, print, and bind sheet music. Furthermore, some copyists are hired specifically because they offer music transcription in addition to the standard responsibilities (Maz, 2023). These individuals offer to transcribe recorded music and deliver *polished sheet music*. Transcribing music copyists often work in film scoring, musical theater, the broader recording industry, and the performance industry. Some also create official sheet music transcriptions for artists or their publishers to sell. Overall, there are few known music copyists who also offer music transcription. Therefore, it is not uncommon for these professionals to transcend several parts of the music industry.

Music Performers and Educators

The performance industry is another prominent field that intersects with music transcription. Performing, whether as an artist or session musician, is becoming an increasingly competitive field. *Opportunity* favors those who show up and deliver strong in the face of limited resources and rehearsal time. Because sheet music is not always available, some gigs require learning musical works from recordings. This scenario is especially common in jazz and popular styles but can occur in other contexts (Green, 2002). Those who want the opportunity must be *prepared to learn* their instrumental parts from recordings. While it is sometimes possible to learn new works by playing along with the recording, transcriptions can reveal additional *detail and nuance* in instrumental parts that may otherwise go unnoticed. Transcriptions also serve as a helpful orientation point, especially during performances with longer setlists and complex or dense arrangements.

Finally, music transcription is relevant to educational environments. As classrooms are becoming increasingly diverse, educators find themselves catering to learners with contrasting needs, interests, and cultural backgrounds (Reza, 2022). With the increasing demand for *inclusive instruction*, inclusivity in education has become an emerging research field. Music classrooms pose particularly interesting challenges because of learner's unique musical interests. When learners pursue music activities, they often show an *intrinsic interest* in learning about the music they listen to daily (Barton, 2018). Learners may expect, consciously or subconsciously, formal music education to cover their *favorite music*. However, sheet music is not always available for the learners' stylistic interests and musicianship level. Music educators who transcribe have an opportunity to make formal music education more inclusive of learners with diverse needs, interests, and cultural backgrounds.

10 A Music Transcription Method

Section Activities

1. Reflecting on your music journey so far, what situations can you think of that would have benefitted from applied music transcription?
2. Thinking ahead, how or in which situations might applied music transcription benefit your music journey?

End-of-Chapter Activity

Applying everything you have learned in this chapter, conduct a Google search to find several music transcription professionals. What parts of the music industry are they active in, and what services do they offer?

Chapter Summary

This chapter covered an introductory definition, emerging methodological inquiries, and several industry applications of music transcription. The field of music transcription has received broad scholarly inquiry, including perspectives from music education, music production, ethnomusicology, and music information retrieval research. Common industry applications of music transcription include arranging, orchestration, performance, copyist work, and music education. The section activities provided opportunities for learners to relate music transcription to their own music journeys. Finally, the end-of-chapter activity provided an opportunity to explore the profiles and services of active music transcriptionists.

Learning Outcomes

The learner should now be able to:

CO 1: Relate to research inquiry in the field of music transcription.
CO 2: Relate to the role of music transcription in the music industry.

Up Next

Chapter 2 covers how to listen to music for the purpose of music transcription.

References

Barton, G. (2018). *Music learning and teaching in culturally and socially diverse contexts: Applications for classroom practice.* Palgrave Macmillan Cham. https://doi.org/10.1007/978-3-319-95408-0
Bhattarai, B., & Lee, J. (2023). A comprehensive review on music transcription. *Applied Sciences, 13*(21), Article 11882. https://doi.org/10.3390/app132111882
Cleland, K. D., & Dobrea-Grindahl, M. (2020). *Developing musicianship through aural skills: A holistic approach to sight singing and ear training* (3rd ed.). Routledge. https://doi.org/10.4324/9780429020230
Del Mar, J. (2023). Mussorgsky, orch. Ravel Pictures from an Exhibition. In *Orchestral masterpieces under the microscope* (pp. 317–331). Boydell & Brewer. https://doi.org/10.1017/9781800106611.044
Doky, N. L. (2018). *Jazz transcription: Developing jazz improvisational skills through solo transcription and analysis.* Alfred Music. ISBN: 978-3-892-21155-6
Gordon, E. E. (2012). *Learning sequences in music: A contemporary music learning theory* (2012 ed.). GIA Publications. ISBN: 978-1-579-99890-5

Gorow, R. (2002). *Hearing and writing music: Professional training for today's musician* (2nd ed.). September Publishing. ISBN: 978-0-962-94967-8

Green, L. (2002). *How popular musicians learn: A way ahead for music education.* Routledge. https://doi.org/10.4324/9781315253169

Kanno, M. (2007). Prescriptive notation: Limits and challenges. *Contemporary Music Review, 26*(2), 231–254. https://doi.org/10.1080/07494460701250890

Kogan, G., & Belsky, S. (2010). *Busoni as pianist* (Vol. 73). University of Rochester Press. https://www.jstor.org/stable/10.7722/j.ctt81q7w

Lerch, A. (2022). *An introduction to audio content analysis: Music information retrieval tasks & applications.* Wiley. https://doi.org/10.1002/9781119890980

Maz, A. (2023). *Music technology essentials: A home studio guide.* Focal Press. https://doi.org/10.4324/9781003345138

McCarthy, D., & Turek, R. (2020). *Singing and dictation for today's musician.* Routledge. https://doi.org/10.4324/9780367814984

Müller, M. (2015). *Fundamentals of music processing: Audio, analysis, algorithms, applications.* Springer Cham. https://doi.org/10.1007/978-3-319-21945-5

Nettl, B. (1964). *Theory and method in ethnomusicology.* Free Press of Glencoe. https://lccn.loc.gov/64016964

Nettl, B. (2015). *The study of ethnomusicology: Thirty-three discussions* (3rd ed.). University of Illinois Press. https://www.jstor.org/stable/10.5406/j.ctt1hj9xkf

Nicholl, M., & Grudzinski, R. (2007). *Music notation: Preparing scores and parts.* Berklee Press. ISBN: 978-0-876-39074-0

Radley, R. (2016). *Reading, writing and rhythmetic: The ABCs of music transcription.* Sher Music Co. ISBN: 978-1-883-21795-2

Reza, F. (Ed.). (2022). *Diversity and inclusion in educational institutions.* Cambridge Scholars Publishing. ISBN: 978-1-527-57638-4

Rona, J. (2022). *The reel world: Scoring for pictures, television, and video games* (3rd ed.). Rowman & Littlefield Publishers. ISBN: 978-1-538-13776-5

Sapiro, I. (2016). *Scoring the score: The role of the orchestrator in the contemporary film industry.* Routledge. https://doi.org/10.4324/9781315857824

Seeger, C. (1958). Prescriptive and descriptive music-writing. The Musical Quarterly, 44(2), 184–195. https://doi.org/10.1093/mq/XLIV.2.184

Sikora, F. (2022). *Jazz harmony: Think - Listen - Play - A practical approach.* Schott Music. ISBN: 978-3-795-74930-9

2 Analytical Listening

Chapter Overview

This chapter covers the foundational listening strategies for notating recorded music by ear. The first section provides a brief introduction to music listening approaches and the layers of music information to be transcribed. The second section then covers targeted listening to three listening dimensions related to music transcription, namely time, frequency, and panorama. Finally, the third section covers the basics of spotting and identifying sound sources, as well as analyzing the heard music information. The section activities help learners explore several listening approaches pertaining to music transcription. In summary, this chapter helps learners understand and apply those listening techniques necessary to transcribe music.

Learning Outcomes

After reading this chapter, the learner will be able to:

CO 1: Locate music information through directed listening.
CO 2: Explain the foundations of auditory analysis in music transcription.

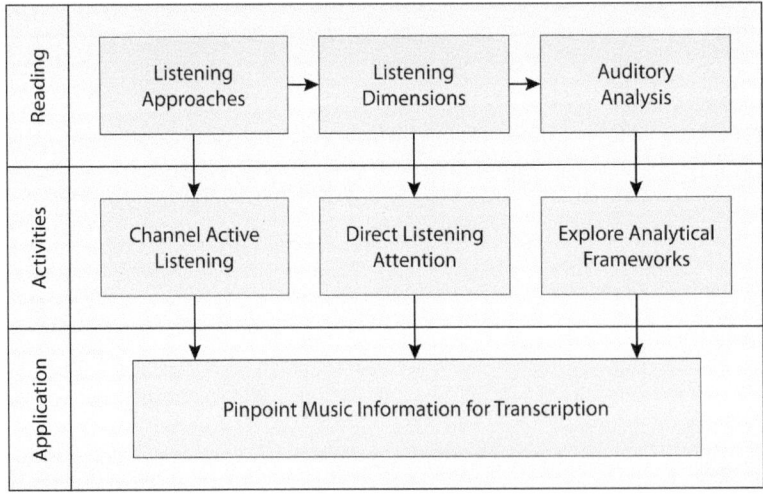

Figure 2.1 Chapter 2 map.

DOI: 10.4324/9781003511946-3

Listening Approaches

There exist many *ways of listening* to the same musical work. Some individuals may listen for personal entertainment, while others listen to participate in an activity. Some listen consciously, while others listen subconsciously. Communities may adopt different listening approaches based on their cultures of practice. Musicians may listen differently than non-musicians. Listening approaches even differ between individual musicians. The list of comparisons is endless. However, at the very foundation, listeners can listen to music *passively* or *actively* (Jorgensen, 2003).

Passive and Active Listening

Passive listening describes contexts in which music takes a background role. For example, consumers might passively listen to background music in a restaurant. As another example, students might passively listen to music while studying. In contrast, *active listening* takes place at the listener's *center of attention*. In this state, the listener's primary thoughts concern the music heard at that time. As a process, music transcription requires the listener's *undivided attention* to the heard music. That is because music recordings hold a wealth of music information that can only be discerned and analyzed through careful listening (Gorow, 2002). Therefore, music transcription requires active listening.

There exist many ways of listening to music actively (Wallace, 2014). Some listeners may focus on the music's overarching narrative message. Others may prioritize arrangement or orchestration parameters including form, dramatic shape, articulations, playing techniques, and instrumentation. Again, others may focus on a recording's performance quality. Finally, some may listen to the balance of frequency registers and other mix engineering aspects in a recording (Corey, 2016). *Listening priorities* vary significantly between *career profiles* and industry fields. For example, audio engineers tend to listen to music differently than session instrumentalists. Also, vocalists may listen to music differently than arrangers. While exact listening strategies vary from person to person, those pursuing music industry careers focus on the listening skills that support their *specific roles*.

Industry Voice: Listening Practices and Scope of Audibility

Andreas: How do you listen to music for transcription purposes?

Greg: I'm listening to the big picture first. If you're giving me a song to transcribe, the first thing I'm going to do is outline the structure. That includes verses, choruses, bridges, intros, interludes, etc . . . Structural outlining streamlines the process. If a verse happens three times, I don't always have to keep transcribing it. I then outline the general harmonic structure. What's going on? What are the chords here? . . . Training yourself to listen this way is something we all can do, not just when transcribing. I remember teaching young people about music years ago, and teaching teachers how to work with young people and getting everybody to listen to the same recording several times, while focusing on different instruments. That skill becomes so essential. The first time you listen to something, it's just a big piece of music. But if you need to understand what the guitar is doing, you might find that, the more you listen, you can actually hear everything

> that's happening in a way that you didn't the first time. You start to hear details. This reminds me of the time when the Beatles remastered some of their recordings in the 80s. I remember sitting with a friend and listening to these records that we knew from earlier, and hearing things we'd never heard before. Because the fidelity or mix had changed, we were able to dig deeper inside the records and finding things we never realized were there. That becomes tremendously fun to do, especially with a piece you know really well, or think you know really well.
>
> Gregory Pliska – Composer, Conductor, & Orchestrator, NYC
> *War Horse, The Infiltrator, NPR's Morning Edition*

Music Information Layers

When transcribing music, the listener should focus on those types of music information *represented in sheet music*. This information includes the pitch and timing of heard notes, notes' sonic properties, and the larger context around these notes (Bhattarai & Lee, 2023). In music transcription, the order in which music information types are notated matters. This book distinguishes between *three types* of music information layers that should be transcribed *sequentially*:

1. Global layers: Meter, time signatures, tempo, and key signatures.
2. Foundational layers: Note timing, length, and pitch, and slash notation.
3. Dependent layers: Articulations, ornamentation, dynamics, chord symbols, and lyrics.

Global layers outline the work's larger structural parameters and provide a *notation framework* for the subsequent layers. Global parameters, particularly those pertaining to metering, exert a significant influence over the sheet music's appearance (Boenn, 2018). As an analogy, global layers could represent a cake form. Next, foundational layers represent the rhythms and pitches of the heard notes. Any audible *music notes* in a recording can be notated through foundational layers. Together, these foundational layers represent the cake that conforms to the shape of the cake form. Finally, dependent layers articulate the *sonic properties* of these music notes in further detail. In analogy, dependent layers describe the cake's scent and color.

Section Activities

1. Articulate what elements you listen to when listening actively. How might your approach to active listening differ from that of your peers?
2. Select a familiar music recording. At a first listen, which music information types stand out to you most intuitively? Articulate ideas to cultivate listening to elements you overlooked initially.

Listening Dimensions

Listening to music is a *multidimensional activity* (Gibson, 2018). The experience is perhaps comparable to a car ride from a driver's perspective. The car drives forward while the driver

a) Full Notation

[musical notation: Hopeful ♩ = 120, 4/4, mf]

b) Dependent Layers

[musical notation with accents, mf]

c) Foundational Layers

[musical notation]

d) Global Layers

[musical notation: Hopeful ♩ = 120, 4/4]

Example 2.1 Music information layers. Turner (2023), "America, America," mm. 17–19, melody, in *Ciao Bambino the Musical*. Transcribed by Andreas Häberlin. Printed with permission of Elizabeth Allen Turner.

observes the horizontal and vertical field of view beyond the windshield. Similar to the car's driving direction, music is listened to from an earlier point in the recording to a later one. In analogy to the vertical field of view, the transcriptionist may temporarily listen to higher or lower notes played in a recording. Finally, the horizontal field of view compares to listening to the left or right speaker. To drive safely, the driver must remain aware of any events unfolding in this three-dimensional space. Similarly, a transcriptionist will *scan* the three-dimensional space to discover any *relevant music information* to be transcribed.

Time, Frequency, and Panorama

As an art form that unfolds over time, a key listening dimension in music is time. Similar to the changing landscape during a car ride, the music information heard in a recording unfolds over the course of that recording. The transcriptionist listens to music information layers and captures their developments over time. For obvious reasons, a specific passage in time can only be transcribed if it is heard. This book refers to the first listening dimension as the *temporal dimension*, and to the listening approach as *horizontal listening* (Sheinberg & Dougherty, 2020).

The second listening dimension refers to snapshots of music information at a specific timestamp in the recording. Similar to the car driver's vertical field of view, a transcriptionist listens to events within the audible frequency range, from low to high. Music notes with

16 A Music Transcription Method

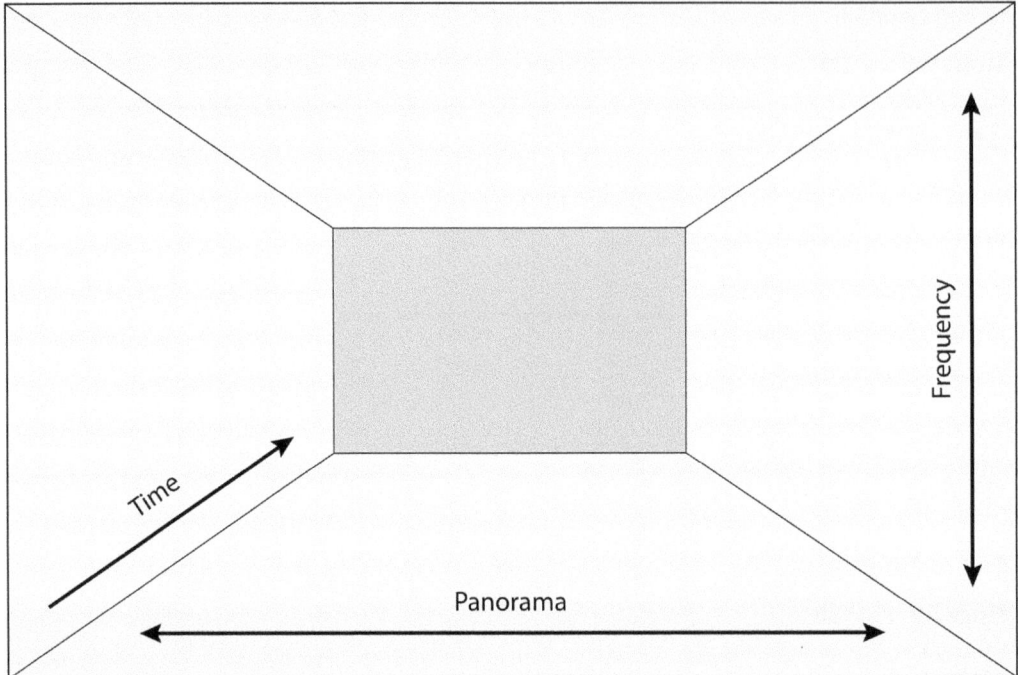

Figure 2.2 Listening dimensions.

different pitches are classified as higher or lower in this frequency range. The transcriptionist must scan the relevant frequency registers at that specific timestamp to determine the presence and pitches of any notes sounding concurrently. This book refers to the second listening dimension as the *frequency dimension*, and to the listening approach as *vertical listening* (Riess Jones et al., 2010).

The third listening dimension focuses on a recording's stereo image. In analogy to the car driver's horizontal field of view, a transcriptionist listens to centered, left-panned, and right-panned events. Panned sounds sound more prominent from the speaker they are panned toward, while centered sounds sound equally prominent from both speakers (Senior, 2018). If checking for the presence of specific sounds in a stereo image, the transcriptionist must scan all relevant locations in the recording's stereo panorama. This book refers to the third listening dimension as the *panoramic dimension*, and to the listening approach as *panoramic listening*.

Targeted Listening

When transcribing music information layers, transcriptionists *listen to* the temporal, frequency, and panoramic *dimensions concurrently*. That is because all audible music notes include some form of rhythm or timed motion, populate a specific frequency register, and a specific panorama position. In analogy, driving a car safely requires monitoring all three visual dimensions concurrently. Because the global, foundational, and dependent layers are linked directly to a recording's audible music notes, transcribing any layers requires listening to these notes and, therefore, targeted listening.

Generally, the busier and more complex a recorded music work is, the more difficult it becomes to *discern* less prominent music notes within a recording. This type of challenge is often attributed to the field of *masking* in psychoacoustics (Fastl & Zwicker, 2007). For example, in a recording that contains a single unpitched percussion instrument, that instrument is easily heard. Although the recorded instrument populates a specific frequency register and panoramic position, the transcriptionist may focus on horizontal listening without any distractions from competing instruments. In contrast, if the same unpitched percussion instrument is placed in a busy arrangement with several competing sound sources, directed vertical and panoramic listening suddenly become key to locating and identifying that instrument in the audio mix.

With the challenges of psychoacoustics in mind, different transcription phases require focusing on listening dimensions differently. Transcriptionists should aim to focus on *one specific task* at a time (Bhattarai & Lee, 2023). At the beginning of a project, it is practical to prioritize the *more prominent* sound sources. These are the sound sources with better discernible rhythms and pitches. In this phase, horizontal and vertical listening guide the transcription of rhythm, melody, and harmony. Subsequent phases then focus on *less prominent* sound sources. Vertical and panoramic listening become progressively more important in locating less discernible rhythms and pitches. Dense or indistinct chord voicings, in particular, require an increased focus on vertical and panoramic listening.

Section Activities

Select a familiar music recording:

1. What instruments and pitches can you hear playing in the low, mid, and high registers?
2. Listen through stereo speakers or headphones. Locate several playing instruments, then describe how they fit into the three listening dimensions.

Auditory Analysis

The previous two sections discussed the importance of targeted listening to locate specific music information in a recording. Naturally, different music parameters require listening to different elements. These elements may stand out easily in less dense arrangements, or may require more focused listening in denser arrangements. Once the transcriptionist has located an element, the final step preceding notation is to analyze and interpret the heard music. At this point, the transcriptionist must *translate* the heard music to *music notation*. The process may include determining the sound source through its sonic characteristics. The process further includes the analysis of music information layers through audiation (Gordon, 2012).

Sonic Characteristics

Musical sound sources can be identified by their unique sonic characteristics that distinguish them from other sound sources. From a vertical listening perspective, a played note consists of a fundamental frequency and its related overtones (Zizza, 2023). The fundamental frequency represents the note's main pitch, while the overtones accompanying the fundamental frequency are higher auxiliary pitches. In combination, the fundamental frequency and its overtones form a note's *timbre*. Together, these characteristics make different sound

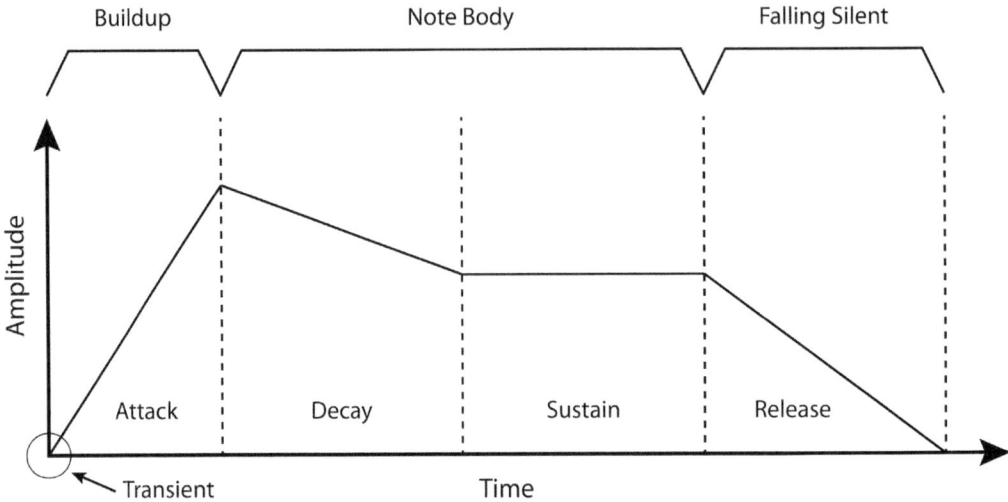

Figure 2.3 ADSR envelope and note segments.

sources *sonically recognizable*. For example, it is easy to differentiate between the contrasting sonic characteristics of a piano and a saxophone.

From a horizontal listening point, sonic characteristics can be framed as a *sequence* of an attack with initial transient, body, and release. At just a few milliseconds long, the *transient* is a short energy burst that represents the played note's initial portion (Dittmar, 2017). The *attack*, which includes the transient, describes the time it takes for the played note to reach its intended volume. A note's attack portion has unique timbral characteristics that help determine the note's sound source. Next, the *note body* represents the played note's main portion. Based on the sound source, the body's volume may or may not decay over time. Finally, the *release* represents the note's end portion, during which the note falls silent.

In music transcription, *sonic characteristics* are important for three reasons. First, the source-specific timbral characteristics help transcriptionists *identify the sound source* in question (Karpinski, 2000; Lee, 2020). Second, timbral characteristics help *identify dynamics*. That is because sound sources played at a louder volume will both sound louder and result in a brighter timbre (McAdams, 2019). Chapter 11 covers the intersection of timbre and dynamics in further detail. Third, note attacks including transients help *locate quieter notes* that are less discernible in a recording. For example, the body of notes played by a harp would be difficult to discern in an orchestral recording. That is because the body of harp notes are naturally quiet in comparison to other orchestral instruments. However, the plucked transients of these harp notes have an increased chance of standing out in a recording. Well-discernible transients facilitate the transcription of notes and rhythms immensely.

Processing Music Information

Once music information has been heard and located, the transcriptionist must *analyze it cognitively* before notating it. Gordon (2012), a music learning theory researcher, frames this process as part of the larger umbrella of audiation. Audiation describes the ability to *process and comprehend* music. For example, a musician might listen to a recording to determine a meter, key signature, and other music information commonly notated. In the context of music listening, a further differentiation is necessary between simple attentive listening and listening to process music. Simple attentive listening describes the event of hearing music without necessarily analyzing music information. In contrast, listening with the intention to process describes the act of making sense of the heard music. The result of listening to process is a *deeper understanding* of the heard music's defining parameters (Abraham, 2020).

The eight different types of audiation collectively cover the *activities* of listening to, reading, writing, recalling, creating, and improvising music (Luce, 2004). Each type includes *musical sensemaking* based on a specific activity type and music source format. Furthermore, the *level* at which each activity is performed is articulated through six progressive audiation stages. Starting with momentary retention of heard music at the first stage, stages two to five cover progressive abilities to analyze, organize, retain, and recall heard patterns. The function of these abilities is comparable to listening to speech. With growing experience, learners can analyze, organize, retain, and recall heard speech parts at *increasing scope and detail*. Finally, the sixth stage describes the ability to anticipate musical patterns based on experience. The ability to predict musical patterns in a specific style indicates mastery of audiation in that style. Overall, all six stages are relevant to fluency in music transcription.

In summary, audiation types describe the type of music activity pursued, while audiation stages describe the transcriptionist's sophistication of inquiry (Feldman & Contzius, 2020). *Musical sensemaking* allows the transcriptionist to analyze those elements discovered through *targeted listening*. To discover these elements, the transcriptionist must familiarize with those music information layers commonly notated in sheet music. Together, a familiarity with music information layers, targeted listening, an awareness of sonic characteristics, and audiation form the foundations of analytical listening. Parts II and III of this book cover concrete strategies to identify, analyze, interpret, and transcribe heard music for transcription purposes.

Section Activities

Select and listen to a familiar music recording:

1. What sound sources can you hear, and how do their sonic characteristics differ?
2. Next, look up Gordon's six audiation stages. Which stage matches your current ability the closest?

End-of-Chapter Activity

Applying everything you have learned in this chapter, listen to an excerpt of a personally significant music recording. Identify several sound sources and describe their location using the three listening dimensions. Then articulate any prominent sonic characteristics in these sound sources.

Chapter Summary

This chapter covered music listening approaches, listening dimensions, and auditory analysis as applicable to music transcription. Transcribing recorded music starts with active and targeted listening to locate the music information in question. The second step includes analyzing music information layers by sonic characteristics and through audiation. The section activities provided learner opportunities to explore the listening skills necessary to locate and analyze music. Finally, the end-of-chapter activity provided an opportunity to explore analytical listening for transcription purposes through a personally significant music recording.

Learning Outcomes

The learner should now be able to:

CO 1: Locate music information through directed listening.
CO 2: Explain the foundations of auditory analysis in music transcription.

Up Next

Chapter 3 covers how to create a context-based transcription setup.

References

Abraham, A. (Ed.). (2020). *The Cambridge handbook of the imagination*. Cambridge University Press. https://doi.org/10.1017/9781108580298

Bhattarai, B., & Lee, J. (2023). A comprehensive review on music transcription. *Applied Sciences, 13*(21), Article 11882. https://doi.org/10.3390/app132111882

Boenn, G. (2018). *Computational models of rhythm and meter*. Springer Cham. https://doi.org/10.1007/978-3-319-76285-2

Corey, J. (2016). *Audio production and critical listening: Technical ear training* (2nd ed.). Routledge. https://doi.org/10.4324/9781315727813

Dittmar, T. (2017). *Audio engineering 101: A beginner's guide to music production* (2nd ed.). Focal Press. https://doi.org/10.4324/9781315618173

Fastl, H., & Zwicker, E. (2007). *Psychoacoustics: Facts and models*. Springer Berlin. https://doi.org/10.1007/978-3-540-68888-4

Feldman, E., & Contzius, A. (2020). *Instrumental music education: Teaching with the musical and practical in harmony* (3rd ed.). Routledge. https://doi.org/10.4324/9780429028700

Gibson, D. (2018). *The art of mixing: A visual guide to recording, engineering, and production*. Routledge. https://doi.org/10.4324/9781351252225

Gordon, E. E. (2012). *Learning sequences in music: A contemporary music learning theory* (2012 ed.). GIA Publications. ISBN: 978-1-579-99890-5

Gorow, R. (2002). *Hearing and writing music: Professional training for today's musician* (2nd ed.). September Publishing. ISBN: 978-0-962-94967-8

Jorgensen, E. R. (2003). *Transforming music education*. Indiana University Press. ISBN: 978-0-25310-958-3

Karpinski, G. S. (2000). *Aural skills acquisition: The development of listening, reading, and performing skills in college-level musicians*. Oxford University Press. https://doi.org/10.1093/oso/9780195117851.003.0001

Lee, S. Y. (2020). *Fundamental physics of sound*. World Scientific. https://doi.org/10.1142/11893

Luce, D. W. (2004). Music learning theory and audiation: Implications for music therapy clinical practice. *Music Therapy Perspectives, 22*(1), 26–33. https://doi.org/10.1093/mtp/22.1.26

McAdams, S. (2019). Timbre as a structuring force in music. In K. Siedenburg, C. Saitis, S. McAdams, A. N. Popper, & R. R. Fay (Eds.), *Timbre: Acoustics, perception, and cognition* (pp. 211–243). Springer Handbook of Auditory Research, 69. https://doi.org/10.1007/978-3-030-14832-4_8

Riess Jones, M., Fay, R. R., & Popper, A. N. (Eds.). (2010). *Music perception* (Vol. 36). Springer New York. https://doi.org/10.1007/978-1-4419-6114-3

Senior, M. (2018). *Mixing secrets for the small studio* (2nd ed.). Routledge. https://doi.org/10.4324/9781315150017

Sheinberg, E., & Dougherty, W. P. (Eds.). (2020). *The Routledge handbook of music signification*. Routledge. https://doi.org/10.4324/9781351237536

Turner, E. A. (2023). America, America [Song]. In *Ciao bambino the musical* [Unpublished manuscript].

Wallace, R. (2014). *Take note: An introduction to music through active listening*. Oxford University Press. ISBN: 978-0-195-31433-5

Zizza, K. (2023). *Game audio fundamentals: An introduction to the theory, planning, and practice of soundscape creation for games*. Focal Press. https://doi.org/10.4324/9781003218821

3 Transcription Setup

Chapter Overview

This chapter covers the different components of a music transcription setup and the criteria for selecting these components. The first section discusses the scope of source types, audio quality parameters, and playback devices. The second section then evaluates how audio output devices, listening environments, and reference tools influence a transcriptionist's listening experience. Finally, the third section discusses the choice of music notation software and peripherals, and how they can be connected to increase transcription effectiveness. The section activities help learners explore and apply various setup components. In summary, this chapter illuminates the role of technology in optimizing a personalized transcription workflow.

Learning Outcomes

After reading this chapter, the learner will be able to:

CO 1: Assess source materials, transcription equipment, and listening environments.
CO 2: Design a conducive music transcription work environment.

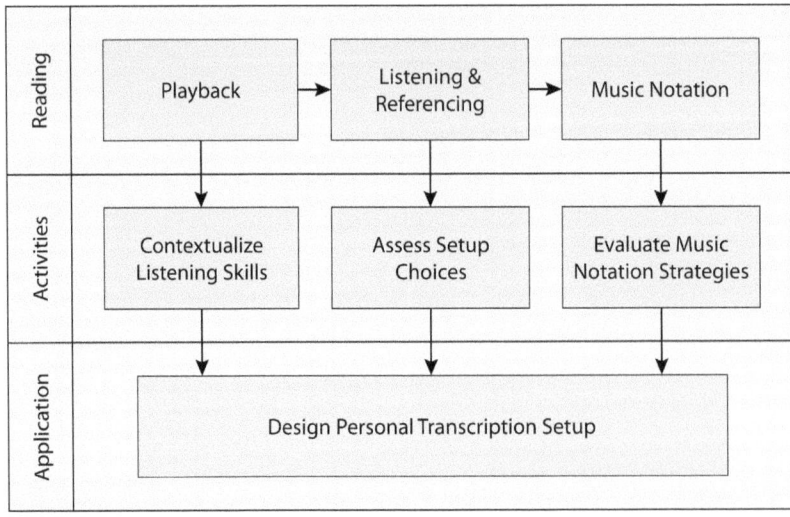

Figure 3.1 Chapter 3 map.

DOI: 10.4324/9781003511946-4

Playback

Analytical listening requires listening to a music recording or performance. For transcription purposes, *recorded music* is preferable because it can be replayed as necessary, allowing the listener to transcribe or proofread one segment at a time. Essentially, recorded music offers transcriptionists a comprehensive and *stable reference point*. Although transcribing music entirely from memory is possible, several limitations should be mentioned: First, it is uncommon to register all the elements of a heard performance simultaneously (Nettl, 1964). Second, of those elements registered, it is uncommon to remember them flawlessly. In contrast, music recordings allow listeners to focus on short segments, transcribe all desired elements in detail, and *replay* the music as often as helpful.

Source Types

Recorded music can be broadly categorized into single-file and multi-file audio sources (Huber et al., 2023). The industry standard audio file formats include .wav, .mp3, and .aiff files. Perhaps the best-known source type, *single-file sources* store an entire music recording in *one audio file*. This format is prevalent in published music, but also common with demo recordings of works in progress. Most music recordings that reach the public are single-file sources. In contrast, *multi-file sources* consist of several audio files that *collectively represent* a music recording. As a common example, the different files may represent individual instruments. This format, known as multitrack or stem sessions, is prevalent in music production environments. Music creatives, including audio engineers, work with multitrack formats to retain surgical creative control over a recording. For example, multitrack sessions allow creatives to replace an instrumental part recorded on a separate audio file. For copyright reasons, access to multitrack sessions is often limited to those collaborators whose work requires access to these sessions.

The context of music production also requires covering musical instrument digital interface (MIDI) files. MIDI is a broadly adopted *digital communication protocol* for music information (Huber, 2020). MIDI files do not hold audio data. Instead, they store quantified music performance data. Prominent examples of MIDI performance data include:

- Pitch, onset timing, and offset timing of each played note.
- The articulation of each played note.
- Changes to a passage's volume.
- Onset and offset timing of the sustain pedal.

In contrast to audio files, which store audio information, MIDI files communicate *music performance instructions* to hardware and software sampler instruments. Music creators use MIDI to capture their musical ideas through MIDI-compatible hardware and software instruments (McGuire & Matějů, 2020). In music production, MIDI files are often found in multitrack digital audio workstation (DAW) sessions.

Audio resolution is also critical to music transcription. This resolution is determined by a recording's sample rate and bit depth (Huber et al., 2023). An audio file's *sample rate* determines the highest frequency the file can capture. Recordings with a sample rate of 44.1 kHz or higher generally cover the *frequency range* of human hearing. Conversely, a sample rate below 44.1 kHz progressively impacts the recording's clarity and overall quality. Next, an audio file's *bit depth* determines the capturable *dynamic range*. A high bit depth will represent quiet and loud sounds closer to their original volume. Conversely, a low bit depth will represent these sounds at a more similar volume. Recordings at 16-bit or 24-bit are considered industry standard. Overall, a higher sample rate and bit depth increase the quality of the recorded audio. For transcription purposes, a sample rate of 44.1 kHz and a bit depth of 16-bit are acceptable audio quality standards. Lower standards will progressively compromise the audible detail and, therefore, the scope of transcription quality. However, higher standards create no audible advantage for music transcription. It should be noted that, if high-resolution files are converted to lower resolutions, the loss in audio quality is permanent. A reconversion to higher settings will not restore the audio quality.

Playback Device

When listening to a musical work for enjoyment, it is common to listen continuously from an earlier point in the recording to a later point. In this scenario, any playback device will work. However, analytical listening for music transcription benefits significantly from a more *granular playback functionality*. Transcriptionists listen to a selected passage repeatedly to retrieve music information. Therefore, the playback device should provide the option to *loop-play* the selected passage with little effort. A second essential feature is *variable playback speed*. Complex passages can be significantly easier to dissect if listening to the recording at a slower playback speed. Next, a less obvious, but equally important feature is *adjustable tuning*. If a recorded work's tuning departs from the international standard of 440 Hz, pitch referencing through tools calibrated to 440 Hz becomes increasingly difficult (Benetos et al., 2019). Playback devices with adjustable tuning can help calibrate recordings and pitch reference tools.

Annotation features are another key consideration for playback devices. The ability to mark sections, measures, and beats as *visual reference points* in a music recording is critical for metering purposes (Collins, 2014). Measures and beats help determine time signatures and tempi throughout the work. Similarly, section markers help determine a work's form. Beyond clarifying *structural parameters*, these visual reference points also help the transcriptionist *locate a specific passage* in both the playback session and the notation program.

Finally, the choice of playback device also depends on the number of audio and MIDI stems available for a project. *Single-file audio sources* work well on any playback device with the mentioned playback and annotation features. The prevalent playback device available for music transcription from single-file audio sources is Transcribe! by publisher Seventh String Software. A similar playback program is the browser-based Tune Transcriber. In contrast, *multi-file sources* with several files playing concurrently benefit from playback

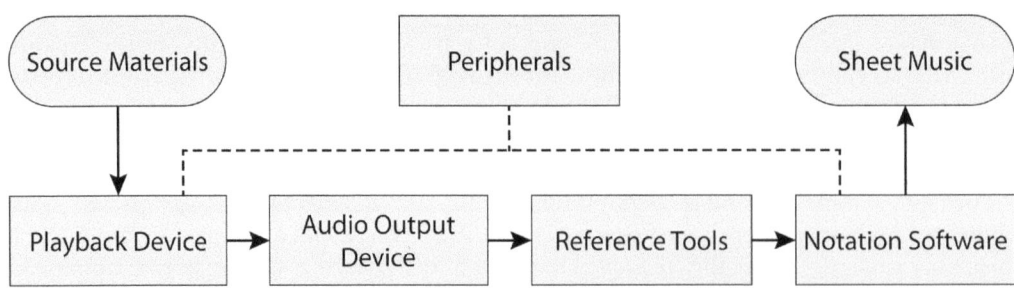

Figure 3.2 Music transcription setup.

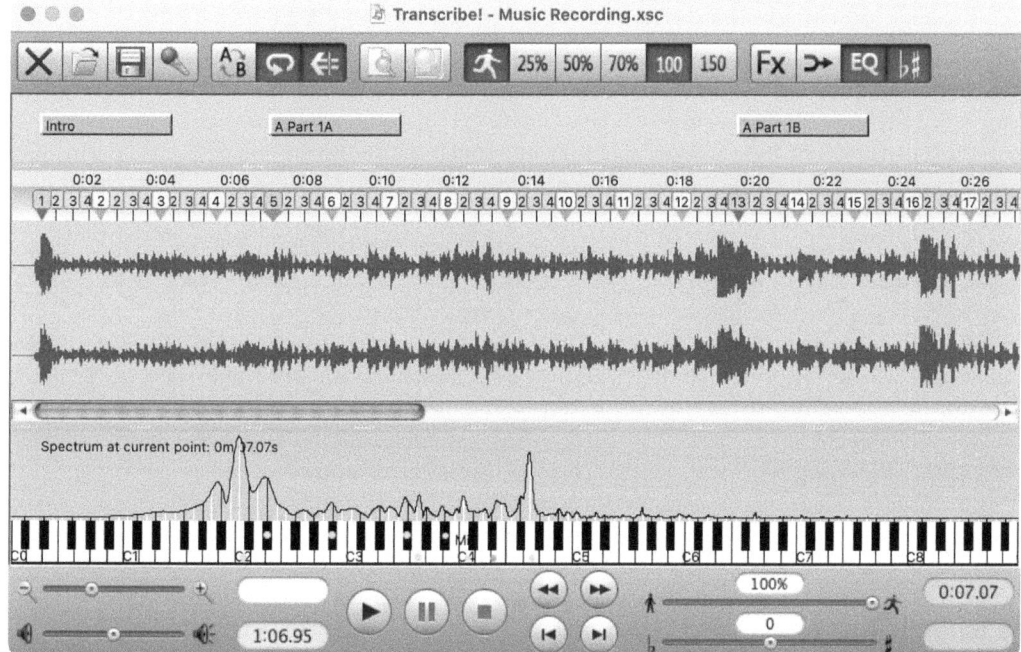

Figure 3.3 Transcribe! (2022) software. Printed with permission of Seventh String Software.

in a DAW. DAWs are capable of playing back multitrack sessions involving both audio and MIDI files. Common commercial DAWs used for transcription from multitrack sessions include Logic Pro, Pro Tools, Digital Performer, and Cubase. While DAWs generally include looping, tuning, and annotation features, their ability to vary playback speed is less flexible compared with Transcribe!

Section Activities

1. Listen to the online audio examples provided. How do different audio quality settings affect your listening experience?
2. Think of a personally relevant transcription project. Which playback device would you use and why?

Listening and Referencing

Several considerations are essential when analyzing music for transcription purposes. In addition to source types and playback devices, transcriptionists must carefully evaluate the audio output device, work environment, and reference tools used in the process. Similar to audio engineering, each *setup decision* impacts the scope of *listening quality possible* (Toole, 2017). For example, choosing a basic playback device will slow down the transcription pace, regardless of the remaining setup. Similarly, choosing a cheap audio output device will make it difficult to hear certain frequency registers reliably, regardless of the remaining setup. Finally, a noisy environment will likely mask quieter details in recorded music. In summary, each setup component should be carefully evaluated.

Audio Output Device and Environment

Music transcription requires an audio output device with a *balanced frequency response* that represents the human hearing range. Devices vary widely in audio output quality. For example, cheap earphones from an airplane will reveal a minimal portion of a music recording's full picture. The bass frequencies may be almost inaudible on this device type. Another consumer product includes high-fidelity devices. These devices emphasize the low and high frequencies while deemphasizing the mid-range (Borwick, 2001). While high-fidelity devices are popular with consumers, their frequency response profiles make it more challenging to discern quieter mid-range parts in music recordings. Overall, a *studio-grade* audio output device is critical to *hearing sufficient detail* in music recordings.

Music transcription tends to expose the ears to *prolonged listening* sessions. In career settings, a transcriptionist may listen to music for an entire workday at a time. To preserve long-term hearing health, it is therefore recommended to listen to music at a generally *low volume* (Dobrucki et al., 2017). In turn, a low listening volume requires a work environment *free of extraneous noise*. The quieter the listening environment, the easier and quicker it is to discern music information from a recording. When setting up a transcription workspace, ample consideration should be given to limiting noise from the following sources:

- Cohabitants, pets, and neighbors.
- Nearby environment.
- Computer fans.
- Household appliances.

The choice of audio output device also impacts the perceived extraneous noise floor. Monitor speakers, while popular in consumer and studio settings, will not reduce extraneous noise floors. Similar to the field of audio sample editing, important details may go unnoticed behind the noise floor if listening through studio monitors. In this context, *headphones* are a more conducive choice for music transcription. Specifically, closed-back headphone models can significantly *reduce* the audible *extraneous noise floor* surrounding the transcriptionist (Collins, 2020). Broadly established entry models for studio-grade closed-back headphones include the Sennheiser HD 280 Pro, Audio-Technica m50x, and Beyerdynamic DT 770 Pro.

Reference Tools

Each piece of heard music information must be compared against a reference before it can be transcribed. The purpose of using reference tools is to ensure that transcribed music information matches the recording. The prevalent elements to reference are pitch and tempo. *Pitch reference tools* include any pitched music instrument, whether acoustic, electric, or virtual. Several features are advantageous for pitch reference tools: First, *polyphonic*

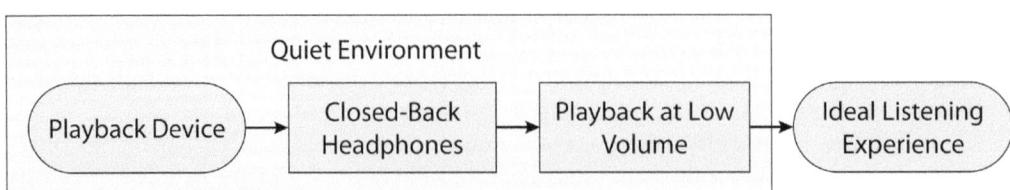

Figure 3.4 Listening quality.

instruments help reference voicings and chord qualities. Second, instruments with large pitch ranges help reference pitches in their actual octave registers. Finally, *non-transposing* pitch reference instruments may help reduce transposition errors when transcribing. By using a non-transposing reference instrument, transcriptionists can both reference and notate a pitch in concert key. All things considered, and in analogy to music theory applications, the *piano* is among the most recommended pitch reference tools (Schmeling, 2011a, 2011b).

As for *tempo referencing*, metronomes and beat mapping software are of note. Metronomes have been a cornerstone of instrumental practice and exist both as physical devices and software programs. The central metronome feature for transcription purposes is the *tap tempo function*. This feature allows tapping a button along the perceived beat to determine a passage's tempo. Some metronomes also calculate the *average tempo* based on the number and frequency of registered taps. Metronomes with a tempo tap feature are ideal for determining the tempo of passages with stable beats per minute (bpm). In contrast, tempo tapping produces less accurate results for passages with fluctuating bpm. In these cases, *beat mapping software* is a more suitable tool. Like tempo tap functionality, beat mapping includes identifying the beats in the selected passage. However, in addition to identifying an average bpm, beat mapping captures the timing of individual beats through beat markers (Piorkowski, 2023). Once the marking is complete, the program can calculate the tempo at any location in the passage and *visualize tempo developments*. Beat mapping functionality can be found in DAWs and Transcribe! In summary, both tempo tap and beat mapping functionality find ample application in music transcription. The choice between these two options depends on the source materials and transcription purpose.

Section Activities

1. Listen to a familiar music recording through a consumer-grade audio output device, then through studio monitor headphones. Also consider listening in quiet and noisy environments. How does your analytical listening experience change?
2. Given your skills and available resources, which reference instrument would you use and why? Which tempo reference tool would you use and why?

Industry Voice: A Personalized Setup

Andreas: What does your music transcription setup look like?

Chris: My preferred tools to notate music are my laptop and a piano keyboard. When I travel, I have a portable number pad, but at home, I have a bigger computer keyboard with a full number pad. I use the number pad to enter note values, and then I use the piano keys to enter pitches. But because I had to work without those tools so many times, I've become pretty fast at entering notes with just a regular laptop keyboard. Sometimes, I'll bring the piano keyboard and my number pad on the road, and I won't even use them, because it's just as fast to use the laptop keyboard. For those with developed piano skills though, it might be faster to just play notes on the piano keyboard, then arrange them in the notation software. I occasionally do that with chords.

Andreas: What workflow considerations are important when creating a sheet music template?

> *Chris:* The main considerations are having the part name and title at the top of the page, and the copyright at the bottom, all ready to go. There is a certain way that I've decided to place these, and I've kept it that way. Placing these text objects takes time, and if you have to do it every single time when you create a new score, that process becomes time-consuming. I just want the fonts and overall appearance set up and ready to go. I have a string quartet template that I use all the time and that allows me to get started quickly. I just put in the title, tempo and other basic information, and then it's ready to go. I use MuseScore.
>
> Chris McQueen – Guitarist and Arranger, Austin, TX
Snarky Puppy, Bokanté, Guitar Note Atlas app

Music Notation

The final part of a music transcriptionist's setup concerns music notation. In this context, music transcription is similar to speech transcription. Both transcription types require *tools to notate* what is heard. However, more importantly, tools are key to establishing an *effective workflow*.

For example, transcribing speech with pen and paper can be considered a dated practice in the context of emerging auto dictation features. Similarly, transcribing music with pen and paper is possible, but tends to take more time than computer-based notation. Based on ease of note entry, formatting, and flexible updates to parts and scores, *digital music notation* has become the prevalent way to notate music (Nicholl & Grudzinski, 2007).

Music Notation Software

Today's *industry standard* for paid music notation software includes Dorico, Sibelius, and Finale. This book acknowledges that Finale's developer has announced the discontinuation of Finale in August 2024. At the time of writing this edition, Finale is still considered a critical part of the music industry. All three notation software options provide *comprehensive functionality* and are used frequently on music industry projects of all scopes. A key difference lies in their *unique workflows*. Although the three programs can produce similar results, the steps and key commands necessary to achieve these results vary considerably between the options. The *learning curve* of these distinct workflows is a likely reason that musicians tend to learn only one of the three programs. However, exceptions exist: By trade, music copyists and engravers are likely to use two or more notation programs to fulfill their clients' needs (Maz, 2023). Chapter 14 explores advanced workflow concepts for music notation.

In music transcription, the *choice of notation software* depends on several factors. For practicality, transcriptionists tend to prefer notation software based on their experience with that software (Maz, 2023). However, the software *preferences of clients and collaborators* are equally important to consider. The industry purpose of music transcriptionists is to notate music quickly, so that musicians can use the sheet music. Some projects require using a specific notation program. Different *parts of the music industry* tend to prefer different notation programs. For example, musical theater productions have a historical preference for Finale. Conversely, Sibelius is slightly more anchored in the film-scoring industry.

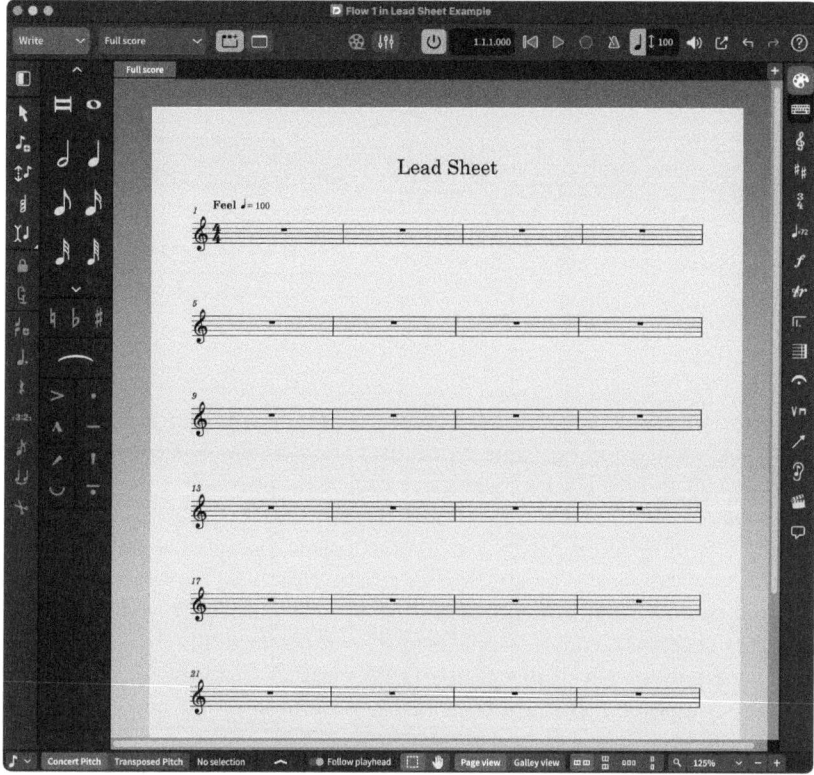

Figure 3.5 Dorico (2024) music notation software. Printed with permission of Steinberg Media Technologies GmbH.

Some transcriptionists specialize in one notation program, while others learn two or more programs. Both pathways can lead to ample industry opportunity. In summary, some transcription *opportunities remain contingent* on specific notation software, while others are more flexible.

Peripherals

Most steps in the transcription process involve using software. Therefore, hardware devices are critical to establishing an *effective workflow*. In the context of music transcription, the main hardware controllers include a computer keyboard and mouse. For a lack of more streamlined notation technology, music transcription is a *manual intensive process* that involves ample clicking and typing (Nowakowski & Hadjakos, 2023). The number of clicks and keystrokes per project adds up significantly, especially with projects of scale and extended work hours. To preserve long-term *hand and wrist health*, an ergonomic computer mouse and keyboard are recommended.

The major notation programs allow users to *enter notes* either step-by-step through a *computer keyboard*, or as a real-time recorded performance through a MIDI keyboard (Huber, 2020). When connected to the notation program, MIDI keyboards allow music note entry through a *physical piano interface*. Some users find MIDI keyboards a more

30 A *Music Transcription Method*

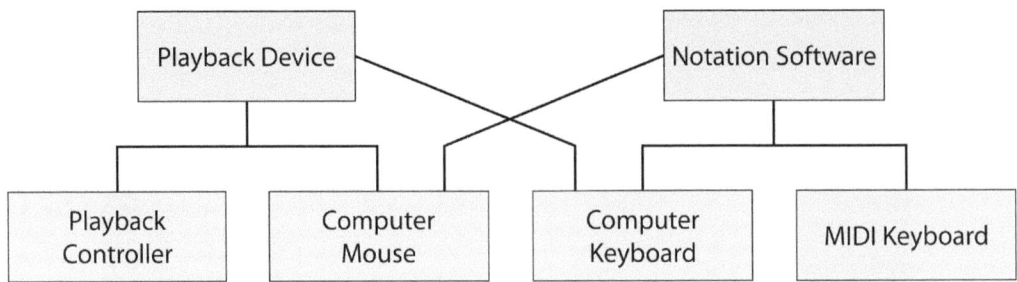

Figure 3.6 Peripherals in music transcription.

intuitive note-entry option than standard computer keyboards. Since note-entry workflows involve highly personal choices, transcriptionists should *experiment* with both MIDI and computer keyboards to find the most effective personal approach.

Finally, *playback controllers* allow transcriptionists to *save time navigating* audio sources. Music transcription requires a concurrent use of playback and notation software. Although both programs are typically within reach, switching between the programs manually interrupts the transcription process. A playback controller reduces the number of manual switches necessary and creates a *smoother workflow*. Playback controllers vary in shape and can be part of MIDI devices or DAW control surfaces. The playback program Transcribe! also supports transcription pedals, a technology commonly used in medical transcription, legal transcription, and similar fields (Diehl, 2012).

Section Activities

1. Research the use of notation programs in your part of the music industry. What trends, if any, do you recognize?
2. Experiment with different note-entry modes in your notation program. Do you prefer using only a computer keyboard or an additional MIDI keyboard? Why?

End-of-Chapter Activity

Applying everything you have learned in this chapter, create a detailed plan for your ideal personal transcription setup. Explain your thought process and choices.

Chapter Summary

This chapter covered source types, equipment, listening environments, reference tools, music notation software, and peripherals related to music transcription. Together, these components form a conducive digital transcription setup. While the book's method remains the same, transcription setups may require context-based adaptations. The section activities provided learner opportunities to explore factors influencing the choice of transcription setup components. Finally, the end-of-chapter activity provided an opportunity to synthesize the different decision-making processes by creating a personally relevant transcription setup.

Learning Outcomes

The learner should now be able to:

CO 1: Assess source materials, transcription equipment, and listening environments.
CO 2: Design a conducive music transcription work environment.

Up Next

Chapter 4 covers the outlining process of a transcription from single-file audio sources.

References

Benetos, E., Dixon, S., Duan, Z., & Ewert, S. (2019). Automatic music transcription: An overview. *IEEE Signal Processing Magazine, 36*(1), 20–30. https://doi.org/10.1109/MSP.2018.2869928

Borwick, J. (Ed.). (2001). *Loudspeaker and headphone handbook* (3rd ed.). Routledge. https://doi.org/10.4324/9780080496177

Collins, K. (2020). *Studying sound: A theory and practice of sound design*. MIT Press. ISBN: 978-0-262-36291-7

Collins, M. (2014). *In the box music production: Advanced tools and techniques for Pro Tools*. Routledge. https://doi.org/10.4324/9780203066362

Diehl, M. O. (2012). *Medical transcription: Techniques and procedures* (7th ed.). Saunders. ISBN: 978-1-437-70439-6

Dobrucki, A., Kin, M. J., & Kruk, B. (2017). Various aspects of auditory fatigue caused by listening to loud music. In S. Hatzopoulos (Ed.), *Advances in clinical audiology* (pp. 167–185). InTech. https://doi.org/10.5772/66203

Dorico (Version 5.1.70.2200) [Computer software]. (2024). Steinberg. https://www.steinberg.net/dorico/

Huber, D. M. (2020). *The MIDI manual: A practical guide to MIDI within modern music production* (4th ed.). Routledge. https://doi.org/10.4324/9781315670836

Huber, D. M., Caballero, E., & Runstein, R. (2023). *Modern recording techniques: A practical guide to modern music production* (10th ed.). Focal Press. https://doi.org/10.4324/9781003260530

Maz, A. (2023). *Music technology essentials: A home studio guide*. Focal Press. https://doi.org/10.4324/9781003345138

McGuire, S., & Matějů, Z. (2020). *The art of digital orchestration*. Focal Press. https://doi.org/10.4324/9780429345012

Nettl, B. (1964). *Theory and method in ethnomusicology*. Free Press of Glencoe. https://lccn.loc.gov/64016964

Nicholl, M., & Grudzinski, R. (2007). *Music notation: Preparing scores and parts*. Berklee Press. ISBN: 978-0-876-39074-0

Nowakowski, M., & Hadjakos, A. (2023). Estimating interaction time in music notation editors. *Proceedings of the 16th International Symposium on CMMR, Tokyo, Japan* (pp. 335–346). https://doi.org/10.5281/zenodo.10113069

Piorkowski, C. (2023). *Scoring to picture in Logic Pro: Explore synchronization techniques for film, TV, and multimedia composers using Apple's flagship DAW*. Packt Publishing. ISBN: 978-1-83763-689-1

Schmeling, P. (2011a). *Berklee music theory: Book 1* (2nd ed.). Berklee Press. ISBN: 978-0-87639-110-5
Schmeling, P. (2011b). *Berklee music theory: Book 2* (2nd ed.). Berklee Press. ISBN: 978-0-87639-111-2
Toole, F. (2017). *Sound reproduction: The acoustics and psychoacoustics of loudspeakers and rooms* (3rd ed.). Routledge. https://doi.org/10.4324/9781315686424

Transcribe! (Version 9.21.0) [Computer software]. (2022). Seventh String Software. https://www.seventhstring.com/

Part II
Process

Part Overview

Chapters 4, 5, 6, and 7 cover the procedural steps of transcribing recorded music by ear. Chapter 4 covers how to outline a transcription and retrieve global music information layers. Chapter 5 covers the transcription of foundational music information layers. Chapter 6 covers the transcription of dependent music information layers. Chapter 7 illustrates several process variants based on different source and target formats. In summary, Part II guides learners through the foundations of transcribing music by ear.

Learning Outcomes

After reading Part II, the learner will be able to:

BO 2: Analyze recorded music for transcription purposes.

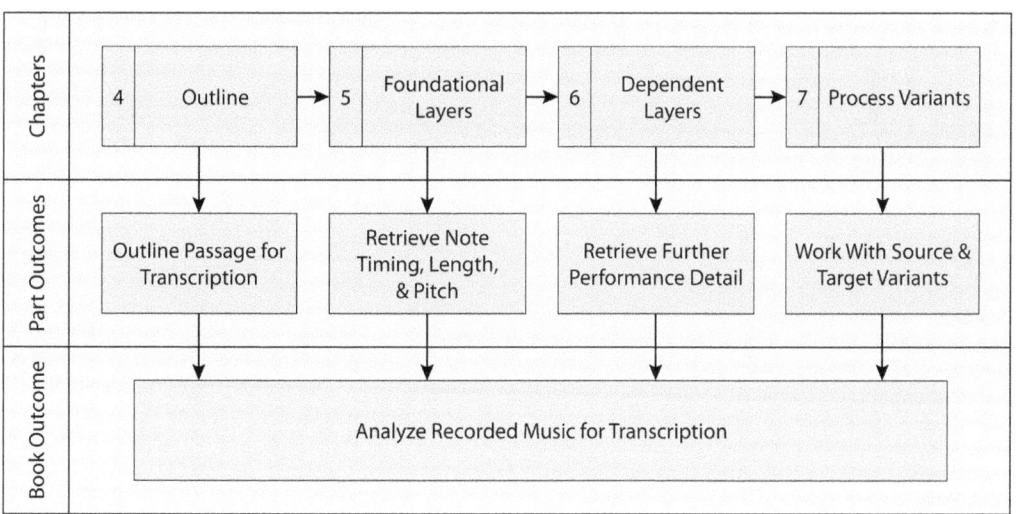

Figure 0.2 Part II map.

DOI: 10.4324/9781003511946-5

4 Outline

Chapter Overview

This chapter covers the procedural steps involved in planning and outlining a music transcription project. The first section discusses how to set a favorable transcription scope based on experience, arrangement complexity, and production quality. The second section then introduces six sheet music formats along with general guidance on selecting a purposeful format for a project. Finally, the third section covers the processes of metering the recording, analyzing global music information layers, and transferring that information to the sheet music file. The section activities help learners practice decision-making in this initial phase. In summary, this chapter explains the considerations for creating a strong fundament in the transcription process.

Learning Outcomes

After reading this chapter, the learner will be able to:

CO 1: Set the transcription scope and sheet music format.
CO 2: Retrieve global music information layers.

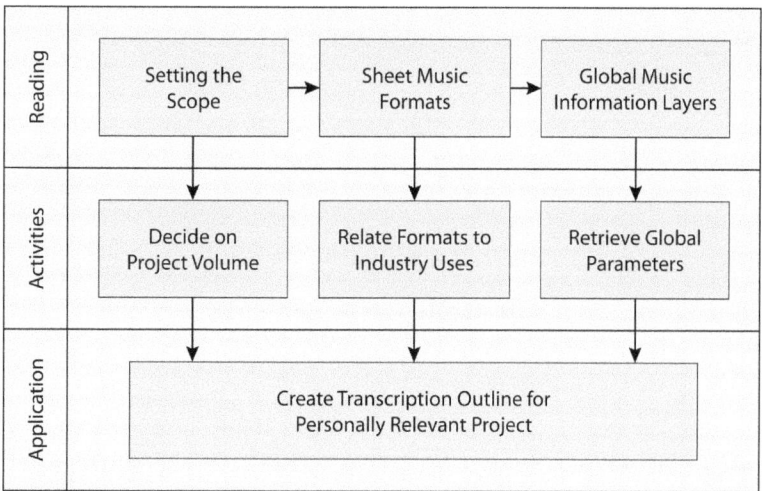

Figure 4.1 Chapter 4 map.

DOI: 10.4324/9781003511946-6

Setting the Scope

The transcription process starts with an *initial listen* to the recording. At this stage, the objective is to *familiarize* with the recording at a *general level*. For the initial listen, any compatible playback device is acceptable. During this initial listen, the transcriptionist should get a sense for the music style, instrumentation, performance quality, mix quality, and general audio quality. Notetaking is secondary. Rather, this general overview helps gauge the project's *scope and limitations*. Following the first listen, the transcriptionist should decide which passage to transcribe, and more specifically, which segments within that passage. This book refers to a passage as an excerpt of the recording. In turn, a segment represents one specific part of a passage that is played by one or several sound sources. The selection of a passage and segments determines the transcription scope. When deciding about a project scope, transcriptionists should factor in their experience with the craft, the complexity of the arrangement, and the recording's production quality (Gorow, 2002).

Transcription Experience

All calibers of transcriptionists will agree that *transcribing music* takes ample time, aural and analytical skills, technology literacy, and prolonged focus. In simple terms, music transcription is an *involved and demanding* activity (Poliner et al., 2007). A large project scope becomes overwhelming quickly, especially for beginning transcriptionists. That is because, in addition to a large workload, many of the skills required for transcription are developed while transcribing. For comparison, imagine a novice mountaineer with little experience attempting to climb Mount Everest.

For *beginning transcriptionists*, a reasonable scope may be just one segment of a few seconds length, with a clearly audible sound source. *Short segments* offer ample opportunity to practice listening and decision-making skills, with a reachable goal on the horizon. With *growing experience* and focus, transcriptionists may then gradually *increase the scope* of new projects, to include longer passages and more segments. Overall, an appropriate transcription scope helps maintain focus and productivity.

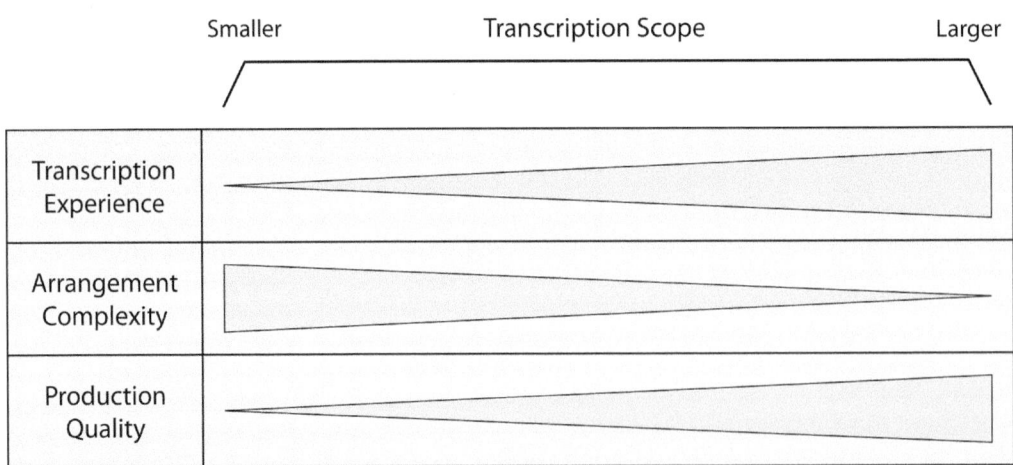

Figure 4.2 Conducive transcription scope.

Arrangement Complexity

Further to the project scope, the complexity of an arrangement also influences the time necessary to transcribe the recording. Naturally, the *more notes* that are played in a passage, the *more time is required* to analyze and notate that passage. For example, a simple melody will take fewer steps to transcribe than the same melody with added ornaments. Also, the more notes that are played concurrently, and the closer their pitches, the more time is required to locate and identify these notes. For example, a single melody takes fewer steps to transcribe than the same melody with harmonization.

Transcribing a *busy arrangement* with many segments and dense voicings requires an *ability to zoom in* and focus on one segment at a time. The ability to distinguish between segments of a busy arrangement develops gradually, with transcription mileage. Therefore, transcriptionists should factor in their *analytical listening skills* when deciding about a *project's scope*. Beginning transcriptionists should start by transcribing clearly audible segments from simple arrangements. With growing experience, transcriptionists may then gradually pursue less audible segments in more complex arrangements.

Production Quality

Further to arrangement complexity, the recording's production quality determines *how clearly music information* is *audible*. The most impactful factors through the production process include:

1. Arrangement quality: How intentional are the musical ideas organized?
2. Performance quality: How intentional did the recording musicians play?
3. Recording quality: How effectively was the performance captured?
4. Mix transparency: How discernible are the segments in the mix?
5. Audio quality: How favorable is the audio file resolution?

Each factor influences the recording's production quality, and therefore also the *time necessary* to locate and retrieve music information (Huber et al., 2023). Note that even just one aspect with *low production quality* will irreversibly *limit the transcription scope*. For example, poor arrangement quality will make it more difficult to discern music information, even if all other production aspects are of high quality. Similarly, a production with poor audio quality also limits the transcription scope, even if the remaining production is of top quality.

Commercially published music generally has favorable production quality standards. In this scenario, music information is *audible* as *clearly* as the style and technology allows. In contrast, it is more difficult to retrieve music information from projects that compromise production values. For example, an early demo recording may contain somewhat organized musical ideas, be performed casually, recorded when inspiration struck, and mixed minimally (Adams, 2016). The conditions in this scenario make it harder to locate played notes and to understand the organization of musical ideas. In summary, transcriptionists should *factor in* a recording's *production quality* when setting the transcription scope.

Section Activities

Select a music recording from YouTube or another music streaming platform:

1. Briefly analyze the arrangement complexity and production quality.
2. Based on your analysis and a self-assessment of your transcription skills, select a passage and one or more segments within to transcribe. Explain your choices.

Sheet Music Formats

After gaining an initial overview of the recording and solidifying the transcription scope, the time is right to *set up the music notation file*. This process includes selecting the sheet music format and customizing instrument staves as necessary. Several considerations should inform the choice of a sheet music format:

- Content: How many staves are necessary to accommodate the selected segments?
- Purpose: Will the transcription be performed as written, or processed further?
- Musicians' backgrounds: Which formats will the musicians read best?

This section covers six distinct sheet music formats as a starting point. Unless a project has specific requirements, it is not necessary to solidify the format at this stage. However, any advance planning helps streamline the transcription process.

Lyric Sheets

Simple charts are common in the *singer and songwriter* industry (Adams, 2016). Perhaps the simplest format is the lyric sheet. The lyrics replace the music notes and, therefore, are the foundational layer. Lyric sheets do not typically include rhythm or pitch information. However, they tend to include *chord symbols* as a harmonic guide. Some lyric sheets also include form labels and implied measure numbers. This format is suitable for musicians who prefer to read lyrics and chord symbols over note-by-note sheet music. Given their stylistic flexibility, lyric sheets are popular with *solo musicians* and *small ensembles*, but less suitable for coordinating larger ensembles.

Lead Sheets

Another format suitable for solo musicians and smaller ensembles is the lead sheet. *Melodies* and *slashes* are the format's foundational layers (Bouchard, 1999). Since lead sheets

Table 4.1 Characteristics of sheet music formats

	Main Content	*Purpose*	*Musicians' Backgrounds*
Lyric Sheet	Lyrics, chord symbols	Stylistically open guide chart	Singer-songwriters, non-readers
Lead Sheet	1 staff: Melody, lyrics, chord symbols, and slash notation	Stylistically approximate guide chart	Readers of groove-based styles
Arrangement	Full detail	Playability by specific line-up	Readers of specific styles
Particell	Full detail, condensed into smallest readable number of staves	Basis for analysis, arranging and orchestration	Arrangers and orchestrators of specific styles
Reduction	As much detail as can be accommodated by a smaller line-up	Playability by smaller line-up	Readers of specific styles
Master Rhythm Chart	2-3 staves: Melodies, voicings, groove, slash notation, cue notes	Navigation and stylistic guidance for rhythm section	Readers of groove-based styles

Intro

| Cm⁷   /B♭ | A♭⁷   G⁷ | Cm⁷   / B♭ | A♭⁷   G⁷ |

Verse 1A

| Cm⁷   /B♭ | A♭⁷   G⁷ | Cm⁷   A♭⁷ | G⁷ |
Fine looks, and   smart with books,   intelligent, classy and fun.

| Cm⁷   /B♭ | A♭⁷   G⁷ | Cm⁷   A♭⁷ | G⁷ |
Warm touch,   attracts much,   you better watch out hun.

Verse 1B

| Cm⁷   /B♭ | A♭⁷   G⁷ | Cm⁷   /B♭ | A♭⁷   G⁷ |
Stunning, the way you walk in the street, the way you rise from every defeat.

| Cm⁷   /B♭ | A♭⁷   G⁷ | N.C. | N.C.   G⁷ |
Marvelous you they   want to be,   think how you'll feel when your name's on the marquee.

Chorus

| Cm⁷   /B♭ | A♭⁷   G⁷ | Cm⁷   /B♭ | A♭⁷   G⁷ |
You've got it,   yeah, you've got it, you've got it all.

| Cm⁷   /B♭ | A♭⁷   G⁷ | Cm⁷   /B♭ | A♭⁷   G⁷ |
You've got it,   yeah, you've got it, you've got it all.

Example 4.1 Lyric sheet with chord symbols and barlines. Turner (2019), "You've Got It All," in *Ciao Bambino the Musical*. Transcribed by Andreas Häberlin. Printed with permission of Elizabeth Allen Turner.

consist of one staff, the space for secondary melodies, chords, and further note-by-note elements is limited. Therefore, *chord symbols* often summarize elements beyond the main melody. Lead sheets describe the arrangement in greater detail than lyric sheets, but still leave *room for creative freedom*. Lead sheets are popular in settings with *improvisation*. Perhaps the best-known collection of lead sheets is the Real Book series.

Master Rhythm Charts

Rhythm section players sometimes perform from a *one-size-fits-all format* to streamline their navigation as a group (Houghton et al., 1994). This format, known as a master rhythm chart, is common in groove-based music and includes two, or sometimes three staves. All performers playing from a master rhythm chart have exactly the same performance information available. The foundational layers include a combination of melodies, voicings, grooves, slash notation, and cue notes. Given the limited staff space, master rhythm charts *prioritize elements* by their *relevance to the work*. This chart type is popular with *groove-based music*. Chapter 7 covers master rhythm charts in more detail.

Example 4.2 Lead sheet. Turner (2019), "You've Got It All," mm. 1–28, in *Ciao Bambino the Musical*. Transcribed by Andreas Häberlin. Printed with permission of Elizabeth Allen Turner.

Example 4.3 Arrangement. Häberlin (2016), *The Dragon Apprentice*, mm. 93–98 (in concert key; woodwinds, percussion, and strings omitted).

Example 4.4 Particell. Häberlin (2020), *Funk Factory*, mm. 127–130 (in concert key; unpitched percussion omitted). Printed with permission of Molenaar Edition.

Arrangements

Perhaps the *most common format* in published sheet music is the arrangement. Arrangements contain dedicated performance instructions for each instrument involved in a musical work. In other words, *each instrument* has its *own part* to play. Line-ups can vary from solo instruments to full symphony orchestras. Arrangements shine through their *detailed performance instructions*, using all music information layers relevant to the work and style (Nestico, 2014). This format is used primarily for performances and recording sessions with a specific line-up. Based on project requirements, transcriptionists may choose to transcribe in detail one specific segment, a passage, or an entire work. Arrangements with rhythm section may also contain a master rhythm chart next to the other parts.

Particells

Similar to arrangements, particells capture a musical work in *rich notation detail*. However, in contrast to arrangements, the primary purpose of particells is to group arrangement elements into *as few staves as possible* (Sevsay, 2013). For example, a harmonized melody played by a three-piece trombone section would be presented on one staff instead of three. This presentation is not intended for performance, but *highlights* the work's *arrangement structure*. Particells are used primarily for music analysis and as a foundation to create an arrangement or orchestration.

Reductions

Finally, some industry scenarios require transcribing a work for a *smaller* line-up *than the original line-up* (Roberge, 1993). The format needed in these scenarios is called a reduction. When creating reductions, the goal is to *preserve the original work* as much as possible, while notating elements *in order of their importance* to the work. Given the limitations of the smaller line-up, some elements of the original work are unavoidably lost. Perhaps the most prominent reduction type is the piano reduction. It is used to substitute larger line-ups during rehearsals. Chapter 7 covers reductions in more detail.

Section Activities

1. Research several examples of the sheet music format you are least familiar with. How might these examples be relevant to the music styles they represent?
2. You are to create a playable transcription of a pop song for musicians you have worked with for a while. Which sheet music format will you use and why?

Global Music Information Layers

Once the transcription scope, playback device and sheet music format are solidified, it is time to retrieve the global music information layers. Global layers act as a *fundamental grid* for subsequent layers and, therefore, have a *significant impact* on the sheet music's *appearance*. It is recommended to spend enough time determining the global layers to build a solid fundament. The process starts with *metering the recording*, followed by retrieving the time signature and metronome mark, and finally the key signature. Note that global parameters

44 *A Music Transcription Method*

can change between sections of a passage or develop within the same section. This chapter covers constant global parameters, while Chapter 9 covers more advanced scenarios with evolving global parameters.

Metering

This first phase entails analyzing the passage's beats and measures. The goal is to determine the total number of measures and their location in the selected passage. In music with a broad appeal, conducive metering should fulfill *two criteria*: First, it should make the beats and measures *countable with ease* – any musician who reads the transcription should feel that it is intuitive to count; and second, the *shortest frequent note values* should be *no shorter than 16th notes* or their *tuplet equivalents* – 32nd notes and shorter values are more difficult to read, and their beams clutter the sheet music's visual appearance. The transcriptionist can control the length of note values by assigning a longer or shorter note value to the metronome mark.

Metering starts with *listening* to the passage's *pulse* and marking the main beats. The transcriptionist may *tap along* the playback with a hand or foot (Radley, 2016). According to Parncutt (1994), the clearest perceivable counting speed falls between 67–150 bpm. For transcription purposes, a conducive counting speed may widen this scope to 55–170 bpm. Values outside the recommended bpm range are less practical to count. If the counting speed falls outside that range, it is recommended to test counting at half or double the speed to fall within the practical range. Two additional guidelines help determine the counting speed: The first guideline is to *envision walking* at the speed of the main beats, taking *one*

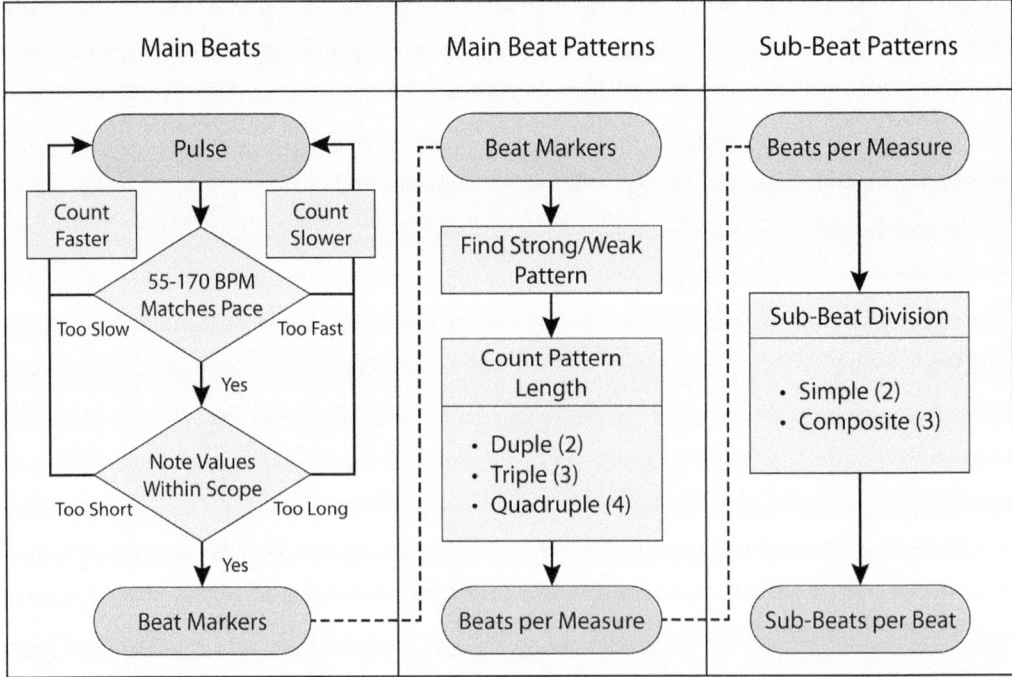

Figure 4.3 Three phases of metering.

footstep per beat – the walking speed should *match* the work's *perceived pace*; and second, the shortest frequent notes should be no shorter than a 6th of the main beat. This criterion reduces the number of short note values that may be impractical to read on paper. While these three guidelines may seem abstract at first, they set the stage for a transcription that is both well countable and readable.

After the main beats are determined, the next step entails finding *recurring patterns* of strong and weak main beats. The guiding concept is that strong beats mark the downbeats of new measures, while weaker beats mark the remaining beats in these measures. With this concept in mind, the transcriptionist should identify the *recurring strong beats* in the passage. This can be done by tapping along the established main beats and accentuating stronger beats. After determining the strong beats, the transcriptionist should then count the *length of recurring patterns*. Each pattern represents one measure and, therefore, should have a strong beat, followed by at least one weak beat. Music with a broad appeal often builds on duple meters, which include two and four-beat patterns, and triple meters, which include three-beat patterns (Kerman & Tomlinson, 2022). Note that this book frames four-beat patterns as quadruple meters. Transcriptionists may *count verbally* or use *conducting patterns* to determine the length of recurring beat patterns (Radley, 2016). Finally, strong beats should be entered as measure markers in Transcribe!, while weak beats should be entered as beat markers.

Once the recurring main beat patterns have been identified, the number and location of measures becomes apparent. To finalize the metering, the focus should shift to the *sub-beat patterns* of the main beats. The goal is to determine if the sub-beat patterns are in *simple or compound meter*. Similar to previous steps, sub-beats can be determined through *verbal counting* (Kerman & Tomlinson, 2022):

- Simple meter denotes a division into two sub-beats and is counted as *1 & 2 &*, and so on.
- Compound meter denotes a division into three sub-beats and is counted as *1 & a 2 & a*, and so on.

Note that, in *some passage*s, the decision between the two meters is *ambiguous*, for example if both simple and compound rhythms are present. In these passages, it is recommended to identify and select the *meter* that is *played more prominently* by the majority of instruments. Also note that swing feels are most often notated in simple meter.

Industry Voice: Laying the Groundwork

Andreas: How do you go about outlining a transcription?

Bob: I always use my ears. Basically, I listen to see if the recording is in duple or triple meter, and if the meter is simple or compound. Sometimes that's hard to figure out and you end up asking the client, "How do you want me to write this? It could be in 3/4 or 6/8." Meter is the first thing I listen for after all these years. Most pop songs are in a basic 4/4, and in that case, I just listen through once to get a feel for where the verses and choruses are, and the bridge, or anything that stands out. Then I usually just take down a chord chart and lay it out on the piano staff, or whatever

> the main instrument is. I'll go through the whole song and lay it out with meters, figure out any rubato parts, looking for anything that's different from a standard pop arrangement. I just lay it out in one part and then I'll fill in the other parts as I go. After I finish the main rhythm part, it's a lot easier to transcribe the rest. That's probably the biggest part of a takedown, just getting it laid out in the notation software you're using. It's also important to account for fermatas. You'll have to decide whether to write for a click track or not. In a click situation, you'll figure out the duration of the space, then insert the appropriate extra bar or beat. What I've learned over the years is that, if I'm having trouble hearing or figuring something out in the recording, everybody else will too. So, I just need to come up with a solution, regardless of what is actually "correct." My solution becomes the new "correct" and that solves the problem. Don't ever stay stuck!
>
> Boh Cooper – Keyboardist and Music Director, Nashville, TN
> *David Foster, Peter Cetera, Rascal Flatts*

Time Signatures and Tempo

With measures, main beat and sub-beat patterns clarified, the moment has arrived to construct the time signature and metronome mark. *Time signatures* are constructed based on the *main beat* and *sub-beat patterns* (Zolper, 2017). Each time signature is accompanied by a *corresponding* note value for the *metronome mark*. For simple meters, the note values of metronome marks commonly represent the time signature's denominator. For compound meters, the note values of the metronome mark are triple the denominator's value.

The transcriptionist may decide between time signatures that are *more common* for contemporary genres with broad appeal, and those that are *less common*. This *choice is discretionary*. The options presented in this chapter are mere suggestions for contemporary music with broad appeal. The intent behind these options is to support readability for a general audience. It is acknowledged that historical notation practices may have favored different combinations of time signatures and metronome marks, and that creatives of the present may have their own notation preferences (Grant, 2014).

Table 4.2 Basic time signatures in contemporary music with broad appeal

Meter Types	Duple (2 beats) Main Beat		Triple (3 beats) Main Beat		Quadruple (4 beats) Main Beat	
Simple						
More Common	2/2	half note	3/4	quarter note	4/4	quarter note
Less Common	2/4	quarter note	3/2	half note	4/8	eight note
Compound						
More Common	6/8	dotted quarter	9/8	dotted quarter	12/8	dotted quarter
Less Common	6/4	dotted half	9/4	dotted half	12/4	dotted half

Once the recording is metered, and once the time signature and beat value are selected, the *final step* is to determine the *metronome mark's bpm value*. Bpm values can be retrieved most accurately by analyzing the tempo in the metered playback session. In Transcribe!, the *compute tempo* function measures the average tempo of any selected passage. Transcribe! is ideal for calculating stable tempi, but less for determining fluctuating bpm values at specific locations. Conversely, conductor tracks in DAWs typically display the bpm value at specific locations, but are less designed to calculate average tempi.

Key Signatures

After the recording is fully metered, including time signatures and tempo, one global parameter remains to be transcribed. Key signatures help musicians *understand a work's tonal center* at a glance. *Well-placed* key signatures make the music *easier to read* and less cluttered visually. With the exception of the film scoring industry, most music styles with a broad appeal have adopted key signatures and benefit from them. Finding a passage's key signature requires listening to the pitches present, then determining which major or minor scale would best *represent* the sum of these *pitches diatonically* (Karpinski, 2000). A pitch reference tool is necessary for this task. The following two frameworks are recommended.

A great approach to *determine key signatures* is through *cadences*. In music with broad appeal, root tones of prominent chords tend to fall on a key's scale degrees (Fox & Weissman, 2013). Following this approach, the transcriptionist will *identify basic chord qualities*, then *relate these qualities* through scale degrees. For reference, Chapter 5 discusses strategies to determine chord qualities. As a simple example, the transcriptionist may identify the chord series F, B♭, C, and F. When related, these chords represent the scale degree sequence I–IV–V–I in the key of F major. The V–I resolution is a particularly helpful reference point as it describes two major chords whose roots are a perfect 5th away from each other. Many examples of cadences exist, both simple and complex. Also note that music with a broad appeal will often, but not always, start or end on the key's tonic.

Although many tonal works build on cadences, some use a *different harmonic framework*. For example, in minimalistic works, *harmony evolves gradually* over time, if at all. As another example, modal music builds more on scale modes than cadences (Mulholland & Hojnacki, 2013). If a search for cadences produces limited or no results, it is worth analyzing which *scales* are *present or approximated* in a passage. Next, the transcriptionist should determine which of the present scales or scale approximations is *most prominent*. That scale's accidentals are possible reference points for a key signature. In other cases, the music's tonal center may develop at such a quick pace that key signatures would be counterproductive to readability. For example, a change of key signature every four measures would likely be considered impractical. In these cases, key signatures may be omitted altogether. Finally, note that key signatures can always be revised at a later time, with a better understanding of the harmonic qualities present.

Transfer to Notation Software

Once the global music information layers are solidified, they can be transferred from the *playback device to* the *notation software*. The process starts with transferring the metering, followed by time signatures, metronome marks, and key signatures. This mainly functional consideration helps the transcriptionist *navigate effectively* between the *metered recording* and *sheet music file*. For example, if transcribing music from a specific measure, jumping to that measure in both playback and notation software becomes a more targeted effort. The transfer of global parameters to the notation software also establishes the project's bigger picture and allows targeting transcription segments more intentionally.

Section Activities

Listen to the online audio examples provided:

1. Meter the recording in Transcribe! Construct a time signature and corresponding metronome mark. Explain your process.
2. After metering the recording, also retrieve the key signature. Explain your decision-making process.

End-of-Chapter Activity

Applying everything you have learned in this chapter, select a personally significant music recording, then decide on a sheet music format, passage, and segment to transcribe. Next, meter the recording and retrieve the global parameters. Finally, set up a sheet music file and transfer the found global parameters to that file.

Chapter Summary

This chapter covered decision-making frames for project scopes, sheet music formats, and for retrieving global music information layers. Together, these components form the transcription outline. A thoughtful and intentional outline supports the countability and readability of the transcription. The section activities provided learner opportunities to explore decision-making during the outline phase. Finally, the end-of-chapter activity provided an opportunity to synthesize the different decision-making processes to create a transcription outline of a personally significant work.

Learning Outcomes

The learner should now be able to:

CO 1: Set the transcription scope and sheet music format.
CO 2: Retrieve global music information layers.

Up Next

Chapter 5 covers the transcription of foundational music information layers.

References

Adams, S. (2016). *The singer-songwriter's guide to recording in the home studio*. Berklee Press. ISBN: 978-0-876-39171-6
Bouchard, J. (1999). *Beginning rock keyboard*. Alfred Music. ISBN: 978-0-882-84979-9
Fox, D., & Weissman, D. (2013). *Chord progressions: Theory and practice for pianists: Everything you need to create and use chords in every key*. Alfred Music Publishing. ISBN: 978-0-739-07056-7

Gorow, R. (2002). *Hearing and writing music: Professional training for today's musician* (2nd ed.). September Publishing. ISBN: 978-0-962-94967-8

Grant, R. M. (2014). *Beating time & measuring music in the early modern era*. Oxford University Press. https://doi.org/10.1093/acprof:oso/9780199367283.001.0001

Häberlin, A. (2016). *The dragon apprentice* [Video]. YouTube. https://www.youtube.com/watch?v=fgq2juo76Pw

Häberlin, A. (2020). *Funk factory* [Instrumental]. Molenaar Edition. https://www.molenaar.com/details/1/20700/en

Houghton, S., Ranier, T., Viapiano, P., & Warrington, T. (1994). *The complete rhythm section*. Warner Bros. Publications. ISBN: 978-1-576-23990-2

Huber, D. M., Caballero, E., & Runstein, R. (2023). *Modern recording techniques: A practical guide to modern music production* (10th ed.). Focal Press. https://doi.org/10.4324/9781003260530

Karpinski, G. S. (2000). *Aural skills acquisition: The development of listening, reading, and performing skills in college-level musicians*. Oxford University Press. https://doi.org/10.1093/oso/9780195117851.003.0001

Kerman, J., & Tomlinson, G. (2022). *Listen* (10th ed.). W.W. Norton & Company. ISBN: 978-1-324-03944-0

Mulholland, J., & Hojnacki, T. (2013). *The Berklee book of jazz harmony*. Berklee Press. ISBN: 978-0-876-39142-6

Nestico, S. (2014). *The complete arranger* (Rev. ed.). Fenwood Music. ISBN: 978-1-502-74511-8

Parncutt, R. (1994). A perceptual model of pulse salience and metrical accent in musical rhythms. *Music Perception: An Interdisciplinary Journal*, 11(4), 409–464. https://doi.org/10.2307/40285633

Poliner, G. E., Ellis, D. P. W., Ehmann, A. F., Gomez, E., Streich, S., & Ong, B. (2007). Melody transcription from music audio: Approaches and evaluation. *IEEE Transactions on Audio, Speech, and Language Processing*, 15(4), 1247–1256. https://doi.org/10.1109/TASL.2006.889797

Radley, R. (2016). *Reading, writing and rhythmetic: The ABCs of music transcription*. Sher Music Co. ISBN: 978-1-883-21795-2

Roberge, M.-A. (1993). From orchestra to piano: Major composers as authors of piano reductions of other composers' works. *Notes*, 49(3), 925–936. https://doi.org/10.2307/898925

Sevsay, E. (2013). *The Cambridge guide to orchestration*. Cambridge University Press. ISBN: 978-1-107-02516-5

Turner, E. A. (2019). You've got it all [Song]. In *Ciao bambino the musical* [Unpublished manuscript].

Zolper, S. T. (2017). *The A to Z of music theory fundamentals: The ultimate workbook for music understanding*. Waveland Press. ISBN: 978-1-478-63296-2

5 Foundational Layers

Chapter Overview

This chapter covers the procedural steps and decision-making frames for transcribing pitch and rhythm. The first section covers the procedures for transcribing the timing, length, and pitch of individual notes. The second section then covers procedures for transcribing percussive, melodic, and harmonic note series, as well as slash notation. Finally, the third section covers a practical roadmap for transcribing foundational layers in order of difficulty. The section activities help learners decide which procedures to use in context to transcribe foundational layers. In summary, this chapter offers a framework for practitioners of diverse backgrounds to transcribe effectively based on their skills and general musicianship.

Learning Outcomes

After reading this chapter, the learner will be able to:

CO 1: Analyze note timing, length, and pitch in recorded music.
CO 2: Retrieve foundational music information layers.

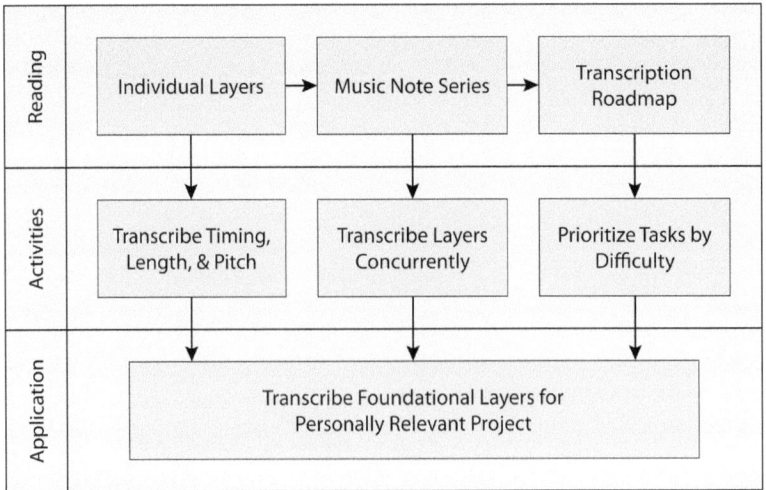

Figure 5.1 Chapter 5 map.

DOI: 10.4324/9781003511946-7

Individual Layers

Once a passage is outlined in both the playback and the notation file sessions, it is time to retrieve the foundational layers. This book defines foundational layers as note timing, length, and pitch. Together, these three layers describe the *basic parameters of notes played*. Although these layers can be transcribed one at a time, it is common to *transcribe* two or all three of them *concurrently*. For example, timing and length are transcribed concurrently for unpitched sound sources. As another example, all three layers are transcribed concurrently for melodies. In other words, all foundational layers relevant to the sound source are typically notated at once. This holds especially true with digital music notation. Given that notation software builds on MIDI functionality, note inputs require timing, length and pitch (Horton, 2022). This section summarizes music dictation approaches for each of the three layers.

Timing

In genres with broad appeal, the majority of note patterns have *perceivable rhythms*. Music transcription *frames the timing* of individual notes in these patterns. Because different rhythmical patterns often play concurrently, it is good practice to focus on the patterns of one sound source at a time. The following steps help determine note timing:

1. Select and play a short phrase on the playback device.
2. While listening, mark the main beats with one hand or foot.
3. At the same time, also mark the rhythmical patterns with a free hand or foot.
4. Dissect the rhythmical patterns through rhythm syllables.
5. Count each note's timing in relation to main beats and sub-beats.
6. Notate the rhythmical pattern.

Rhythm syllables are the prevalent strategy to break down rhythmical patterns into *countable units*. Musicians typically learn rhythm syllables during music theory or ear training courses. In context of transcription, musicians may recall internalized syllables and match them to the heard patterns. Several rhythm syllable systems exist, and preferences vary between cultures and musicians (Houlahan & Tacka, 2015). With *growing experience*, transcriptionists will increasingly *recognize rhythmical patterns intuitively*. At this later point, rhythm syllables take a background role and become more relevant for proofreading.

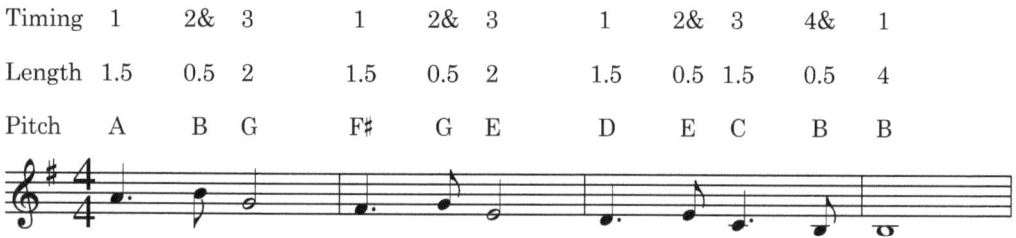

Example 5.1 Foundational layers. Häberlin (2024), *Reverie in G Major*, mm. 1–4, melody.

Length

Rhythm syllables establish the timing of notes and, for notes matching basic note values, also their length. However, it is important to understand that no rhythm system captures rhythmical detail exhaustively (Varley, 2005). One shortcoming is the absence of guidance on counting rests and tied-over notes. Although this absence is insignificant when reading sheet music, it creates challenges when transcribing sheet music. That is because transcriptionists must *determine* the *length of rests* and *tied-over notes* by ear. Perhaps the most practical system to count note endings is the Traditional American System (TAS), which numbers the beats and sub-beats in each measure. This system helps transcriptionists determine on which beat or sub-beat a note ending falls. The following steps are recommended:

1. Play the selected phrase, mark main beats, and use TAS rhythm syllables.
2. Focus on the ending portion of notes.
3. Count each note's ending in relation to main beats and sub-beats.
4. Transcribe the note, then adjust its duration to match the note ending.

Several practices affect the way that *note length* is notated. In a *basic scenario*, each note's length is written at its *full value*. In an orchestral context, notes with a longer natural decay may also be notated as basic note values with the instruction "let ring" (Sevsay, 2013). If note endings are prominent, they can be indicated through a dampening or choke symbol. This practice is particularly common with percussion instruments, but also with harp, piano, and pizzicato techniques. Chapters 6 and 10 cover length-based articulations in further detail.

Pitch

Most notes in genres with broad appeal include pitch. *Pitches* are transcribed for *individual notes*, *melodies*, *or harmony*. The process of determining pitch is similar to determining note timing and length, but requires *different analytical skills*. In fact, pitch and rhythm detection are two independent skills (Krumhansl, 2000). The following steps outline how to determine pitch:

1. Select and play a short phrase or a chord on the playback device.
2. While listening, match the heard pitches through vocalization. Vocalize in the closest possible octave register.
3. Determine the pitch of the first note. Using a pitch reference tool is helpful.
4. Analyze the remaining pitches. Using solfège and pausing playback is helpful.
5. Notate the pitches in their original octave register.

In Western music cultures, *solfège* is perhaps the most *established approach* to analyze pitches. Solmization is a strategy that *associates note pitches with syllables* and can be used to analyze intervals between notes (Andrianopoulou, 2019). After determining the first note's pitch, the transcriptionist may use solfège to *analyze the intervals* present in the phrase or chord. Once learned, solmization reduces the need for pitch reference tools and helps speed up the workflow of those with relative pitch. Two solfège systems are popular in Western music: *Fixed do* uses fixed syllables for pitches, while *movable do* labels pitches based on their position in the key's scale. Those transcriptionists with relative pitch should explore which system works best for them. Finally, those with perfect pitch may use any way to determine pitches, including their ability to name pitches directly.

Section Activities

Listen to the online audio examples provided:

1. How are note timing, length, and pitch relevant for each example?
2. Transcribe each example. Evaluate the effectiveness of your process.

Music Note Series

Transcribing *one note at a time* is time-consuming. Imagine counting the timing and using a pitch tool for every single note. Although possible, this approach *slows down the process*. The approach also treats notes individually, rather than as phrases or chords. For both, *workflow and musical reasons*, notes should be *transcribed as series* whenever possible. Transcribing note series helps interpret individual notes in their surrounding context (Gorow, 2002). Short series of a few notes are ideal for this purpose. Longer phrases become less memorable, which makes them more difficult to transcribe as a note series.

Throughout their journeys, musicians *familiarize with* a growing number of *musical phrases* and chords. When transcribing, musicians will *match the heard music to the* phrases and chords they already know. The process can be intentional or subconscious. If the transcriptionist is already familiar with a heard music note series, the series may reveal itself and can be *transcribed without further analysis*. Naturally, those with more mileage in music know more phrases. In this context, transcription gradually becomes more intuitive with growing aural skills (Cleland & Dobrea-Grindahl, 2020). This section offers strategies to transcribe music as note series.

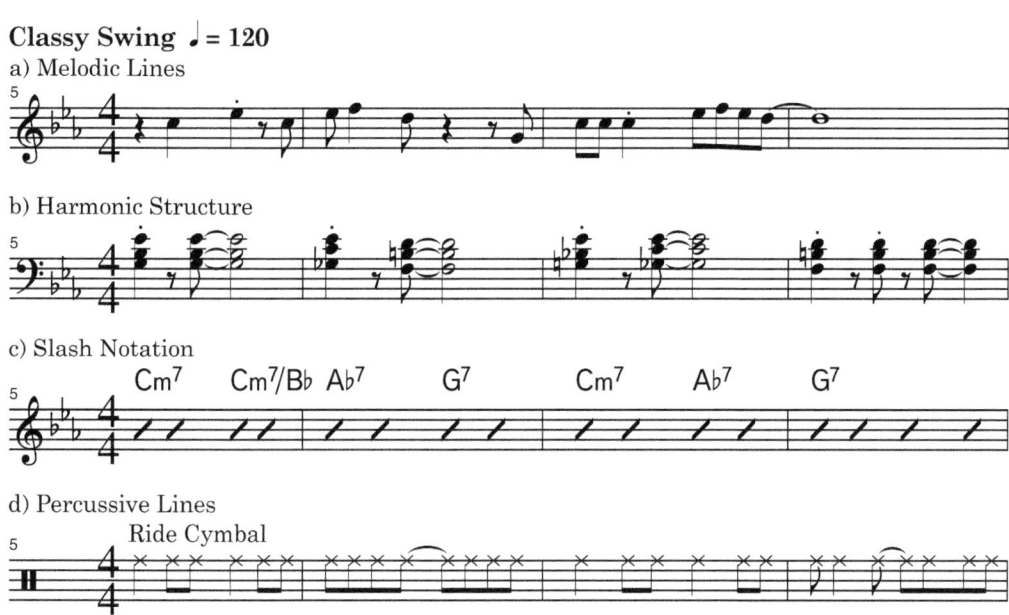

Example 5.2 Transcribing music note series. Turner (2019), "You've Got It All," mm. 5–8, in *Ciao Bambino the Musical*. Transcribed by Andreas Häberlin. Printed with permission of Elizabeth Allen Turner.

54   A Music Transcription Method

Percussive Lines

Instruments without a defined pitch are notated primarily by their *note timing* and *note length*. These instruments include acoustic drums, electronic drums, as well as unpitched percussion for bands, orchestras, and ethnic percussion. *Pitch information* for unpitched percussive instruments typically only describes the instrument's *approximate register*, for example high tom or low tom. Therefore, individual unpitched instruments are typically notated on the same line or space in the percussion staff (Sevsay, 2013). The following steps help transcribe percussive lines:

1. Listen to the selected phrase.
2. Analyze note timings for the phrase.
3. Analyze note lengths as necessary. Check for rests and potentially tied-over notes.
4. Transcribe both note timing and length for each note in the phrase.

For continuity, the preceding instructions summarize the referencing and marking necessary to transcribe these layers. Note that the steps to transcribe note timing and length remain the same. However, when transcribing note series, both *timing and length* should be *analyzed before* the *series is notated*.

Melodic Lines

Perhaps the *most memorable music elements* for the general public are melodies. Melodies are monophonic note series that are often exposed and performable with reasonable efforts. These characteristics explain, at least in part, why melodies tend to be memorable (Halpern & Bartlett, 2010; Perricone, 2000). Transcriptionists may use *melodic memorability* to their *advantage*. Melodies are transcribed like percussive lines, but with added pitch information. To transcribe melodies, one should:

1. Listen to the selected phrase.
2. Analyze the following two in the order preferred:
   a. Note timings and note lengths in the phrase.
   b. The pitch of each note in the phrase.
3. Transcribe note timing, length, and pitch for each note in the phrase.

Given that note timing, length, and pitch are transcribed concurrently, transcribing melodies takes slightly more effort than percussive lines. Rhythm and pitch can be analyzed in any order preferred by the transcriptionist. *Findings* of rhythm and pitch analyses *should be memorized*, then *transcribed together*. Overall, these steps apply to lead melodies, secondary melodies, basslines, and generally any distinguishable monophonic lines with rhythm and pitch.

Industry Voice: Breaking into Broadway

Andreas: When did you first get started transcribing, and what was it like?
Erin: I didn't get started in transcription until I started writing my own music. And I realized that you have to transcribe what's on your mind. Part of my

> writing skill is actually notation. So I notate as I write, but that's not everybody's process. Some people play their instrument instead. I use notation as part of my skill, because I'm not a piano player. Then I got further into that world, which led me to start working on other people's projects, people who don't notate, which is actually the most common for Broadway. Transcription is a totally separate skill from writing. And so I come in when the writers feel that they have a good draft. Someone will hire me to write down the first draft of the score. That's basically how you break into what I do in the Broadway industry. You talk to several music directors, and usually your first chance will be transcribing a score for a week-long workshop or similar. So my first chance in the industry was to notate a score from a voice memo with an out-of-tune piano.
>
> *Andreas:* What parts of the craft have become easier for you over time?
>
> *Erin:* I think what's become easier is melodic retention. I used to be able to remember only a bar of music at a time for the melody. I would listen to it once or twice to get it in my ear, then sing or play it back, and I would notate it from there. Today I can retain, depending on the meter, four to eight bars from one or two listens. You'll notate that, then go back and listen. If everything's correct, you can move on to the next phrase. So I think the ability to memorize longer chunks of music in short-term memory makes the process easier, because you don't have to continually listen back to the recording. You can hear it, write it down, and move on. The more you have to listen to something, the longer it's going to take you, because music is time.
>
> Erin J. Reifler – Music Assistant, NYC
West Side Story, The Great Gatsby, Shucked

Harmonic Structure

The *most sophisticated note series* to transcribe are vertical pitch series, commonly referred to as chords. Chords consist of several notes with *different pitches played concurrently*. Two aspects are noteworthy. First, distinguishing individual notes from a chord is a more involved task (Radley, 2016). For comparison, imagine trying to discern one speaker from a large group of speakers. Second, although chord tones are played concurrently, they can only be vocalized one at a time. The following steps help transcribe harmonic structure:

1. Listen to the selected chord.
2. Match the chord's bottom and top notes through vocalization.
3. Determine the pitches of both notes. Using a pitch reference tool is helpful.
4. Transcribe the two notes.
5. Locate the chord tones between the bottom and top notes. Using solfège is helpful:
    a. Test sing suspected notes to determine if they are present.
    b. Or test play suspected notes on a keyboard, together with established notes.
6. Transcribe the internal chord tones.

Chord series can also be *transcribed more sequentially*: Using the *melodic lines approach*, transcribe the most prominent note of each chord in the sequence. Then repeat the *harmonic structure steps* for each chord in the sequence to determine its remaining notes. Finally, identifying harmonic intervals is considered difficult primarily because the inner chord tones tend to be quieter or otherwise less discernable than the outer chord tones. That is why bottom and top notes are considered great starting points to determine chord voicings (Radley, 2008).

Slash Notation

In some scenarios, music segments are transcribed as *approximate guidelines* rather than detailed instructions. This is common for parts that include improvisation, for example, solos or accompaniment parts. The standard way to convey these guidelines is slash notation, accompanied by chord symbols and textual performance instructions (Feist, 2017). Slash notation differentiates between time and stop time slashes. *Time* describes a groove with a *degree of improvisation* that follows harmonic and rhythmic guidelines. Conversely, *stop time* describes hits with *fixed timing and length* that follow harmonic guidelines. Both time and stop time slashes use chord symbols as guidance, but leave the *choice of voicings* up to the performers. The following steps help transcribe slash notation:

1. Select a passage with a groove or solo.
2. To start, mark the corresponding sheet music part with slashes.
3. Play back the passage and listen out for any prominent synchronized hits.
4. Mark these hits with *stop time* slashes.
5. Add chord symbols and textual performance instructions.

The selected segment should be describable through *basic chord symbols*. Note that chord symbols are limited to *simplified summaries of actual voicings* (Chen et al., 2020). Chord symbols may occur every few measures or beats, but, for readability, should change no more than one to three times per measure. If a passage's harmonic qualities change on every beat or sub-beat, that passage will be more readable if transcribed note by note. Also note that Chapter 6 covers chord symbol transcription, and Chapter 7 covers slash notation for rhythm charts.

Section Activities

Listen to the online audio examples of the note series provided:

1. Which strategy would you use to transcribe each series?
2. Transcribe each example. Evaluate the effectiveness of your process.

Transcription Roadmap

It is common to feel unsure how to start transcribing foundational layers. Each transcription project is different and provides *many possible starting points*. A large amount of music information can become overwhelming quickly (Sikora, 2022). To maintain personal motivation and a sense of direction, it is helpful to *prioritize elements* that are transcribable within reasonable time. A proven strategy is to transcribe the *most audible elements first*, then gradually move on to the less audible elements. The most audible elements are usually those *perceived most intuitively* by the listener. Transcribing the most audible elements first creates a solid foundation to which any less audible elements can be added gradually.

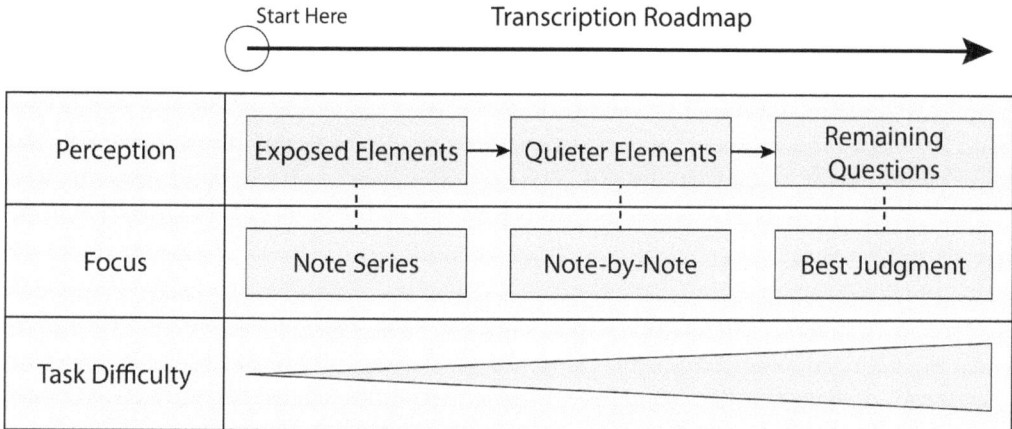

Figure 5.2 Prioritizing tasks by difficulty.

Exposed Elements

Different musicians tend to intuitively *listen to different elements* in the same music recording. This holds true even if elements in a recording are similarly exposed. For example, a vocalist might intuitively listen to vocal melodies, while a bass player might focus on a recording's bassline. Of course, these habits are only stereotypical tendencies, and the same musicians may very well notice other elements first. However, with the natural tendencies in mind, it is recommended to listen to the selected passage, identify the *most prominent element* and *transcribe it first*. Often, but not always, these most prominent elements are exposed melodies or percussive lines.

Individual listening preferences are secondary, as long as the chosen first element is clearly audible to the transcriptionist. With *growing experience*, transcriptionists become more *actively aware* of other audible elements in recordings (Wallace, 2014). With that awareness comes the ability to *choose elements* to transcribe *more intentionally*. After notating the most prominently heard element, the transcriptionist can proceed with the next most prominent audible element. The process is repeated until all relevant exposed elements are transcribed.

Quieter Elements

Sooner or later, every transcriptionist reaches a point where the *remaining elements* to be transcribed become *ambiguous* (Sikora, 2022). This moment is accompanied by uncertainty about the heard elements. It may be unclear which pitches or rhythms are present in a segment. It may even be unclear if certain instruments are played at all. This situation is *completely normal* in music transcription and is no reason for concern. Instead, the situation marks an *opportunity for developing* one's listening skills further. Elements can be difficult to discern for several reasons, including:

- Some notes are played quieter than others.
- A sound source is mixed at a low volume.
- A sound source is panned to the side.
- The mix in the selected passage is busy.
- The notes are encapsulated in dense voicings.

Once this point is reached, it is recommended to *examine* the quieter elements at a *slower pace* and with *increased focus*. Instead of analyzing one phrase or chord at a time, it may be helpful to analyze one note at a time. It may also be worth slowing down the recording to magnify individual notes even further. Both strategies slow down the transcription pace and take more time. However, these strategies allow a *closer examination* of elements that would otherwise be difficult to discern.

Remaining Questions

Even when transcribing segments one note at a time, *some elements* may *remain ambiguous*. Transcriptionists will encounter this situation during all stages of their careers. The situation is very common, and there is no ground for concern if some elements do not reveal themselves. Perhaps the most common reason is that some elements are masked in the mix and cannot be discerned sufficiently by ear (Hepworth-Sawyer & Hodgson, 2016). This is a natural limitation. Another common reason is a transcriptionist's unfamiliarity with the instruments and style in question. Transcription experience grows gradually, when successfully transcribing unfamiliar styles, instruments, or patterns. Whenever ambiguous transcription segments remain, it is important to *accept* that some music information *cannot be reliably retrieved* in that moment.

At this point, the transcriptionist has *two options*. The first option is to complete missing information through a *simplified interpretation* of what notes might be present (Klapuri & Davy, 2006). This approach is common with arrangers who are looking to complement missing information with arrangement techniques. The second option is to interpret any audible traces on the recording and *notate the suspected notes*. This forensic approach is more common with those transcriptionists who value a note-by-note representation of a recorded work. Overall, option one prioritizes practicality and legibility while option two prioritizes original detail.

Section Activities

Select and listen to a familiar music recording:

1. Which elements stand out to you the most?
2. Which elements do you find difficult to hear clearly?

End-of-Chapter Activity

Applying everything you have learned in this chapter, build on the transcription outline you created during the final activity in Chapter 4. Using the techniques and roadmap discussed, transcribe all foundational layers in the selected segment.

Chapter Summary

This chapter covered the transcription of individual layers, music note series, and a roadmap for retrieving foundational music information layers. To produce timely results, it is helpful to start transcribing the most clearly audible elements first, followed by less distinguishable elements. Whenever practical, it is recommended to transcribe notes series rather than individual notes. The section activities provided learner opportunities to practice transcription and self-evaluation related to foundational layers. Finally, the end-of-chapter activity provided an opportunity to transcribe the foundational layers of a personally significant music recording.

Learning Outcomes

The learner should now be able to:

CO 1: Analyze note timing, length, and pitch in recorded music.
CO 2: Retrieve foundational music information layers.

Up Next

Chapter 6 covers the transcription of dependent music layers.

References

Andrianopoulou, M. (2019). *Aural education: Reconceptualising ear training in higher music learning*. Routledge. https://doi.org/10.4324/9780429289767
Chen, T.-P., Fukayama, S., Goto, M., & Su, L. (2020). Chord jazzification: Learning Jazz interpretations of chord symbols. *Proceedings of the 21st International Society for Music Information Retrieval Conference* (pp. 360–367). https://doi.org/10.5281/zenodo.4245444
Cleland, K. D., & Dobrea-Grindahl, M. (2020). *Developing musicianship through aural skills: A holistic approach to sight singing and ear training* (3rd ed.). Routledge. https://doi.org/10.4324/9780429020230
Feist, J. (2017). *Berklee contemporary music notation*. Berklee Press. ISBN: 978-0-876-39178-5
Gorow, R. (2002). *Hearing and writing music: Professional training for today's musician* (2nd ed.). September Publishing. ISBN: 978-0-9629496-7-8
Häberlin, A. (2024). *Reverie in G major* [Unpublished manuscript].
Halpern, A. R., & Bartlett, J. C. (2010). Memory for melodies. In M. Riess Jones, R. Fay, & A. Popper (Eds.), *Music perception*. Springer handbook of auditory research, 36 (pp. 233–258). Springer. https://doi.org/10.1007/978-1-4419-6114-3_8
Hepworth-Sawyer, R., & Hodgson, J. (Eds.). (2016). *Mixing music*. Routledge. https://doi.org/10.4324/9781315646602
Horton, P. (2022). The evolution of music notation software. In A. Sutherland, J. Southcott, & L. de Bruin (Eds.), *Revolutions in music education: Historical and social explorations*. Lexington Books. ISBN: 978-1-66690-705-6
Houlahan, M., & Tacka, P. (2015). *Kodály today: A cognitive approach to elementary music education* (2nd ed.). Oxford University Press. ISBN: 978-0-190-23577-2
Klapuri, A., & Davy, M. (Eds.). (2006). *Signal processing methods for music transcription*. Springer New York. https://doi.org/10.1007/0-387-32845-9
Krumhansl, C. L. (2000). Rhythm and pitch in music cognition. *Psychological Bulletin, 126*(1), 159–179. https://doi.org/10.1037/0033-2909.126.1.159
Perricone, J. (2000). *Melody in songwriting: Tools and techniques for writing hit songs*. Berklee Press. ISBN: 978-0-634-00638-8
Radley, R. (2008). *The "real easy" ear training book: A beginning/intermediate guide to hearing the chord changes*. Sher Music. ISBN: 978-1-883-21761-7
Radley, R. (2016). *Reading, writing and rhythmetic: The ABCs of music transcription*. Sher Music. ISBN: 978-1-883-21795-2
Sevsay, E. (2013). *The Cambridge guide to orchestration*. Cambridge University Press. ISBN: 978-1-107-02516-5

Sikora, F. (2022). *Jazz harmony: Think – Listen – Play – A practical approach*. Schott Music. ISBN: 978-3-795-74930-9

Turner, E. A. (2019). You've got it all [Song]. In *Ciao bambino the musical* [Unpublished manuscript].

Varley, P. C. (2005). *An analysis of rhythm systems in the United States: Their development and frequency of use by teachers, students, and authors; and relation to perceived learning preferences* [Doctoral dissertation, University of Missouri]. UMSL Graduate Works. https://irl.umsl.edu/dissertation/622

Wallace, R. (2014). *Take note: An introduction to music through active listening*. Oxford University Press. ISBN: 978-0-195-31433-5

6 Dependent Layers

Chapter Overview

This chapter covers the procedural steps and decision-making frames for transcribing dependent music information layers. The first section covers procedures for transcribing dependent layers associated with individual notes and short patterns. The second section then covers procedures for transcribing dependent layers associated with phrases and sections. Finally, the third section covers a roadmap for practitioners to transcribe dependent layers while ensuring an effective workflow and transcription consistency. The section activities help learners transcribe dependent layers as relevant in their respective contexts. In summary, this chapter offers guidance for practitioners to enhance transcribed foundational layers with additional performance instructions and nuance.

Learning Outcomes

After reading this chapter, the learner will be able to:

CO 1: Analyze dependent music information layers associated with notes, phrases, and sections.
CO 2: Retrieve dependent music information layers.

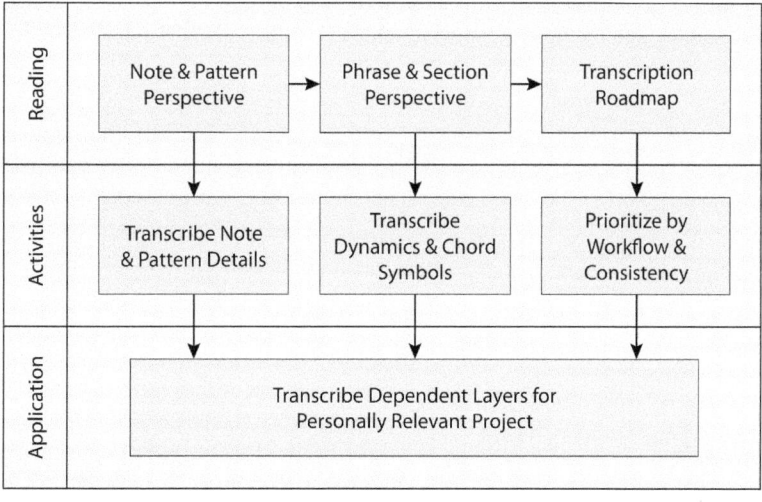

Figure 6.1 Chapter 6 map.

DOI: 10.4324/9781003511946-8

Note and Pattern Perspective

Rhythm and pitch form the foundation of music notes. They describe when a note is to be played and what its primary frequency is. Building on these foundational layers, several *further parameters* affect the way in which notes and patterns are notated. For example, individual notes are performed with different emphasis, length, and developing pitch. As another example, certain note series are grouped as ornaments to indicate which pitches are to be played, and at what pace (Feist, 2017). Finally, lyrics shape the character of vocal parts. This section covers *articulations, ornamentation,* and *lyrics*. Note that Chapter 11 covers dependent layers more specific to instruments and timbre.

Transcribing *dependent layers* requires a familiarity with their sound and common notation. Without knowledge of articulations or ornaments, a transcriptionist may not recognize these layers, or may feel unsure how to notate them. Also, transcriptionists unfamiliar with vocal notation practices may be unsure how to notate lyrics. Similar to the journey of arrangers and orchestrators, a great way to *familiarize with the sound* of dependent layers is through *score study* (Nestico, 2014). Specifically, transcriptionists should listen to published recordings while following the corresponding score. While listening, transcriptionists should analyze the sound and notation of articulations, ornaments, and lyrics. Note that score study for dependent layers requires sheet music that matches the recording note by note.

Articulations

Beyond rhythm and pitch, each *individual note* is performed with a certain *emphasis and intent*. Some notes blend into their phrase while others stand out, not through their timing or main pitch, but through the way they are articulated (Gould, 2011). For comparison, imagine a photograph showing a group of friends. Some friends have similar haircuts, while others have unique haircuts. The photograph captures the variety of these haircuts. In analogy, articulation symbols capture the similar and unique *characteristics of neighboring notes*. This book covers three articulation aspects:

- Emphasis: A note's initial attack strength in context.
- Length: A note's actual duration in relation to its note value.
- Pitch: Any changes to the note's main pitch over time.

Articulations can be combined across different aspects (Fetherolf, 2019). For example, a note may be played with distinct emphasis, held specifically for its full duration, and fall in pitch. Some combinations even have their own symbols. The articulation shading subsection in Chapter 10 (pp.117–118) covers several common combinations. In summary, articulation symbols can be used to capture those characteristics that *make a note stand* out from its immediate context. Note that this section covers a general overview of articulations. This book acknowledges that further articulations exist, and that different parts of the music industry interpret articulations based on their culture of practices.

Further to describing individual notes in more detail, *purposefully placed articulations* also *increase* the sheet music's *readability*. Perhaps most importantly, length articulations communicate note durations with increased granularity while keeping note values visually simple. Length articulations can be used to simplify the duration of shorter note values. Furthermore, it is also more effective and accurate to capture note emphasis primarily through accents rather than dynamic marks. That is because emphasis describes the note's initial attack strength, while dynamic marks describe the overall volume present.

Ornamentation

Western music notation recognizes certain *series of music notes* as ornaments (Bonnici et al., 2018). These note series are considered common building blocks in Western music. Ornaments are *notated prescriptively*, in visually simplified ways, to make them *recognizable by the reader*. Two categories are worth mentioning: First, several ornament types condense recognizable note series into abbreviated notation – examples include trills, tremolos, and mordents; and second, several ornament types streamline the appearance of rhythmic patterns – popular examples include grace notes and arpeggios. Overall, purposefully placed ornaments *increase readability* and help musicians understand the sheet music more intuitively.

Transcribing ornamentation entails *recognizing heard patterns* as ornaments. Therefore, the transcriptionist must be familiar with the different ornaments, their sound, and how they are notated. For comparison, imagine spotting a circle shape and drawing it without knowing what a circle is. Learning how to recognize and notate ornaments is a skill that grows with stylistic experience and general musicianship. It is *common to revise* transcribed

Emphasis				Marcatissimo
Label	None	Accent	Marcato	Marcatissimo
Intensity	None	Some	Ample	Maximum
Length				
Label	Tenuto	Neutral	Staccato	Staccatissimo
Duration	Full, With Intent	Full	Short	Very Short
Pitch				
Label	Fall	Doit	Plop	Scoop
Direction	Down	Up	Down	Up
Note Portion	Ending	Ending	Start	Start

Figure 6.2 Matrix of common articulations and their sound.

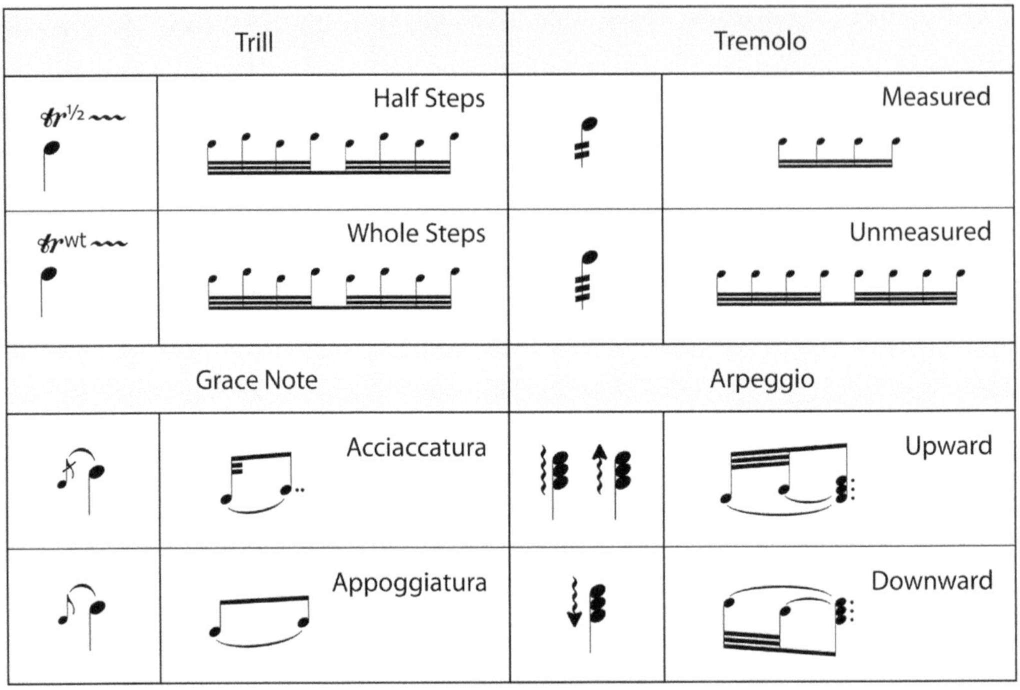

Figure 6.3 Common ornamentations and their sound.

note series and determine whether the *most appropriate choice* is ornamentation or literal notation. In analogy with broader readability guidelines, ornamentation is best used if its presence helps *convey note patterns with clarity* (Gould, 2011).

Lyrics

Another dependent layer associated with individual notes or patterns are lyrics. Lyrics are different from narrated text in that they are *anchored rhythmically*. They may be sung, spoken, or a mix of both. The transcription process is very similar to text-based dictation. Transcriptionists listen to short phrases at a time and notate the heard words. In addition, each *syllable* must be *allocated* to its *corresponding note or phrase*. When transcribing lyrics, the listening focus falls on *phonetics* (Nowacka, 2023). The goal is to recognize each word as a whole, and to determine each syllable's timing and length. During this process, it is common to make rhythmical and tonal adjustments to the vocal melody, so that it aligns with the lyrics.

Whenever *written lyrics are available*, it is recommended to reference these while transcribing. Some transcriptionists may take for granted the ability to understand heard lyrics phonetically. However, several factors impact how well heard lyrics are understood. First, a recording's production quality determines the clarity at which recorded words were spoken and mixed (Moylan, 2020). Second, language proficiency determines one's ability to understand lyrics phonetically. For commercially published music, lyrics are often available in *online databases*. In other cases, *clients or collaborators* may have written lyrics available. While referencing available lyrics, transcriptionists should *watch out for any discrepancies* between available and heard lyrics.

Section Activities

Examine the online audio and corresponding sheet music examples provided:

1. Add any articulations that you feel will enhance the reader's understanding of the transcription.
2. Circle and name any ornaments you can identify.

Phrase and Section Perspective

Some dependent layers apply more to individual notes and short patterns, while others apply more to selections with longer durations. Often but not always, dynamics are associated with *phrases and sections*. In genres with broad appeal, dynamic markings capture the *overall dynamics* and *dynamic developments* present in a section. Chord symbols are another layer relevant to phrases and sections. *Chord symbols summarize* the *harmonic qualities* present in the selection (Chen et al., 2020). This section covers the transcription of dependent layers associated with sections and phrases.

Similar to the layers discussed earlier, transcribing phrase and section-based layers requires a *familiarity* with their *sound and underlying theory*. To familiarize with dynamics, the transcriptionist may again listen to a published orchestral recording while following its conductor score (Sevsay, 2013). It is recommended to absorb the sound of different dynamic marks, as well as *crescendo*s and *diminuendo*s. In contrast to dynamics, chord symbols require a more abstract understanding of harmony. The associated skills are perhaps best learned as part of formal music theory and ear training courses.

Industry Voice: Capturing the Sound of an Era

Andreas: How do you approach transcribing dynamics and articulations?
Greg: There's a big debate about over-articulating music and under-articulating it. I think part of that debate depends on the style of the time. Truthfully, where we are now in the scoring world, everything is kind of quiet sounding and sustained, with very little vibrato. There's a lot more texture like circular bowing, sul ponticello, and sul tasto. I think technology affects how composers are writing, because of the sample libraries that are coming out. We didn't really see these string effects five or ten years ago, but now we're hearing them a lot more often. People are using them in different ways, and the way to transcribe articulations now has a lot to do with the way that composers are writing. On one side, you've got the very minimalist music that doesn't really use a lot of articulations. This side is really about pads and soundscapes. The other side is more like John Williams, with intricate articulations that never repeat the same way. John likes to write the phrase one way the first time it happens, then modify it every following time. This practice can lead to a lot of questions with musicians. Music preparation houses are basically training people to look for patterns, but in this instance, you're then asking them to ignore these very patterns. It's really difficult to know which road to take. There are so many different

66 *A Music Transcription Method*

> ways to notate ideas that it really does bleed into transcription, because the psychology of seeing and playing music is really important.
>
> Gregory Jamrok – Partner at Fine Line Music Service, Los Angeles, CA
> *Oppenheimer, The Last Repair Shop, Beetlejuice Beetlejuice, Star Trek: Discovery*

Dynamics

Beyond rhythm and pitch, music is performed at a certain volume that develops over time. Some of these fluctuations are conscious performance decisions, while others happen subconsciously. The more intentionally dynamics are performed, the more *directed and apparent* they become to the listener. For example, an original orchestral soundtrack for a feature film will likely include prominent and *intentional dynamic developments*. In contrast, a rough first demo recording of a song idea will likely show less intentional, and potentially less prominent dynamic developments. These cases illustrate the significance of intentional performance on transcription (Hepworth-Sawyer, 2008).

Dynamics can *unfold over any timespan*, including sections, phrases, and sustained notes (Moylan, 2020). From a *section perspective*, dynamics include markings that describe a section's *general volume*, and any gradual *dynamic changes* ending at a different volume. At the *phrase level*, one can think of dynamics that *fluctuate* up and down, but remain within the section's general volume. Perhaps the most common phrasing dynamic is a crescendo hairpin at the phrase beginning, followed by a diminuendo hairpin toward the phrase end. The audible effect is similar to that of a car approaching and passing by

Example 6.1 Dynamics in sections, phrases, and sustained notes. Häberlin (2016), *The Dragon Apprentice*, mm. 1–2, 69–74, and 78–81.

the listener. Finally, dynamic developments can also occur as *swells on individual notes*. However, note-based dynamic developments are limited to instruments that can control the volume while the note is sustained. Chapter 11 covers dynamics in a more orchestral context.

When transcribing dynamics, it is recommended to *identify* any general *section dynamics first*. For example, the section in question may be played *f* or *p*. Any longer crescendos or diminuendos that result in a new section dynamic should also be transcribed at this time. Based on the established section dynamics, the transcriptionist can *then screen* for any *phrasing-based dynamic developments*. These can be marked with hairpins and further dynamic marks to indicate the scope of dynamic development. Note-based dynamic developments can also be transcribed at this time. Overall, this sequence of steps helps coordinate longer and shorter dynamic developments.

Chord Symbols

Music with broad appeal follows *harmonic guidelines* that make a work memorable and playable. *Note-by-note parts instantiate* these harmonic guidelines. In other words, any reading musician can play note-by-note parts, even with limited or no theoretical knowledge of harmony. In contrast, *chord symbols summarize* harmonic guidelines (Chen et al., 2020). To play from chord symbols, musicians must understand the underlying harmonic concepts. The same theoretical understanding is required when transcribing chord symbols. Transcriptionists determine the notes played in a passage, then summarize these notes as chord symbols.

Chord symbols are essentially snapshots of the harmonic qualities present at any specific location in the work. The *foundational harmonic qualities* in tonal music are the root, 3rd, 5th, 6th, and 7th chord tone. In analogy, foundational qualities could be described as a birthday cake's base. *Extension qualities* may further add combinations of the 9th, 11th, and 13th chord tone. Extension qualities could be described as the icing on the birthday cake. Together, foundational and extension chord tones frame the harmonic qualities present in any specific location (Sikora, 2022). When transcribing chord symbols, transcriptionists essentially look for these chord qualities. The following steps help transcribe chord symbols:

1. During playback, find the onset of a new chord quality.
2. Analyze the harmonic structure present. Chapter 5 explains this process.
3. Align the identified pitches to find the chord's root position.
4. Analyze the harmonic qualities present.
5. Notate the chord symbol.

Note that it is important to get a *general feel* for the *timing of chord changes*. If transcribing chord symbols directly from the recording, the chord tones are temporarily memorized or held on a reference instrument for analysis. The piano is the ideal reference instrument to analyze chord qualities, given its capability to sustain any number of notes played together. Once all notes are identified, they can be *sequenced vertically*, starting with the root and ending with the highest chord tone interval. The sequence is then *analyzed for harmonic qualities* (Levine, 1995). Specifically, each present chord tone's quality is analyzed. For example, the sequence may include a minor 3rd, perfect 5th, and a minor 7th. Following the analysis, the harmonic qualities are then attributed to the most suitable chord symbol. At

68 A Music Transcription Method

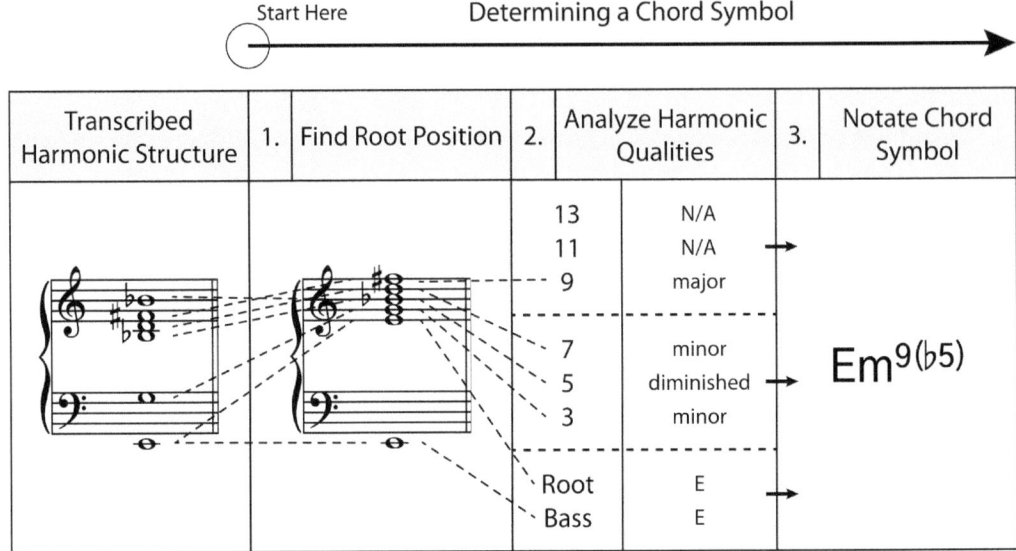

Figure 6.4 Deconstructing harmonic qualities.

the beginning of one's transcription journey, transcribing chord symbols is a more experimental process. With *growing experience*, the process becomes *more intuitive*. Chapter 10 covers advanced decision frames for chord symbol notation.

Section Activities

Examine the online audio and corresponding sheet music examples provided:

1. Add the heard dynamics at the section, phrase, and note level.
2. Transcribe the chord symbols. Evaluate the effectiveness of your process.

Transcription Roadmap

Chapter 5 covers a roadmap to transcribing foundational layers, starting with the most exposed elements and gradually working toward quieter elements. With foundational layers, the goal is to transcribe segments in order of ease, then use best judgment to answer any remaining questions at the end. A similar system applies to *dependent layers*. However, this roadmap is more based on *transcription focus and pace*. Dependent layers require listening to a range of parameters. Those parameters associated with individual notes and short patterns can be transcribed together with foundational layers. In contrast, parameters associated with phrases and larger sections are better transcribed after all foundational layers are notated.

Together with Foundational Layers

At the time of transcribing *pitch and rhythm*, the transcriptionist focuses strongly on *short patterns and individual notes* of phrases (Gorow, 2002). Each note receives ample attention at the moment it is transcribed. However, once the transcriptionist moves on to the next pattern or note, the previous notes are quickly erased from short-term memory. Revisiting

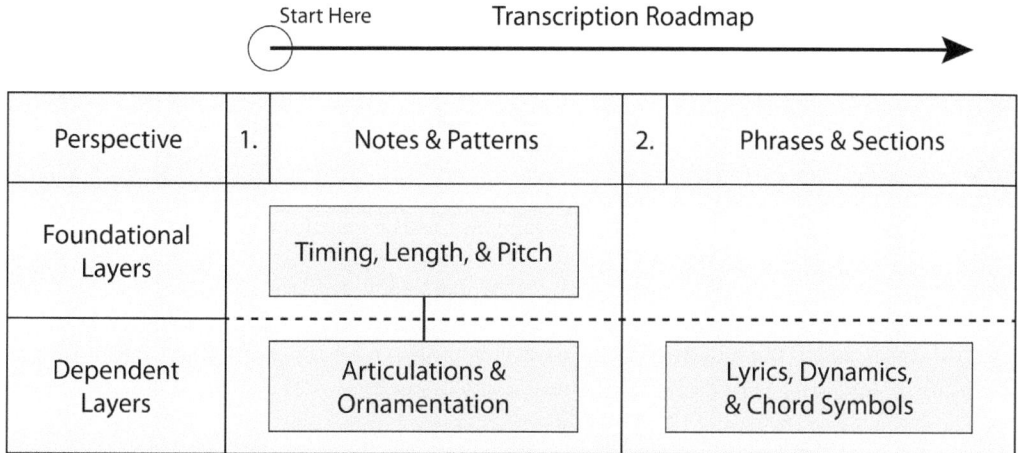

Figure 6.5 Prioritizing layers for workflow and consistency.

transcribed notes to analyze and notate further detail takes additional time. Therefore, it is recommended to transcribe note-based and pattern-based *dependent layers concurrently* with foundational layers. This includes *articulations* for individual notes and *ornaments* that represent short patterns.

Lyrics are an exception to this rule. Although lyrics are often anchored with individual notes or short patterns, they are better *notated after transcribing foundational layers*. Two reasons are noteworthy. First, transcribing lyrics requires a different listening and analytical focus than transcribing notes (Nowacka, 2023). Transcribing both notes and lyrics concurrently impacts the focus on transcription quality. Second, *entering lyrics* into notation software is more *effective if pursued separately* from transcribing notes. That is because notation software is designed to work quickest if the processes are pursued separately. For comparison, imagine a car driving on a road. The road must be paved before the car can drive on it. However, ideally, the car and the paver vehicle will never drive on the same road at the same time.

After Foundational Layers

Transcribing dependent layers associated with *phrases or sections* requires a *larger overview*. That is because these layers evolve over longer note series. For example, transcribing section dynamics requires listening to the entire section rather than one note. Similarly, transcribing chord symbols requires listening to one or several phrases for context (Sikora, 2022). Without this additional context, it would be difficult to transcribe dynamics and chord symbols accurately. Therefore, *dynamics and chord symbols* are best transcribed by *listening to longer selections* at a time. In contrast, foundational layers are transcribed with attention to individual notes and, therefore, require listening to shorter selections at a time.

Given the difference in focus and pace, *dynamics and chord symbols* are best transcribed *after the foundational layers* are completely notated. This approach groups tasks that require listening to audio selections of similar length. In other words, the transcriptionist can *focus more on similar tasks* at the same time. Similar to proofreading in music engraving, this approach also helps reduce errors from multi-tasking dissimilar tasks (Fetherolf, 2019). In summary, transcriptionists should start with foundational layers, accompanied by articulations and ornamentation as relevant. Thereafter, lyrics, dynamics and chord symbols should be transcribed one at a time.

Section Activities

Examine the online audio and corresponding sheet music examples provided:

1. Update the existing sheet music with ornamentations and articulations. Describe the effort involved with adding these details after transcribing foundational layers.
2. Add dynamics to the existing sheet music. Then describe how, if at all, adding dynamics required updating your previously notated articulations.

End-of-Chapter Activity

Applying everything you have learned in this chapter, build on the transcription you created during the final activities in Chapters 4 and 5. Using the techniques and roadmap discussed, transcribe all applicable dependent layers in the selected segment.

Chapter Summary

This chapter covered the transcription of dependent music information layers associated with individual notes, phrases, and sections, as well as a practical roadmap for retrieving dependent layers. Transcribing articulations and ornamentation concurrently with rhythm and pitch increases time-efficiency and consistency of results. Conversely, lyrics, dynamics, and chord symbols should be transcribed after notating the foundational layers to streamline the process and support consistency. The section activities provided learner opportunities to practice transcription and decision-making related to dependent layers. Finally, the end-of-chapter activity provided an opportunity to transcribe the dependent layers of a personally significant music recording.

Learning Outcomes

The learner should now be able to:

CO 1: Analyze dependent music information layers associated with notes, phrases, and sections.
CO 2: Retrieve dependent music information layers.

Up Next

Chapter 7 covers several variants to the transcription of global, foundational and dependent layers.

References

Bonnici, A., Abela, J., Zammit, N., & Azzopardi, G. (2018). Automatic ornament localisation, recognition and expression from music sheets. *DocEng '18: Proceedings of the ACM Symposium on Document Engineering,* Article 25. https://doi.org/10.1145/3209280.3209536

Chen, T.-P., Fukayama, S., Goto, M., & Su, L. (2020). Chord jazzification: Learning Jazz interpretations of chord symbols. *Proceedings of the 21st International Society for Music Information Retrieval Conference* (pp. 360–367). https://doi.org/10.5281/zenodo.4245444

Feist, J. (2017). *Berklee contemporary music notation*. Berklee Press. ISBN: 978-0-876-39178-5

Fetherolf, D. (2019). *The G Schirmer manual of style and usage* (4th ed.). G. Schirmer. https://www.classicalondemand.com/products/manual-of-style

Gorow, R. (2002). *Hearing and writing music: Professional training for today's musician* (2nd ed.). September Publishing. ISBN: 978-0-962-94967-8

Gould, E. (2011). *Behind bars: The definitive guide to music notation*. Faber Music. ISBN: 978-0-571-51456-4

Häberlin, A. (2016). *The dragon apprentice* [Video]. YouTube. https://www.youtube.com/watch?v=fgq2juo76Pw

Hepworth-Sawyer, R. (Ed.). (2008). *From demo to delivery*. Routledge. https://doi.org/10.4324/9780080928432

Levine, M. (1995). *The Jazz theory book*. Sher Music. ISBN: 978-1-883-21704-4

Moylan, W. (2020). *Recording analysis: How the record shapes the song*. Focal Press. https://doi.org/10.4324/9781315617176

Nestico, S. (2014). *The complete arranger* (Rev. ed.). Fenwood Music. ISBN: 978-1-5027-4511-8

Nowacka, M. (2023). Lyrics as a means of raising phonetic awareness: Transcription, pronunciation, and descriptive phonetics combined. In A. Henderson & A. Kirkova-Naskova (Eds.), *Proceedings of the 7th International Conference on English Pronunciation: Issues and Practices* (pp. 199–213). Université Grenoble-Alpes. https://doi.org/10.5281/zenodo.8225365

Sevsay, E. (2013). *The Cambridge guide to orchestration*. Cambridge University Press. ISBN: 978-1-107-02516-5

Sikora, F. (2022). *Jazz harmony: Think – Listen – Play – A practical approach*. Schott Music. ISBN: 978-3-795-74930-9

7 Process Variants

Chapter Overview

This chapter covers several context-based variants to the transcription process. The first section outlines common source and target formats, their characteristics, and how they integrate with the transcription process. The second section then explains how to transcribe global, foundational, and dependent layers from the audio and MIDI stems of multi-file sources. Finally, the third section explains how to transcribe to target formats with limited sheet music space, namely reductions and rhythm charts. The section activities help learners explore common process variants of music transcription. In summary, this chapter demonstrates how to navigate the intricacies of transcribing different types of source and target formats.

Learning Outcomes

After reading this chapter, the learner will be able to:

CO 1: Transcribe from multitrack sessions.
CO 2: Transcribe to compact sheet music formats.

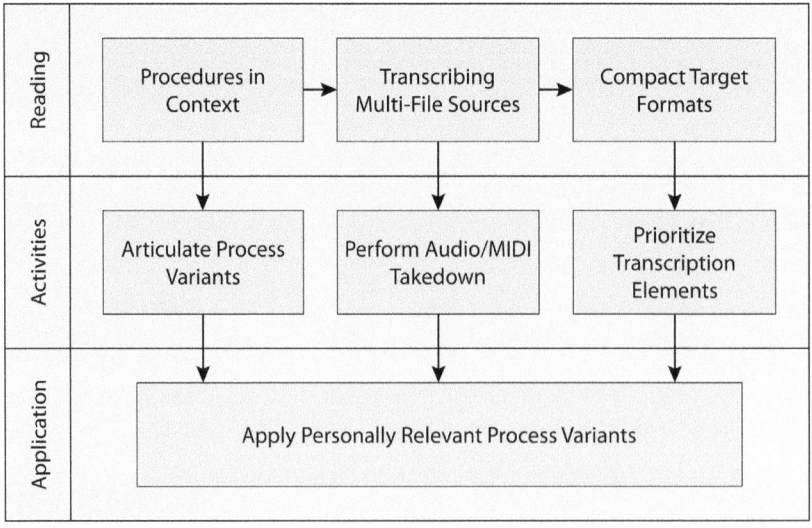

Figure 7.1 Chapter 7 map.

DOI: 10.4324/9781003511946-9

Procedures in Context

Chapters 4 to 6 describe the general *procedures to transcribe music* information layers from audio recordings. The transcription of global, foundational, and dependent layers is relevant to all project types. Framing the music through global parameters, then gradually adding further notation layers ensures a systematic process. However, although the method remains the same conceptually, the transcription tools and decision-frames *change based on the context*. Specifically, the *source format* determines which playback device is most effective for the project. Furthermore, a project's *target sheet music format* determines what music information should be prioritized, and how it should be notated.

Source Formats

As discussed in Chapter 3, some projects require transcribing from a *single audio file*, while others require transcribing from several stems. Single-file sources hold the recording of an entire work in one audio file. While single-file sources are compact and practical, they only allow listening to the *fixed mix* on that file (Savage, 2014). The inability to listen to isolated individual sound sources naturally *limits the transcription scope*. To extract as much detail as practical, single-file sources are best played in Transcribe! That is because Transcribe! offers advanced playback functionality to magnify details in the recording. Particularly helpful features include variable playback speed and a spectrum analyzer that indicates possible notes played.

In contrast to single-file sources, *multi-file sources* consist of individual audio or MIDI stems that *collectively hold the recording* of a work. Each stem contains a smaller part of the entire work, for example, a single sound source or a smaller group of sound sources (Huber et al., 2023). When listening to individual stems, transcriptionists can *distinguish* between the present sound sources *with increased accuracy*. Therefore, multi-file sources are preferable for transcribing recordings with large line-ups or dense arrangements. However, to meter and listen to multi-file sources effectively, transcriptionists must work in a DAW environment. DAWs allow transcriptionists to organize and listen to audio and MIDI stems based on the project's needs.

Target Formats

The choice of sheet music format shapes, to an extent, the music notation decision-frame. *Detailed transcriptions* of arrangements and particells focus more on *note-by-note information*. In this case, note-by-note transcription is a priority, with the possible exception of improvisational parts. Next, *reduction formats* require a similar decision-frame as note-by-note transcriptions. The main difference is that reduction formats can *accommodate fewer parts* and voices than the recorded line-up (Kregor, 2010). Transcribing to a reduction format requires fitting as many elements into a smaller line-up as practical, while prioritizing these elements by importance.

Finally, *rhythm charts* differ from both note-by-note transcriptions and reductions. Rhythm charts serve as a performance roadmap with some improvisational freedom. Performers of rhythm charts make *discretionary accompaniment choices* while following the arrangement structure (Ranier, 1994). To help performers do so, rhythm charts should include:

- The most recognizable note-by-note segments played by rhythm instruments.
- A summary of the groove as time and stop-time notation.
- Any segments from other sound sources that the rhythm section should interact with (Nestico, 2014).

74 *A Music Transcription Method*

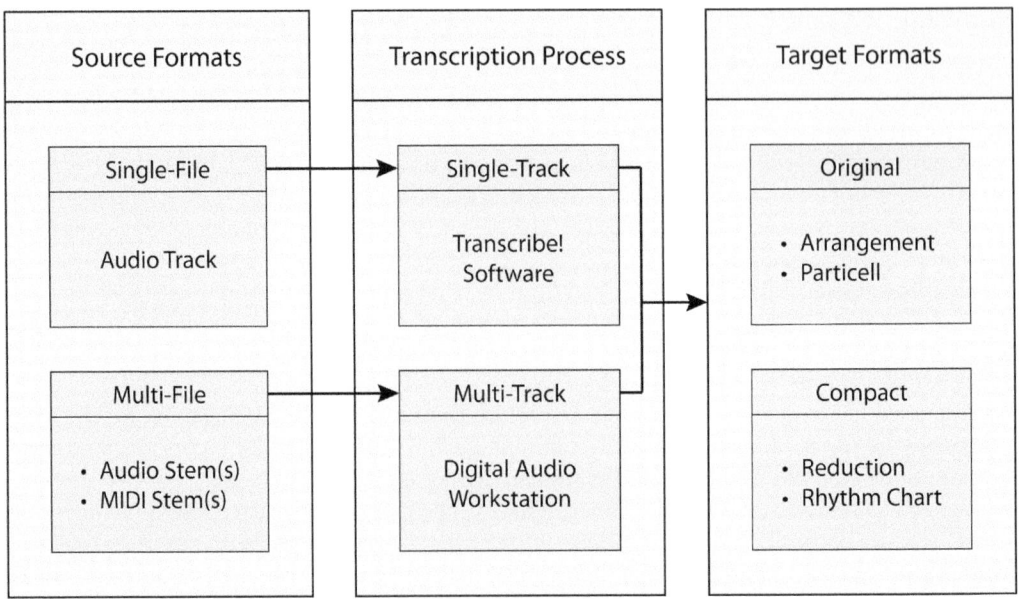

Figure 7.2 Format variants in context.

Rhythm charts differ widely in appearance. Notation on a grand staff is practical, but some musicians also use one or, occasionally, three staves for rhythm charts. In summary, rhythm charts are defined by the content that the involved parties want to see, rather than by a standardized appearance.

Section Activities

Examine the online source file examples provided.

1. Describe the transcription scope and limitations of each source format example.
2. Decide for a sheet music target format. Then explain how you would apply the corresponding notation approach to the heard elements.

Transcribing Multi-File Sources

This format is prevalent in settings involving *music writing and production* (Harding, 2019). Many creatives develop their musical ideas in DAW software. Music transcription becomes relevant if and once these ideas are to be recorded by other musicians. In these cases, transcriptionists *translate the production* in its current state *to sheet music*. Any stems relevant to the recording session will be transcribed. The sheet music then serves as a performance guide for recording musicians. Overall, the transcription process remains similar, but uses DAW software to play back multiple files synchronized and concurrently.

Global Layers

In contrast to single-file sources, multi-file sources *may include bpm and metering information*. This information can be stored in a DAW session or MIDI stems (Huber, 2020). Similarly,

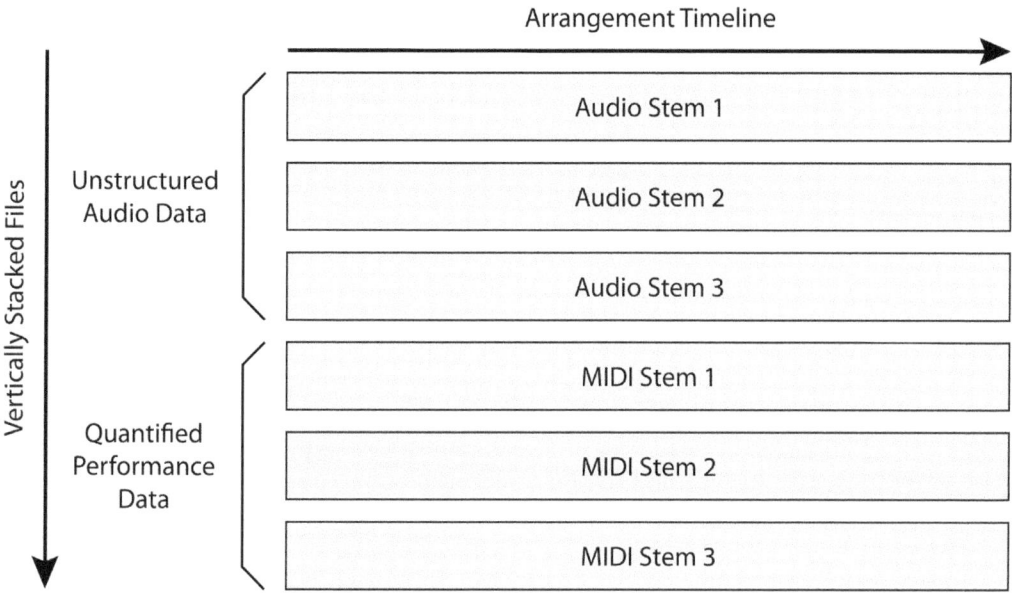

Figure 7.3 Generic abstract of a DAW session with vertically stacked audio and MIDI stems.

audio stems can store a single bpm value in their file metadata, but will not store metering information (Szeto, 2019; Truedell, 2007). When receiving multi-file sources for takedown, transcriptionists can expect one of *several scenarios*. The multi-file sources may arrive:

- In a DAW session, fully metered.
- In a DAW session, partially metered or unmetered.
- As exported stems, with metered MIDI file(s) or bpm metadata in audio file(s).
- As exported stems, without metering.

If a multi-file source arrives *without metering information*, the transcriptionist will need to *add metering manually* (Sapiro, 2016). This process follows the metering decision-frame discussed in Chapter 4, but the metering steps vary slightly between the different DAWs. Similar to single-file sources, it is possible to transcribe multi-file sources without metering. However, without a reference grid, the project becomes more susceptible to transcription errors and inconsistencies.

In a common scenario, *creatives* will sometimes *meter their projects* in a less conducive way. For example, they may set the bpm at double or half the value ideal for notation. Creatives may do this to create a specific click track for recordings, or simply for *personal preference*. Many further examples exist. When receiving multi-file sources with non-optimized metering for notation, it is good practice to address any changes deemed necessary with the creative party in advance. That is because re-metering may offset the measure numbers between the original DAW session and the sheet music. Mismatching measure numbers becomes an issue when the involved parties want to reference specific measure numbers between the DAW session and the sheet music, for example, during a recording session (Sharon et al., 2015).

Industry Voice: Orchestration in Film Scoring

Andreas: What is the role of an orchestrator in the film scoring industry?

Tracie: In essence, my job is to take the composer's vision for the score and bring it to life. My job in practice is to take the composer's ideas, mostly in the form of MIDI data, and turn it into sheet music that can be read and performed as intended. The job is highly collaborative, but every composer has a different preference on how collaborative they want to be with their music. Sometimes, composers dictate exactly what they want, down to dynamic and articulation preferences, but other times a composer will just send me a "sketch" of their ideas and ask me to use my best judgment to make it fit with the ensemble available. It takes experience from listening and arranging for all the different instrument groups to create the right idiomatic ideas to realize the composer's vision. In this way, orchestration can be very methodical, but it can also be very artistic depending on how much freedom you have to work with their ideas.

Andreas: What's your usual project timeline for takedown?

Tracie: It varies really widely. There have been times when the session starts at 3 pm, and I received a four-minute full orchestra action cue at 2 pm, but I wouldn't say that's the norm! Either way, the speed has to be there. The most important thing is having a consistent process for how to compartmentalize the takedown and find a way to meet the deadline. Beyond transcription skills, it helps to have a strong knowledge base around tech and the ability to optimize your workflow via macros and other time-saving features, to enhance your ability to work quickly and accurately. When deadlines aren't as tight, I would say I typically get around two weeks to turn over a full-length feature film score, including all takedowns, so even on the more relaxed timelines, you have to be fast!

Tracie Turnbull – Composer & Orchestrator, LA
Star Trek: Strange New World, *Still: A Michael J. Fox Movie*, *Migration*

Foundational and Dependent Layers

Some stems contain one sound source only, while others contain grouped sound sources (Huber et al., 2023). As an example, a stem with a single sound source may contain a trumpet part, while a stem with grouped sound sources may contain the higher brass instruments of a recording. The main advantage of working with *multi-file audio sources* is that the transcriptionist can listen to *individual or grouped sound sources* in a more isolated manner. To do so, the transcriptionist simply chooses the stem or stems to *play back in isolation*. It is significantly easier to hear an isolated segment play from an individual audio stem than it is to discern the same segment in a busy stereo mix. Overall, transcribing foundational and dependent layers from audio stems follows the same process covered in Chapters 5 and 6. The main difference is that the playback device is a DAW.

Multi-file sources may also include *MIDI stems* instead of, or in addition to, audio stems. In standard DAW sessions, MIDI stems primarily send *performance instructions* to *virtual instruments* (Thompson, 2018). The virtual instruments then perform the received instructions and return the performance as an audio signal. Creatives use virtual instruments to sketch out and listen to their musical ideas without the need to engage other musicians (Maz, 2023). Since many DAW users work with virtual instruments, MIDI stems are vastly common in digital music production.

In comparison, *MIDI data* captures performance instructions in *quantifiable detail*, while *audio data* captures the performance itself in *rich detail*. MIDI data can only capture simplified, abstract performance parameters (Huber, 2020). For example, MIDI data could describe the timing and length of a note, but not its exact tone color. Transcriptionists use MIDI stems to help extract the more quantifiable performance detail. The following message types are most relevant for music transcriptionists:

- Note Events: Timing, duration, pitch, and attack strength of each note.
- Pitch Bend: Change of played notes' pitch over time.
- Continuous Controllers (CC): Change of played notes' sound over time.
- Aftertouch: Change of played notes' sound over time.

Note events cover the music information needed to transcribe foundational layers. Similarly, dependent layers are mainly covered through pitch bend, CCs, and aftertouch messages. The attack strength of each note, known as velocity, also informs dependent layers. In summary, *MIDI stems hold* much of the *music information* that transcriptionists would usually retrieve by ear. Therefore, MIDI stems may serve as a *shortcut* for the sometimes time-consuming process of music transcription from audio files.

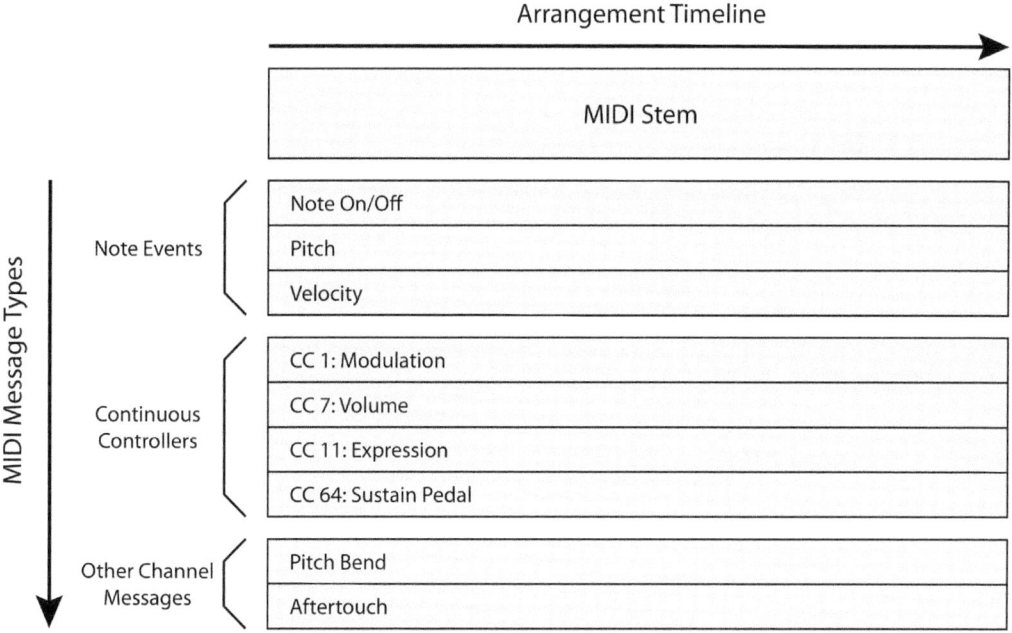

Figure 7.4 Generic abstract of a MIDI stem and examples of MIDI message types it may contain.

78 *A Music Transcription Method*

MIDI stems contain no audio information by themselves. However, for music transcription, it is critical to reference the music as envisioned by the writer. Although *MIDI data* suggests how a segment should be notated, only the audio source can confirm the details of note timing, length, pitch, and dependent layers. Therefore, MIDI data should always be *referenced together with audio data*. Writers who transcribe their own MIDI sketches may simply listen to the virtual instrument playback as an audio reference. However, if someone other than the writer transcribes the music, they may not have access to the writer's specific virtual instruments (Au-Yeung, 2022). In this case, the writer should consider creating audio stems from the available MIDI data and intended virtual instruments. The creation of audio stems from MIDI data is a *prevalent practice* in the *recording industry*.

There are *two ways to transcribe* from MIDI stems. The first option is to *transfer MIDI data manually* and note-by-note, just like transcription from audio files. In this case, the transcriptionist will look at each MIDI note while listening to it, then analyze and notate it. This approach is more thorough and detailed, but also more time-consuming. In contrast, the second option entails cleaning up the MIDI data within the DAW, then *importing the MIDI data* into the notation software. As a process, MIDI cleanup quantizes the timing and duration of MIDI notes to common rhythmical values (Sapiro, 2016). The process may also include removing extraneous MIDI notes that do not produce a sound or were recorded by mistake. If the cleanup is performed correctly, this second option can save ample time transcribing foundational layers, especially with larger projects.

Section Activities

Examine the online multi-file source examples provided:

1. Articulate the remaining steps necessary to outline the global layers.
2. Perform a MIDI cleanup where applicable, then transfer your results to a notation software. Share your decision-frames and challenges.

Compact Target Formats

Musicians have different uses for music transcription. Some scenarios require a note-by-note transcription that preserves the original detail as closely as possible. This comprehensive approach provides more performance insights, but also requires more sheet music space. Other scenarios require *fitting recorded music* to a *narrower format* for a specific purpose. This second approach is often used to perform existing music with a smaller line-up. Sheet music formats that require adaptation include reductions, lead sheets, and master rhythm charts (Houghton et al., 1994; Kregor, 2010). The latter two can be collectively labeled as rhythm charts.

Table 7.1 Feature comparison of compact target formats

Characteristics	*Reduction*	*Rhythm Chart*
Objective	Preserve original work	Create performance guide
Prioritize elements by	Significance to original work	Function in the arrangement
Fill sheet music as much as	Idiomatic to play	Helpful to navigate

Reductions

It is very common for musicians to *arrange existing music* for a *smaller line-up*. A prominent example is piano-vocal songbooks of new pop albums that help vocalists perform songs with a pianist instead of a larger ensemble. The same concept applies to any smaller ensemble wishing to play a work written for a larger ensemble. A reduction describes the process of adapting an original work for a smaller line-up (Roberge, 1993). Across the industry, most transcribing musicians will create a reduction of a recorded work at some point in their careers.

Reductions generally use the same procedures as note-by-note transcriptions. The only difference is that reductions have *limited space available* to accommodate the elements of the original arrangement. For example, consider a reduction of a symphonic work to a single piano. Given the significant difference in forces, some elements will unavoidably be cut during the reduction process (Štšura, 2021). To preserve the original work as far as practical, segments should be *transcribed in order of their significance* to the work. This approach prioritizes a work's most important elements over the elements one might listen to most intuitively. As a general guideline for reductions, transcriptionists may prioritize elements in the following order:

1. Leading melody or pattern.
2. Primary accompaniment.
3. Secondary accompaniment.

There are *two* paths to transcribe a recorded work as a reduction. First, one may transcribe the entire work *note-by note*, *then reduce* the transcription subsequently. This approach allows for more thorough decision-making but also requires more time to complete. Alternatively, one may perform the *reduction while transcribing* the work. This second approach requires more upfront decision-making, but may produce quicker results. The choice of approach depends on several factors, including personal preference, experience, expectations of other parties, and time available. Finally, note that musicians will often tweak the orchestration of reductions to enhance the overall reduction quality. For example, a piano reduction may treat a timpani tremolo as an octave tremolo with applied sustain pedal (Štšura, 2021). Countless creative examples exist beyond this book's functional scope.

Rhythm Charts

Some works are performed entirely note-by-note, while others include improvisation. In genres with broader appeal, improvised segments typically include solos and accompaniment. Improvised solos tend to offer increased creative freedom, which is in part due to their leading role in passages. Conversely, improvised accompaniment tends to follow more coordinated guidelines (Nestico, 2014). After all, the role of accompaniment, fixed or improvised, is to accompany a work's leading melodies. In groove-based genres, *accompanying instrument groups* are called the rhythm section. These groups may include keyboards, guitars, bass, drums, and percussion. Rhythm sections often play from rhythm charts, which include *up to four primary components*:

- Fixed elements: Note-by-note segments, to be played as written.
- Time and stop-time: Guidelines for improvised accompaniment.
- Cues: Segments from other sound sources, to be factored into improvised accompaniment.
- Solos: Improvised leading segment.

Example 7.1 Reduction. Willis (2016), "Solitude," mm. 65–72, on *See Us Through*. Transcribed by Andreas Häberlin. Printed with permission of Michelle Willis.

Example 7.2 Master rhythm chart. Turner (2019), "You've Got It All," mm. 1–20, in *Ciao Bambino the Musical*. Transcribed by Andreas Häberlin. Printed with permission of Elizabeth Allen Turner.

Rhythm sections may play from individual or collective sheet music parts (Houghton et al., 1994). *Individual parts* prioritize *instrument-specific* performance instructions, while *collective parts* prioritize the *elements most central* to the rhythm section as a group. Collective parts then utilize the remaining space on the sheet music for instrument-specific performance instructions. The choice of format is often based on the preferences of involved parties, budget available, and delivery timeframe. Individual parts include ample instrument-specific detail, but tend to take more time to create than master rhythm charts. In contrast to individual parts and master rhythm charts, lead sheets accommodate less performance information, but tend to take significantly less time to create.

Rhythm charts provide both improvisational frameworks and note-by-note parts as necessary. A great starting point is to *notate time slashes* in any measures with a perceivable groove. Slashes simply indicate that a groove is present over the marked beats (Ranier, 1994). The *first few measures* of a new or audibly changing *groove* should also be notated in detail, so that musicians can familiarize with the groove. Grooves will often, but not exclusively, change at the beginning of new sections in a work. Next, the second step entails notating any *important hits* marked by all sound sources. These hits may replace time slashes or populate still empty measures. For each hit in question, the transcriptionist must decide whether to notate:

- Stop-time: For hits in rhythmical unison with approximate voicings.
- Note-by-note: For hits in rhythmical unison that require exact voicings.

Fast-evolving harmonic progressions that frequently change once per beat or quicker are best transcribed note-by-note.

Once the most prominent hits are captured, the next step is to notate any *characteristic patterns* played by individual rhythm section instruments. These include the patterns that *make the recorded work recognizable*. Both sections with existing slashes and empty sections in the sheet music should be screened for characteristic patterns. Finally, once time, stop-time, fixed elements, and characteristic patterns are notated, any remaining untouched time slashes can be enriched with *additional instructions* as helpful. For example, the transcriptionist may consider adding *cue note*s from other segments. Cue notes help performers embellish important compositional elements at their discretion (Feist, 2017). Another common example is to mark measures with *instrumental fills*.

Section Activities

Select and listen to a familiar, groove-based music recording:

1. Plan a reduction of the materials to a personally relevant line-up. Articulate your process and priorities.
2. Plan a rhythm chart for a personally relevant line-up. Justify your choice of sheet music format and notation components.

End-of-Chapter Activity

Applying everything you have learned in this chapter, find a personally relevant project that requires using a process variant. Outline your transcription approach, then transcribe the work. Finally, reflect on your process and challenges encountered.

Chapter Summary

This chapter covered the application of the transcription process to multi-file sources, reduction target formats, and rhythm chart formats. All variants of the transcription process generally follow the same procedures, but use context-specific tools and decision-frames. The presented process variants find broad application across the music industry. The section activities provided learner opportunities to familiarize with process variants and their involved music notation decision-frames. Finally, the end-of-chapter activity provided an opportunity to apply process variants to a personally significant transcription project.

Learning Outcomes

The learner should now be able to:

CO 1: Transcribe from multitrack sessions.
CO 2: Transcribe to compact sheet music formats.

Up Next

Chapter 8 covers the practical potential and limitations of music notation.

References

Au-Yeung, J. (2022). *Music for film and game soundtracks with FL Studio: Learn music production, compose orchestral music, and launch your music career*. Packt Publishing. ISBN: 978-1-803-24559-1

Feist, J. (2017). *Berklee contemporary music notation*. Berklee Press. ISBN: 978-0-876-39178-5

Harding, P. (2019). *Pop music production: Manufactured pop and boybands of the 1990s*. Routledge. https://doi.org/10.4324/9781351189798

Houghton, S., Ranier, T., Viapiano, P., & Warrington, T. (1994). *The complete rhythm section*. Warner Bros. Publications. ISBN: 978-1-576-23990-2

Huber, D. M. (2020). *The MIDI manual: A practical guide to MIDI within modern music production* (4th ed.). Routledge. https://doi.org/10.4324/9781315670836

Huber, D. M., Caballero, E., & Runstein, R. (2023). *Modern recording techniques: A practical guide to modern music production* (10th ed.). Focal Press. https://doi.org/10.4324/9781003260530

Kregor, J. (2010). *Liszt as transcriber*. Cambridge University Press. ISBN: 978-0-521-11777-7

Maz, A. (2023). *Music technology essentials: A home studio guide*. Focal Press. https://doi.org/10.4324/9781003345138

Nestico, S. (2014). *The complete arranger* (Rev. ed.). Fenwood Music Co. ISBN: 978-1-502-74511-8

Ranier, T. (1994). *Piano in the rhythm section*. Alfred Music. ISBN: 978-1-576-23994-0

Roberge, M.-A. (1993). From orchestra to piano: Major composers as authors of piano reductions of other composers' works. *Notes, 49*(3), 925–936. https://doi.org/10.2307/898925

Sapiro, I. (2016). *Scoring the score: The role of the orchestrator in the contemporary film industry*. Routledge. https://doi.org/10.4324/9781315857824

Savage, S. (2014). *Mixing and mastering in the box: The guide to making great mixes & final masters on your computer*. Oxford University Press. ISBN: 978-0-19-992932-0

Sharon, D., Spalding, B., & McDonald, B. (2015). *A cappella*. Alfred Music. ISBN: 978-1-4706-1667-0

Štšura, M. (2021). *Translating twenty-first century orchestral scores for the piano: Transcription, reduction and performability* [Doctoral dissertation, Royal College of Music]. Research Online. https://doi.org/10.24379/RCM.00001897

Szeto, K. (2019). Metadata standards in digital audio. In M. Khosrow-Pour (Ed.), *Advanced methodologies and technologies in media and communications* (pp. 242–262). IGI Global. http://doi.org/10.4018/978-1-5225-7601-3.ch020

Thompson, D. M. (2018). *Understanding audio: Getting the most out of your project or professional recording studio* (2nd ed.). Berklee Press. ISBN: 978-1-495-02875-5

Truedell, C. (2007). *Mastering digital audio production: The professional music workflow with Mac OS X*. Wiley. ISBN: 978-0-470-16576-8

Turner, E. A. (2019). You've got it all [Song]. In *Ciao bambino the musical* [Unpublished manuscript].

Willis, M. M. (2016). Solitude [Song]. On *See us through*. https://open.spotify.com/track/5uPRCzNLUFHVPEHNmnY0gT

Part III

Interpretation

Part Overview

Chapters 8, 9, 10, and 11 cover several advanced decision frameworks for music transcription. Chapter 8 covers the practical scope and limitations of music notation. Chapter 9 covers interpretation scenarios of global music information layers. Chapter 10 covers interpretation scenarios of foundational and dependent music information layers. Chapter 11 covers orchestrational aspects of music transcription. In summary, Part III helps learners evaluate several advanced aspects of music transcription.

Learning Outcomes

After reading Part III, the learner will be able to:

BO 3: Evaluate contextual music notation decisions.

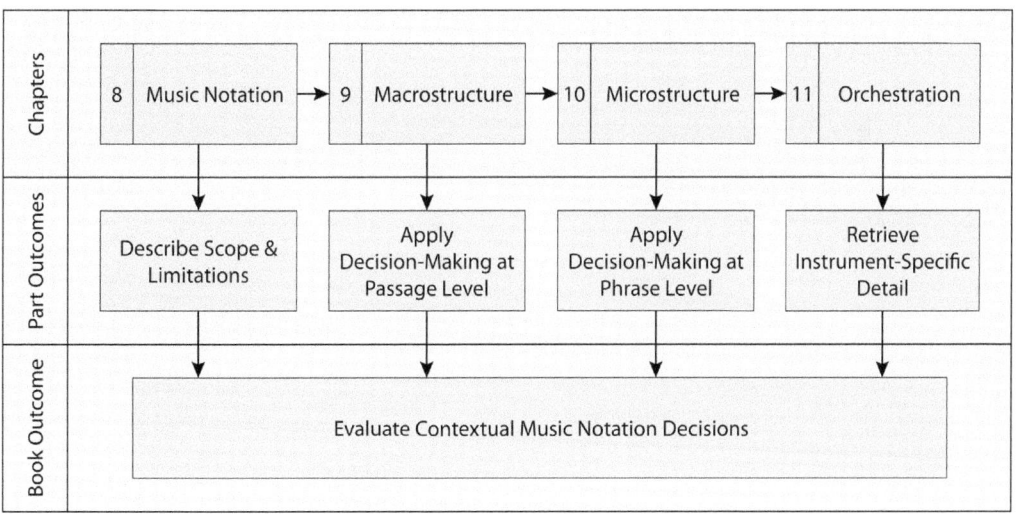

Figure 0.3 Part III map.

8 Music Notation

Chapter Overview

This chapter covers the scope and limitations of prescriptive music notation in an applied industry context. The first section covers the readability, articulacy, and conceptual clarity of transcribed music notation. The second section then covers two dimensions of notation detail and their integration with each other. Finally, the third section provides a decision framework to determine a context-specific level of transcription detail. The section activities help learners understand the scope of notation detail and practice decision-making on a case-by-case basis. In summary, this chapter provides high-level strategies to create effective sheet music with respect for a work's production stage, improvisational components, and musicians' backgrounds.

Learning Outcomes

After reading this chapter, the learner will be able to:

CO 1: Articulate the practical scope and limitations of music notation for music transcription.
CO 2: Evaluate notation detail levels in applied industry contexts.

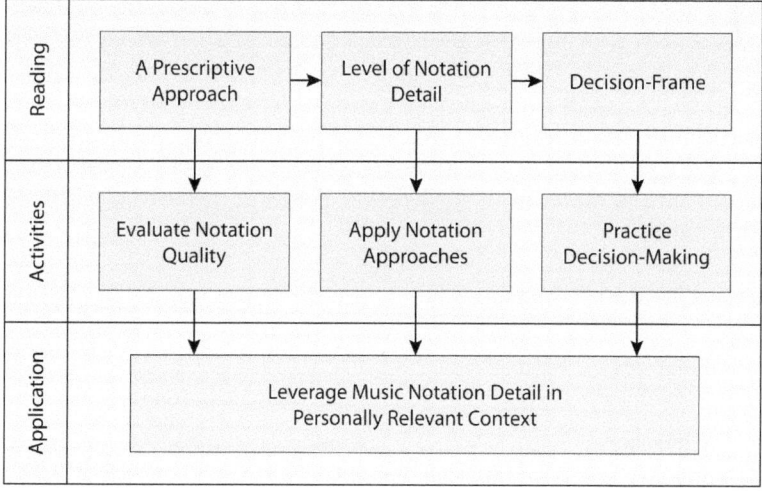

Figure 8.1 Chapter 8 map.

DOI: 10.4324/9781003511946-11

A Prescriptive Approach

In contemporary Western music with a broad appeal, sheet music is created primarily for playing and educational purposes. The notation approach for this type of sheet music is known as *prescriptive music notation*. Prescriptive music notation provides quantifiable performance instructions that help musicians *reproduce a musical work* through performance (Kanno, 2007; Seeger, 1958). In the context of this book, these performance instructions include global, foundational, and dependent layers of music information. When transcribing with a prescriptive framework, it is good practice to consider the sheet music's readability, articulacy, and conceptual clarity. Prescriptive music transcription entails *simplifying a heard performance* through symbolic notation, while preserving important performance details.

Readability

The importance of music engraving during transcription cannot be overstated. Proper attention to *engraving practices* can make the difference between *readable* and difficult-to-read sheet music. General considerations include conducive note spacing, fonts, and notation object sizes. At the phrase level, notation conventions for pitch and rhythmical values have a major impact on readability too (Gould, 2011). Further to music engraving, several transcription practices also have a major impact on readability. The following considerations are most important:

- Countable metering that falls between 55–170 bpm.
- Time signatures that highlight stressed beats and downbeats of new form parts.
- Rhythmical accompaniment note values that fall within whole notes and 16th notes.

Most importantly, transcription must establish a metric grid and align all transcribed notes to it. Without following these guidelines, sheet music quickly becomes difficult to read.

A great way to *familiarize with readability* is to import and *examine raw MIDI data* in a notation software (Kalmanovitch, 2008). Raw MIDI data are somewhat comparable to a chaotic discussion where participants talk over each other. To hear what each participant has to say, they must be allocated a dedicated time window to speak without competing voices. The added structure makes it easier to follow the overall conversation. In analogy, each MIDI note must be assigned its exact place in time and length in alignment with the metering. If done with precision, the MIDI data can be imported into notation software and will look readable. However, even small quantization errors will misalign notes from the meter grid. As a result, the imported MIDI will look unpresentable in notation software.

Table 8.1 Practical notation

Aspect	Impact on Notation
Readability	Is readable with ease
Articulacy	Captures performance nuances
Conceptual clarity	Feels intuitive to understand

Example 8.1 Readability in comparison. Häberlin (2024), *Reverie in G Major*, mm. 1–4.

Articulacy

The *depth of prescriptive notation detail* in dependent layers is equally as important as its readability. Beyond foundational layers, each note is to be played with a certain *energy and technique*. Notation that captures these details helps musicians understand how individual notes should be articulated in the work's larger context (Zolper, 2017). Common ways to add articulacy include capturing:

- Phrasing slurs and phrasing dynamics.
- A few accentuated notes within a phrase.
- Playing techniques with timbral effects.
- Pitch effects.

The *importance of articulacy* is comparable to reciting poetry. If a poem is read aloud with a monotonous voice, it is likely still recognizable as a work, but its charm will be missing. However, if the poem is recited with a dynamic narrative voice, the vocal nuances and contrast make the poem come alive in the listener's mind. In context of music transcription, the poem's words represent the foundational layers, while the speaking voice represents the dependent layers. To preserve a recording's performance nuances, dependent layers should be articulated in as much detail as is *practical to read and play* (Gorow, 2002). Although not all listeners understand what makes a performance lively, most can discern between a lively and monotonous performance.

Conceptual Clarity

Further to readability and articulacy, the hallmark of *practical sheet music* is that it conveys musical concepts with clarity (Miller, 2014). Practical notation should not only be easy to read, but also *intuitive to understand* at a glance. To this point, conceptual clarity also benefits readability. Transcribing with conceptual clarity is a two-phase process. Beyond transcribing individual notes, transcriptionists will almost inevitably discover further structural elements while listening, for example:

- Global: Form labels, section length, tonal center.
- Foundational: Rhythmical patterns, segments with improvisation.
- Dependent: Dynamic developments, phrase length, chord qualities, ornaments.

When recognizing a structural element, it should be notated in an *intuitively understandable* way for the reader. Perhaps the most effective way is to find *common notation symbols* that summarize and explain structural elements visually, at a glance. For example, form labels should reflect the work's underlying structure, rather than just numerate form parts. Similarly, notation should differentiate between section dynamics and phrasing dynamics. Note that previous experience with structural elements from transcription and applied music theory helps discover these elements. A great way to learn about conceptual clarity is to *study sheet music and recordings* in the relevant music industry field.

Section Activities

Compare the different transcription takes of the same recording provided in the online resources:

1. Evaluate each take's general readability.
2. Evaluate the articulacy and conceptual clarity of the different takes.

Level of Notation Detail

Recorded music can be transcribed at *different resolutions*. Two dimensions are of interest. First, the transcriptionist may choose to notate a passage *note-by-note*, or summarize heard notes through *slash notation*. Note-by-note transcriptions enable a detailed reconstruction of the recording, while slash notation enables an approximate reconstruction. Based on the chosen notation path, the transcriptionist may then decide whether to transcribe the recording in *detail or simplify* it. This decision affects both foundational and dependent layers. Although slash notation itself can be considered simplified notation, it can still include either detailed or simplified performance instructions. Of course, middle grounds exist for both dimensions.

Example 8.2 Notation detail in comparison. ii–V7–I progression, improvised and transcribed by the author.

92 A Music Transcription Method

Note-by-Note or Summarized

Prescriptive music notation may include *fully notated parts* that stipulate every note to be played. This approach is perhaps comparable to a choreographed ballet performance. The choreography details every movement and its pace. Ballet dancers are expected to perform the work exactly as choreographed, with attention to every detail. In analogy, note-by-note transcriptions represent a more binding notation form. Musicians are expected to *perform every note as written*. This approach to music notation is common in classical settings, concert and symphonic bands, film scoring, official songbooks, solo transcriptions, and any other settings requiring note-level detail.

Conversely, *slash notation summarizes* heard parts *conceptually*, rather than note-by-note. The result is comparable to a roadmap with guiding instructions. The roadmap keeps the traveler on track, but leaves smaller decisions within those guidelines up to the traveler. In analogy, slash notation provides a *degree of freedom* over what to play, as long as the performer adheres to the chord symbols and stop time notation. Further guidelines may also indicate solo and accompaniment roles, as well as stylistic detail. Slash notation is common with rhythm sections and any ensembles that improvise (Houghton et al., 1994).

Detailed or Simplified

Music transcription is comparable to drawing an object from observation. The heard music represents the object, while the transcription represents the drawing. The painter must decide whether to draw the object in rich detail or as a simplified abstract. Similarly, the transcriptionist must decide whether to *capture subtle nuances* in music information layers *or to notate a simplified version*. However, a key difference between observational drawing and music transcription is the role of the grid as a reference tool in the process. Grids are an optional, temporary reference tool in observational drawing. The grid helps painters approximate object proportions while maintaining a degree of freedom. Conversely, in music transcription, the global music information layers form a required, permanent grid with specific metering. All foundational and dependent layers must conform to the metric units of this grid.

In music transcription, foundational and dependent layers are quantized to fit the global metric grid. *Smaller* and *less common metric units* can offer additional performance detail, but come at the *cost of clarity and readability*. Examples of this granular level of notation detail can be observed in classical serialism. A historically significant work is composer Olivier Messiaen's etude *Mode de valeurs et d'intensités* (Covington, 1980). Conversely, *simple metric units* offer less performance detail, but are *easier to read*. Lead sheets are among the most representative examples of simplified notation. The real book series of jazz music is perhaps the most established collection of simplified transcriptions in Western music with a broader appeal.

An Integrated Approach

Together, the *notation approach* and extent of *performance detail* captured define a transcription's *level of notation detail*. Music may be transcribed note-by-note with a stronger or lesser degree of performance detail. It may also be transcribed in summary notation, again at a certain level of performance detail. For consistency, the degree of performance detail should remain the same within a transcribed work. This means that a work's foundational and dependent layers are transcribed using the same attention to detail throughout the process. For example, if note endings are quantized to 8th-note increments, then this practice should apply throughout the transcription. Similarly, if both lightly and heavily accentuated notes are marked with the same accent symbol, then this practice should apply throughout the transcription. Countless analogous examples exist.

Finally, some transcriptions combine *full notation and summary notation*. In other words, these works include both segments to be played note-by-note, and segments to be improvised with specific guidelines. The combination allows musicians to reproduce the same arrangement of a performance, but express their musical ideas with *increased freedom during slash notation* segments (Lowell & Pullig, 2003). This scenario is common with jazz and pop rhythm sections, big bands, and any larger ensembles with improvisational components. An advantage of this approach, especially for larger ensembles, is that it offers *improvisation opportunities* within a *coordinated framework*. The songbooks of the band Snarky Puppy illustrate this notation approach and how it translates to large ensemble performances.

Section Activities

Select a familiar, groove-based music recording:

1. Select a passage and create a detailed note-by-note transcription.
2. Next, create a simplified and summarized transcription of the same passage. Compare the music information layers between both transcriptions.

Decision-Frame

Sooner or later on their journey, every transcriptionist will arrive at the question of *how much notation detail is appropriate*. Because the music industry is a vast and diverse landscape, there is no simple answer to that question. An appropriate level of notation detail is best determined through a *project-based framework*. Although transcription in the music industry seeks to streamline notation, an appropriate level of detail depends on several factors. The framework presented in this section considers a project's production stage, improvised segments, and musicians' backgrounds. Chapters 9 and 10 instantiate this framework with concrete and applied examples.

Production Stage

This first criterion examines the source materials. Transcriptions can happen at any stage in the music production process. For example, a songwriter may need sheet music based on a *rough song demo*. At this production stage, the demo will contain a *sketch of unpolished ideas* (Farquharson, 2007). Unpolished productions articulate music information with less intent and consistency. For example, a recording's tempo and dynamics may fluctuate intermittently. Similarly, chord voicings and rhythmical patterns may vary unpredictably. Transcriptions of early stage productions typically *summarize and simplify* the music's core ideas. The goal is to capture and clarify the most relevant music information. Dependent layers with little to no substance can be omitted for rough demos. This approach helps both performers and producers grasp the arrangement's *core elements*.

As a contrasting example, an established artist may need band sheet music to perform their latest *commercially released song* on tour. The goal in this case is to help performers

94 *A Music Transcription Method*

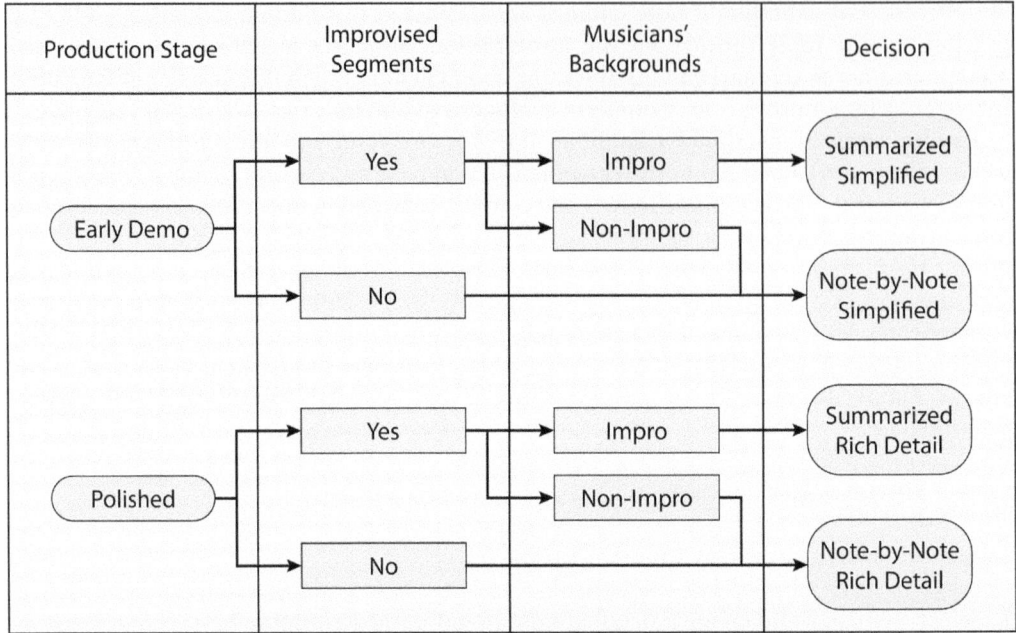

Figure 8.2 Deciding about notation detail.

reproduce the recording as closely as practical. At this stage, the recording contains the *final artistic product* in all its detail. It can be assumed that the captured musical ideas are performed with intention and consistency. Consequently, all relevant music information layers should be transcribed in ample detail. In this case, the sheet music format should have enough staves to accommodate the transcription in *comprehensive notation detail*. Note that any production stage between unpolished demo and commercial release is possible. Transcriptionists should always evaluate the work's production stage before deciding which music information layers to transcribe, and in how much detail.

Improvised Segments

A second criterion concerns how to notate improvised segments in sheet music. *Contemporary music styles* with broad appeal often encourage a *degree of discretionary expression* and spontaneity during performances (Burton & Snell, 2018). This freedom can manifest in several ways, including as improvised solos, accompaniment, aleatory, or fills. In this scenario, musicians exercise *spontaneous creativity*, typically over foundational and dependent layers. In contrast, other situations may stipulate all music information layers. In other words, the notes, expression, and the pace at which the notes should be played are described in detail. In these contexts, which include *classical music*, listeners will expect to hear music *reproduced note-by-note* (Alperson, 2014). In this scenario, performers may exercise a *subtler degree of spontaneous creativity*, typically through their personal interpretation of tempo and dependent layers.

With both scenarios in mind, the transcriptionist should *determine* the *presence of improvised segments* in the selected passage. This skill requires at least some stylistic familiarity with the work in question. Upon discovering an improvised segment, one must *decide* whether the notation should grant *improvisational discretion* or require a *detailed reproduction*. Remember that transcribed passages can include note-by-note and slash notation segments concurrently. As is common in arrangements, one segment may be fixed, while the other one is improvised (Lowell & Pullig, 2003). Overall, note-by-note segments promote a sense of structure, while improvised segments promote a sense of spontaneity. If uncertain about the right approach, it is good practice to inquire about the *expectations and preferences* of those *musicians* using the sheet music.

Industry Voice: Transcribing with the Band in Mind

Andreas: How do athletic band directors use music transcription?

Dylan: With many collegiate bands, the work of band directors is divided between instructional, administrative, and creative work. The creative work is very much about writing custom arrangements for the halftime shows that we perform, and also for custom marching band drill formations. A big part of my summer is really about understanding what's relevant in terms of contemporary pop music, and what's the cultural milieu of the time. And then, together with my colleagues and some student input, I'll design the shows. For example, we recently did a country hits show because of Beyonce's new crossover country album, which took the world by storm. I wrote all the custom arrangements to that marching band show. One of the reasons that we transcribe and arrange in-house is so that we can tailor the music specifically to our students. As a smaller to medium-sized private school, the Tulane University Marching Band has just over 100 members. In any given year, we have fluctuations in terms of how many trumpet and tuba players we have, for example, and the skill level of those players. By creating custom arrangements in house, we can really cater toward the skill and ability levels of our students and to the instrumentation that we have. The process also gives us a great deal of creative license, meaning we write idiomatically for the instruments, then translate the music into something really exciting for the crowd. The arrangements must be playable by avocational music students, because most of my students are not music majors. These students are not necessarily studying music. They're doing music as a co-curricular activity. Basically, I need to write music that is achievable for the players, but also exciting to listen to. Those are two of the core tenets.

Dylan Parrilla-Koester – Assistant Director of Bands, New Orleans, LA
Tulane University Bands

Musician's Background

There exist many ways to learn and perform music (Ake, 2002; Hallam et al., 2014). The background of those musicians involved in a project is a *determining factor* for *music notation decisions*. The *stylistic familiarity* and ways of learning to play new works *differ significantly between musicians*. For example, a musician may be a strong note-by-note reader with some experience playing fully notated jazz, but limited experience with slash notation. This type of musician will thrive sightreading or learning from fully notated music. However, if presented with slash notation, this musician type may need more time to learn the work, or may refuse to play it altogether.

In contrast, a musician may be *versed in improvising* from lead sheets with chord symbols, but have limited experience playing sophisticated note-by-note arrangements. This musician type will excel performing with *improvisational guidelines in familiar styles*. In other words, the musician will use the guidelines as a reference point while adding their own musical ideas to the performance as deemed appropriate (Baerman, 2016). However, if presented with fully notated arrangements that need to be followed note-by-note, this musician type may need more time to learn the work.

Further combinations of reading, improvisational, and *stylistic expertise* exist. Some musicians are even equally skilled in improvising and reading note-by-note arrangements. In summary, a project's level of *notation detail has significant impact* on the performance quality. Before transcribing a real-world project, transcriptionists should *familiarize* with the *involved musicians' backgrounds*. With this knowledge, sheet music can be optimized for those musicians and ultimately facilitate a high-quality performance.

Section Activities

Select a groove-based music recording from YouTube:

1. Determine the production stage of the music recording.
2. Identify any improvised segments. Then think of a recent collaborator and their music background. How would you notate the passage for this collaborator?

End-of-Chapter Activity

Applying everything you have learned in this chapter, find a personally significant music recording and select a specific passage. Next, determine an appropriate level of notation detail. Then transcribe the passage with the prescriptive notation framework in mind.

Chapter Summary

This chapter covered prescriptive music notation, levels of notation detail, and a decision-frame for notation detail as related to music transcription. Prescriptive sheet music quantifies recorded music in a way so that musicians can read and understand the work. The appropriate level of notation detail differs based on a recording's production stage, presence of improvised segments, and the performing musicians' backgrounds. The section activities provided learner opportunities to evaluate different levels of notation detail and their use in an industry context. Finally, the end-of-chapter activity provided an opportunity to practice notational decision-making based on a personally relevant work.

Learning Outcomes

The learner should now be able to:

CO 1: Articulate the practical scope and limitations of music notation for music transcription.
CO 2: Evaluate notation detail levels in applied industry contexts.

Up Next

Chapter 9 covers several interpretation scenarios of music transcription at the passage level.

References

Ake, D. (2002). *Jazz cultures*. University of California Press. https://doi.org/10.1525/9780520926967

Alperson, P. (2014). Musical improvisation and the philosophy of music. In G. E. Lewis & B. Piekut (Eds.), *The Oxford handbook of critical improvisation studies, volume 1* (pp. 419–438). https://doi.org/10.1093/oxfordhb/9780195370935.013.001

Baerman, N. (2016). *The complete Jazz keyboard method*. Alfred Music. ISBN: 978-1-470-63516-9

Burton, S., & Snell, A., II. (2018). *Ready, set, improvise! The nuts & bolts of music improvisation*. Oxford University Press. ISBN: 978-0-190-67592-9

Covington, K. (1980). Visual perception vs. aural perception: A look at mode de valeurs et d'intensités. *Indiana Theory Review*, 3(2), 4–11. https://www.jstor.org/stable/24046005

Farquharson, M. (2007). *Writer. Producer. Engineer. A handbook for creating contemporary commercial music*. Berklee Press. ISBN: 978-0-876-39053-5

Gorow, R. (2002). *Hearing and writing music: Professional training for today's musician* (2nd ed.). September Publishing. ISBN: 978-0-962-94967-8

Gould, E. (2011). *Behind bars: The definitive guide to music notation*. Faber Music. ISBN: 978-0-571-51456-4

Häberlin, A. (2024). *Reverie in G major* [Unpublished manuscript].

Hallam, S., Cross, I., & Thaut, M. H. (Eds.). (2014). *The Oxford handbook of music psychology* (2nd ed.). Oxford Academic. https://doi.org/10.1093/oxfordhb/9780198722946.001.0001

Houghton, S., Ranier, T., Viapiano, P., & Warrington, T. (1994). *The complete rhythm section*. Warner Bros. Publications. ISBN: 978-1-576-23990-2

Kalmanovitch, T. (2008). *"Indo-Jazz fusion": Jazz and Karnatak music in contact* [Doctoral dissertation, University of Alberta]. Education & Research Archive. https://doi.org/10.7939/r3-zw5n-zs96

Kanno, M. (2007). Prescriptive notation: Limits and challenges. *Contemporary Music Review*, 26(2), 231–254. https://doi.org/10.1080/07494460701250890

Lowell, D., & Pullig, K. (2003). *Arranging for large jazz ensemble*. Berklee Press. ISBN: 978-0-634-03656-9

Miller, R. J. (2014). *Contemporary orchestration: A practical guide to instruments, ensembles, and musicians*. Routledge. https://doi.org/10.4324/9781315815008

Seeger, C. (1958). Prescriptive and descriptive music-writing. *The Musical Quarterly*, 44(2), 184–195. https://doi.org/10.1093/mq/XLIV.2.184

Zolper, S. T. (2017). *The A to Z of music theory fundamentals: The ultimate workbook for music understanding*. Waveland Press. ISBN: 978-1-478-63296-2

9 Macrostructure

Chapter Overview

This chapter covers several context-specific decision frameworks for transcribing global music information layers. The first section covers form labels, navigation signs, and the effect of repeated sections on the scope of notation detail possible. The second section then covers time signature changes, pickups and inserts, and more complex metering situations. Finally, the third section covers common types of feels, tempo developments, tempo suspensions, and their notation. The section activities help learners apply contextual decision-making when transcribing form, time signatures, and tempo. In summary, this chapter offers several frameworks to transcribe musical works with respect for their style and industry-specific context.

Learning Outcomes

After reading this chapter, the learner will be able to:

CO 1: Evaluate contextual notation decisions about global music information layers.
CO 2: Integrate procedural transcription skills with contextual decision-making.

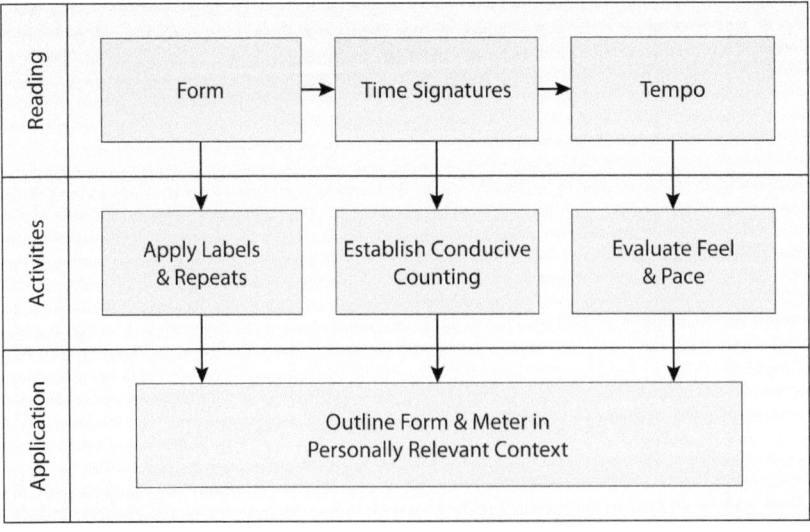

Figure 9.1 Chapter 9 map.

DOI: 10.4324/9781003511946-12

Form

It is good practice to mark the beginning of new sections while metering source materials. New sections tend to bring an audible change to the arrangement, which may be based on any combination of music information layers. The goal with placing *section markers* at these locations is to make the work's form more *visually apparent* (Fayte, 2008). Section markers may also be placed at the beginning of longer phrases and phrase extensions. Once the metering is complete, section markers may be transferred to the notation file as temporary *double barlines* to support navigation while transcribing. Double barlines may also be added permanently to help musicians navigate the *arrangement structure*.

Labels

Further to double barlines, a work's form is often implied through *rehearsal marks* to facilitate navigation (Gould, 2011). Conventions for rehearsal mark formats vary widely. Different parts of the industry have established their own guidelines. The following cases do not usually require labels named after the form:

- Film scoring sessions: No rehearsal marks.
- Classical line-ups: Progressive letters or numbers.
- Musical theater: Measure numbers as rehearsal marks.

In contrast, *groove-based music styles* with broad appeal tend to *label rehearsal marks* after the work's form parts. The labeling often follows the two prevalent form types in these styles: the *pop song form* and the *binary form*. In groove-based styles, musicians tend to be conscious of the work's form while performing (Sikora, 2022). For example, rhythm section players may vary their accompaniment between a verse, pre-chorus, and chorus. Similarly, a music producer may articulate specific musical ideas for each form part in a song.

Just like generic rehearsal marks, *labeling practices* with form names may follow *progressive lettering and numbering*. The level of detail appropriate depends on the context. Informal settings often benefit from simple alphabetical or numerical labeling. In contrast, settings with higher stakes, including studio sessions and performances following a specific arrangement structure, may benefit from alphanumerical labeling. Finally, if the form part names are not apparent upon initial listening, these labels may be added later in the transcription process. Transcribed lyrics and chord progressions are especially helpful in determining form part names (Nobile, 2020).

Navigation Signs

Sheet music can be transcribed in full or compacted length. *Full-length notation* allocates *dedicated space* for each played note. In this case, performers can play the sheet music

Table 9.1 Form-conscious rehearsal marks

Labeling Scheme	Pop Song Form	Binary Form
Alphabetical	Verse A, Verse B, Chorus ...	Part A, Part B ...
Numerical	Verse 1, Chorus 1, Verse 2 ...	Part 1, Part 2 ...
Alphanumerical	Verse 1A, Verse 1B, Verse 2A ...	A-Part 1, B-Part 1, A-Part 2 ...

from beginning to end without making any repetition-based jumps. In analogy to reading a book with straightforward narrative, it is easy to follow the form in sheet music with full-length notation. Overall, this approach requires more notation space, but *captures any variations* in repeating sections. Full-length notation is often found in contexts that require an arrangement played note by note and measure by measure. Prominent examples include film scoring and album recording sessions with session musicians, as well as live performances with click tracks (Piorkowski, 2023).

Conversely, *compacted length notation* allocates a shared notation space to repeating sections. In this case, performers follow navigation signs to play the sheet music from beginning to end. These signs require performers to *jump from one section to another* at a specific point in the sheet music. In analogy to reading a gamebook, it takes more effort to successfully follow the form in compacted sheet music. This approach *captures fewer variations* in repeating sections, but saves notation space (Feist, 2017). Apart from saving paper and reducing page turns, compacted length notation is common in contexts where decisions about repeating form parts are made in the moment. Examples include musical theater, improvisation-centric works, and music at worship events.

Including navigation signs is only effective if the transcriptionist is actively aware of the work's form. If pursuing *compacted notation*, and it becomes clear during the process that form parts are unsuitable for repetition, the sheet music may lose overall consistency. To prevent this outcome, it is recommended to treat each transcription as *full-length notation initially*. Any suspected repetitions of parts can be temporarily marked in the notation file. The transcriptionist can start by transcribing the first occurrence of each part, then compare the results to suspected repeating parts. This approach preserves any non-repeating material that should be notated. Once the potential for compacted notation becomes clear, the transcriptionist can notate the *necessary directives* and *delete any excess measures* from the notation file.

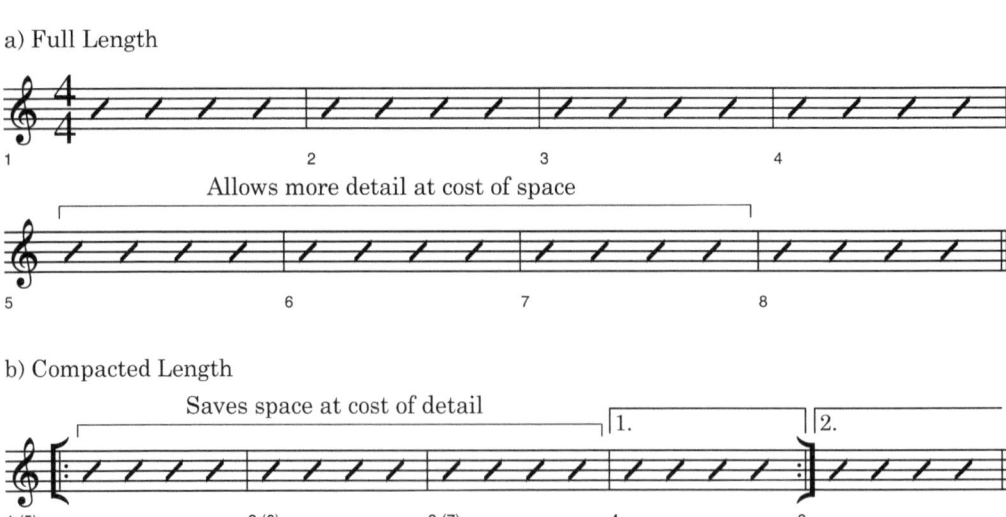

Example 9.1 Full and compacted length notation in comparison.

Section Activities

Select and listen to a familiar music recording:

1. Analyze the form and justify a labeling approach for rehearsal marks.
2. Evaluate the use of navigation signs. In which cases would it make sense to use compacted notation, and why?

Time Signatures

To establish conducive metering, it is recommended to *meter the entire recording* during the transcription outline, even if the intent is to transcribe only a short passage. A fully metered recording provides the *best possible overview* to determine time signatures. This approach is especially valuable in situations when the transcriptionist is unclear about metering. Common examples of metering challenges include measure markers that sound out of place during playback, or measures that do not seem to align with a given time signature. These challenges are common and affect transcriptionists at all career stages (Tan et al., 2017).

Situations with *unclear metering* require increased *attention to sub-beat grouping* (Tan et al., 2017). The objective is to group beats in a way to make the music as clear to count as possible. Using the metering framework covered in Chapter 4, transcriptionists can meter the recording in an exploratory fashion to determine the *clearest way to count* the music. Once an initial pulse and downbeat are identified, the transcriptionist will continue counting beats until the end of the recording, or until the present counting system does not apply anymore. At this point, the transcriptionist must determine any changes to the pulse, the location of the next downbeat, and any possible time signature changes. With growing experience, transcriptionists will determine clear counting patterns and time signatures more intuitively.

Industry Voice: Musical Ideas and Methodology

Andreas: Raven Music Editions publishes piano-vocal songbooks from metal artists. What considerations are important when transcribing into this format?

Martin: The transcriptions, or rather arrangements in this case, are founded on the motivation to transmit the essential musical idea to the largest possible group of consumers and music lovers. The harmonic analysis is thus also very important, because it allows other instruments, for example guitars, to play along as well. The "piano reduction," especially from operatic and orchestral scores has a long historical foundation, in the sense that it was essential for soloists to practice with. Some of these reductions are living their own lives as well and are performed more frequently at concerts than the actual original.

Andreas: How should we listen to music for transcription purposes?

Martin: The transcription methodology is by definition rather subjective (whatever works for the transcriber, works), but the classical methodology is of course to break down the music into its core elements: Meter, tempo, key,

> and rhythm. Then probably picking out the melody first, then the base line, then the harmonies. The middle part of a musical construction is of course the most difficult. I remember transcribing by ear the big band version of Bernstein's *West Side Story* some years ago. Some of the chords have nine different notes in them. That was quite the sport. When listening to music actively, one should ideally do the opposite of breaking down, rather unite it internally. Music is a language of integration and unification.
>
> Martin Romberg – Classical Composer, Norway/France
CEO of *Raven Music Editions*

Pickup and Insert Measures

Sections with established time signatures occasionally include a few *extra beats* that do not match the metric grid. If metered at the established time signature, these extra beats will shift unstressed *notes* to the downbeat. As a result, the sheet music feels less intuitive to play (Ashley & Timmers, 2017). Extra beats may occur as pickup phrases at the very beginning, or as inserts anywhere in the work. To restore and *preserve stressed downbeats*, the extra beats should be *grouped into a separate measure* with its own signature. This practice ensures that the music feels natural to count.

When metering, transcriptionists should monitor continuously for any *extra beats* that shift unstressed notes to downbeats. Extra beats are often *discovered by surprise*, especially when metering unfamiliar works. When discovering extra beats that shift the balance, the transcriptionist should first *identify the closest succeeding downbeat*. This downbeat should restore the time signature preceding the extra beats. Next, the extra beats should be counted and framed as a measure with a separate time signature. Note that pickup measures should always be shorter than the succeeding measures (Franceschina, 2015). Conversely, insert measures can be of any length that is convenient to count.

Section-Based Changes

When new sections build a *stronger contrast* to previous sections, they may also include new time signatures. New time signatures between sections are often part of a metric modulation (Gordon, 2009). In contrast to insert measures, these *new time signatures persist* for at least several measures, a section, or longer. Transcribing section-based time signature changes follows the same approach covered in Chapter 4. However, the transcriptionist should *meter each section* with a suspected time signature change *individually*. In other words, the two sections are treated as separate units.

Like with pickup and insert measures, it is important to determine the time signature that *frames the new section best*. The process includes metering, then selecting a time signature and corresponding tempo mark. In contrast to works with a single time signature and tempo, works with section-based changes are simply *metered section by section*. Whenever the present metering does not match a new section, the transcriptionist should analyze that section separately. Thereafter, a metric modulation text can be added to describe how the previous and present meter relate rhythmically (Gould, 2011). Overall, the metering framework remains the same, but it is applied to shorter parts of the work at a time.

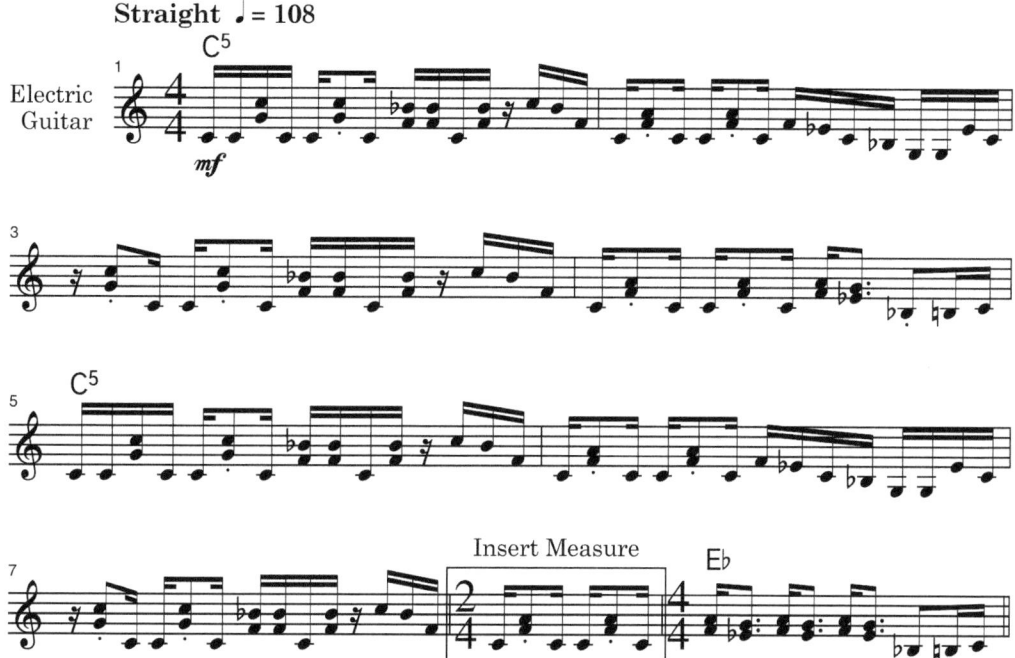

Example 9.2 Occasional time signature changes. Lanzetti (2022), Coney Bear, mm. 1–9, on *Empire Central*. Transcribed by Andreas Häberlin. Printed with permission of Robert J Lanzetti.

Complex and Mixed Meter

Finally, some sections are counted in less straightforward ways. For example, neighboring beat groups may contain uneven numbers of sub-beats, which results in *main beats with different length*. This type of meter is known as non-isochronous (Hesselink, 2022). When housed in the same measure, uneven beat groups add up to *complex time signatures*. Determining complex time signatures follows the same process as identifying simple time signatures. After identifying the recurring downbeats, the transcriptionist will *group the heard sub-beats* into simple and compound groups and determine which time signature captures the recurring beat pattern best.

In a similar case, the distance between downbeats may change every measure, or every few measures. Affected measures differ in length and therefore require a new time signature. These *frequent time signature changes* are also known as *mixed meter* (Hesselink, 2022). Like in other metering scenarios, the first step is to identify downbeats. With mixed meters, these *downbeats* occur, at least initially, at *less predictable* intervals. Once the downbeats are identified, the transcriptionist can count each measure's total number of beats and allocate time signatures accordingly.

Section Activities

Select and listen to a familiar music recording:

1. Start a transcription outline by adding an initial time signature and pickup measure if applicable.
2. Screen for any suspected time signature changes, then analyze and notate these.

104 *A Music Transcription Method*

Example 9.3 Time signatures for complex and mixed meter. Brock (2022), Way Home, mm. 41–48, on *Dirty Mindz*. Transcribed by Andreas Häberlin. Printed with permission of Secret Fort Publishing.

Tempo

Beyond metering, several further aspects are key to *capturing the counting and flow*. Metronome marks describe the initial tempo, and any tempos established at a later point in the work. In genres with broad appeal, metronome marks often include instructions about the music's feel. More gradual tempo developments are captured as *accelerando*s and *ritardando*s. Finally, some passages may show no perceivable pulse. If no conducive pulse is found, transcriptionists should capture the temporary suspension of the tempo instead. This section covers several *decision frames* related to transcribing tempo information.

Feel

Metronome marks frequently include further performance instructions. These instructions summarize *performance nuances as broader guidelines* and eliminate the need to notate these nuances literally, which would clutter the sheet music appearance. Feel guidelines provide the context necessary to interpret the music in a *specific style* or with a *certain energy* (Hartenberger & McClelland, 2020). Without these guidelines, performers are left unclear how to interpret the sheet music. The prevalent *feel* categories include:

- Rhythmic: Straight, swing 8ths, swing 16ths, shuffle, freely, rubato.
- Expression: With excitement, melancholically, joyfully.
- Genre: Rock, pop, jazz, country.
- Timing: Laidback, mechanically, pushed.

Perhaps the most concrete instructions are the *rhythmic feel and timing*. These instructions clarify how the sheet music is to be *interpreted rhythmically*. A straight feel indicates that all notes are to be played at their specified timing and duration. In contrast, swing delays the timing of even sub-beats in each beat group, resulting in groups with longer beats and shorter offbeats. Freely describes broad rhythmical discretion, while rubato limits rhythmical discretion to the phrase level. Finally, laidback and pushed feels describe the micro-timing between instruments (Pedersen, 2013). For example, drums and bass may play slightly behind other members of the rhythm section to create a laidback feel. Because *timing-based feels are subtle*, they are noticed more intuitively if at all.

In genres with a broad appeal, there exist *no fixed rules* for the use of *feel instructions*. Each industry, and sometimes even the local scene, has adopted its own notation preferences for feels. Categories can be combined as helpful to convey the work's feel. However, *musicians' backgrounds* should be factored in at the transcription outline stage. For example, classical musicians tend to play swing more authentically if reading note-by-note, while musicians of groove-based genres tend to prefer summary notation (Corcoran et al., 2022). Similarly,

a) Note-by-Note

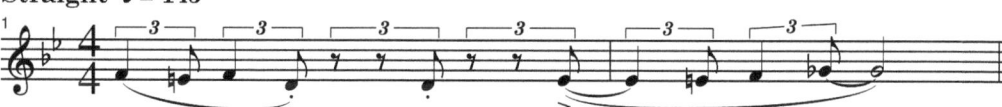

b) Summary Notation

Example 9.4 Swing feel: Note-by-note versus summary notation. Häberlin (2024), *Key West Special*, mm. 1–2, melody.

106   A Music Transcription Method

genre descriptors are only effective if the musicians are *familiar with the genre* in question. Finally, timing-based feels should be reserved for advanced performers.

Developments

A recorded work's *tempo may vary over time*. Some of these variations are intentional, while others occur as natural fluctuations. For example, a passage may slow down intentionally for added emphasis. As another example, a new section may jump to a new tempo to support a change in musical character. In contrast, subtler fluctuations are typically the result of recording the work without a click track (Owsinski, 2016). In any case, the transcriptionist's objective is to *summarize tempo developments* in the *simplest terms possible*.

Continuous tempo developments include *accelerando*s and *ritardando*s. Their effects typically become audible a few beats into the development. Note that beat mapping may expose continuous tempo developments too, in a visualized way. Continuous tempo developments may *start and end anywhere* on beats or between. Transcriptions that will be performed to a click track should honor these start and end points exactly (McGuire, 2019; Mynett, 2017). In all other cases, it is recommended to simplify:

- Start points should fall on downbeats, or halfway into measures.
- End points should fall on the last beat of a measure, or a beat that suspends the tempo.

The end point should also include a new tempo mark that indicates if the succeeding passage will be played slower, faster, or return to the same speed as the passage preceding the tempo development.

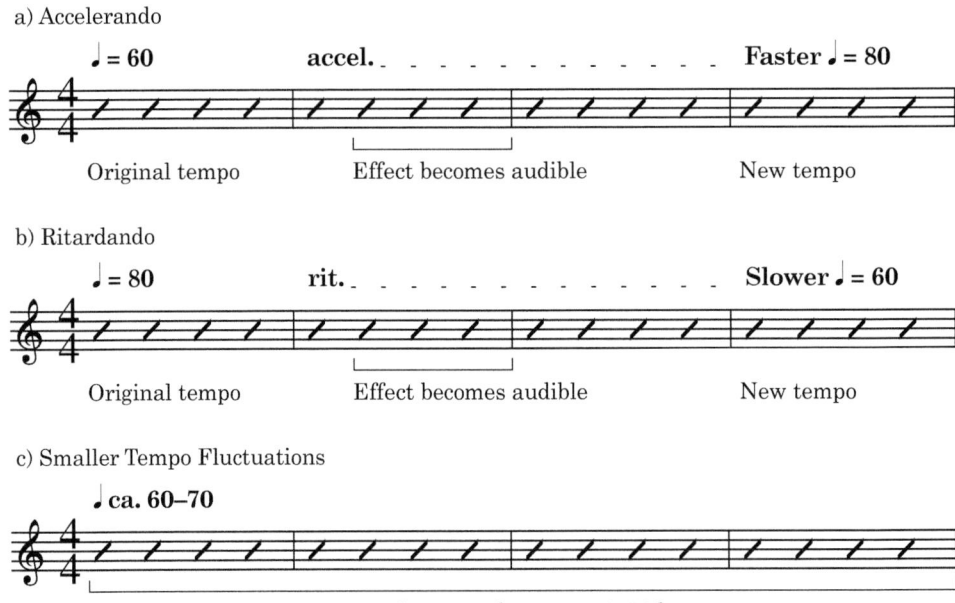

Example 9.5 *Accelerando*, *ritardando*, and smaller tempo fluctuations.

In contrast, *instantaneous tempo developments* are immediately audible unless the change is subtle. In these cases, the transcriptionist may simply *compute the new tempo* over a few measures. Often, but not always, instantaneous developments mark the beginning of new sections. Finally, fluctuating tempo developments simply describe a tempo that varies by a few bpm across a passage. Tempo fluctuations can be subtle and sometimes inaudible. If spotted, it is acceptable to compute the average tempo across the passage and include a "ca." in the metronome mark. Note that subtle tempo fluctuations differ from rubato. Rubato denotes more intentional and pronounced, phrase-based tempo fluctuations (Hartenberger & McClelland, 2020).

Suspensions

In passages with longer sustained notes or rests, the *pulse* sometimes appears *temporarily suspended*. In other words, the previously established pulse does not seem to apply to the present section. These cases suggest the use of fermatas and caesuras to describe the temporary suspension (Labuta & Matthews, 2023). *Fermatas* describe a temporary hold *on the beat* they are placed. These beats may include both notes and rests. Conversely, *caesuras* describe a temporary hold *between beats*. Caesuras denote a brief moment of silence, coordinated across all instruments. Fermatas and caesuras are best used in measures that would otherwise require complex time signatures or unnatural tempo changes.

Tempo suspensions manifest as *metric incontinuities* (London, 2012). They may be discovered during initial metering or later in the transcription process. Before notating a suspension, it is recommended to *try counting* the selected measure based on the established metering in adjacent measures. For example, the transcriptionist may count beats forward or backward to check if the pulse applies to the measure in question. This approach helps *contextualize the metering* in places that are rhythmically unclear. If applied metering from adjacent measures does not clarify the passage in question, then it is worth considering the use of a fermata or caesura.

If using a suspension, one should start by *locating* the *next clear downbeat*. This step helps frame the measure in question. Next, all perceivable beats preceding, hitting, and succeeding the suspension should be marked. The goal is to *gradually corner* the suspended beat. If the measure with the suspended beat matches the present time signature, a fermata is the likely choice. Conversely, if counting a prolonged rest introduces an additional beat to the measure, a caesura should replace this rest to preserve the time signature (Brooks, 2013). Transcriptionists with conducting experience are encouraged to explore the *most concise way of conducting* the section in question, then applying the beating pattern to the metering.

Section Activities

Select and listen to a familiar music recording:

1. Analyze the feel, then justify how you would label it and why.
2. Screen for any tempo developments and suspensions, then analyze and notate these.

Example 9.6 Fermatas and caesuras. Turner (2022), "Everything is Fine," mm. 85–93, in *Ciao Bambino the Musical*. Transcribed by Andreas Häberlin. Printed with permission of Elizabeth Allen Turner.

End-of-Chapter Activity

Applying everything you have learned in this chapter, find a personally significant music recording and create a transcription outline. Notate those form parameters, time signatures, and tempo parameters that you find most conducive.

Chapter Summary

This chapter covered form parameters, time signatures, and tempo parameters as related to music transcription. The covered strategies encourage listeners to explore global music information layers from an in-depth auditory perspective. The decision-frames discussed help listeners contextualize their analyses. The section activities provided learner opportunities to practice decision-making about global music information layers. Finally, the end-of-chapter activity provided an opportunity to practice decision-making on a personally relevant work.

Learning Outcomes

The learner should now be able to:

CO 1: Evaluate contextual notation decisions about global music information layers.
CO 2: Integrate procedural transcription skills with contextual decision-making.

Up Next

Chapter 10 covers several interpretation scenarios of music transcription at the phrase and note level.

References

Ashley, R., & Timmers, R. (2017). *The Routledge companion to music cognition*. Routledge. https://doi.org/10.4324/9781315194738
Brock, Z. D. (2022). Way home [Instrumental]. On *Dirty mindz*. Secret Fort Publishing. https://open.spotify.com/track/07cpVHhFh4uv2TwOm9pEng
Brooks, J. (2013). Invisibility's beat: Ralph Ellison, rhythm, and cinema's blind field. In J. H. Hoogstad & B. S. Pedersen (Eds.), *Off beat: Pluralizing rhythm* (pp. 149–168). Brill. https://doi.org/10.1163/9789401208871_011
Corcoran, C., Stupacher, J., & Vuust, P. (2022). Swinging the score? Swing phrasing cannot be communicated via explicit notation instructions alone. *Music Perception, 39*(4), 386–400. https://doi.org/10.1525/mp.2022.39.4.386
Fayte, B. (2008). *The complete home music recording starter kit: Create quality home recordings on a budget!* Pearson Education. ISBN: 978-0-768-68756-9
Feist, J. (2017). *Berklee contemporary music notation*. Berklee Press. ISBN: 978-0-876-39178-5
Franceschina, J. (2015). *Music theory through musical theatre: Putting it together*. Oxford University Press. ISBN: 978-0-199-99954-5
Gordon, E. E. (2009). *Rhythm: Contrasting the implications of audiation and notation*. GIA Publications. ISBN: 978-1-579-99784-7
Gould, E. (2011). *Behind bars: The definitive guide to music notation*. Faber Music. ISBN: 978-0-571-51456-4
Häberlin, A. (2024). *Key West special* [Unpublished manuscript].
Hartenberger, R., & McClelland, R. (Eds.). (2020). *The Cambridge companion to rhythm*. Cambridge University Press. https://doi.org/10.1017/9781108631730
Hesselink, N. (2022). *Finding the beat: Entertainment, rhythmic play, and social meaning in Rock music*. Bloomsbury Academic. ISBN: 978-1-501-39299-3
Labuta, J. A., & Matthews, W. (2023). *Basic conducting techniques* (8th ed.). Routledge. https://doi.org/10.4324/9781003183617
Lanzetti, R. J. (2022). Coney bear [Instrumental]. On *Empire Central*. Bobbylanz Music. https://open.spotify.com/track/7IF6HT1xgH3tpqyxFZZTmq
London, J. (2012). *Hearing in time: Psychological aspects of musical meter* (2nd ed.). Oxford University Press. https://doi.org/10.1093/acprof:oso/9780199744374.001.0001
McGuire, S. (2019). *Modern MIDI: Sequencing and performing using traditional and mobile tools*. Routledge. https://doi.org/10.4324/9781351263849
Mynett, M. (2017). *Metal music manual: Producing, engineering, mixing, and mastering contemporary heavy music*. Routledge. https://doi.org/10.4324/9781315750071
Nobile, D. (2020). *Form as harmony in rock music*. Oxford University Press. ISBN: 978-0-190-94835-1

Owsinski, B. (2016). *The music producer's handbook* (2nd ed.). Rowman & Littlefield. ISBN: 978-1-4930-8366-4

Pedersen, B. S. (2013). Aesthetic potentials of rhythm in Hip Hop music and culture: Rhythmic conventions, skills, and everyday life. In J. H. Hoogstad & B. S. Pedersen (Eds.), *Off beat: Pluralizing rhythm* (pp. 55–70). Brill. https://doi.org/10.1163/9789401208871_005

Piorkowski, C. (2023). *Scoring to picture in Logic Pro: Explore synchronization techniques for film, TV, and multimedia composers using Apple's flagship DAW*. Packt Publishing. ISBN: 978-1-837-63689-1

Sikora, F. (2022). *Jazz harmony: Think – Listen – Play – A practical approach*. Schott Music. ISBN: 978-3-795-74930-9

Tan, S.-L., Pfordresher, P., & Harré, R. (2017). *Psychology of music: From sound to significance* (2nd ed.). Routledge. https://doi.org/10.4324/9781315648026

Turner, E. A. (2022). Everything is fine [Song]. In *Ciao bambino the musical* [Unpublished manuscript].

10 Microstructure

Chapter Overview

This chapter covers several context-specific decision frameworks for transcribing foundational and dependent music layers. The first section covers strategies to capture repetition in grooves and other recurring patterns. The second section then covers the vertical and horizontal scope of chord symbols, and how to set this scope conducively for transcription. Finally, the third section covers several aspects of capturing nuance in phrasing, namely through melismas and articulation shading. The section activities help learners apply contextual decision-making when transcribing repetition, chord symbols, and note-level contrast. In summary, this chapter offers guidance on transcribing foundational and dependent layers with a readable level of granularity.

Learning Outcomes

After reading this chapter, the learner will be able to:

CO 1: Evaluate contextual notation decisions about foundational and dependent layers.
CO 2: Integrate procedural transcription skills with contextual decision-making.

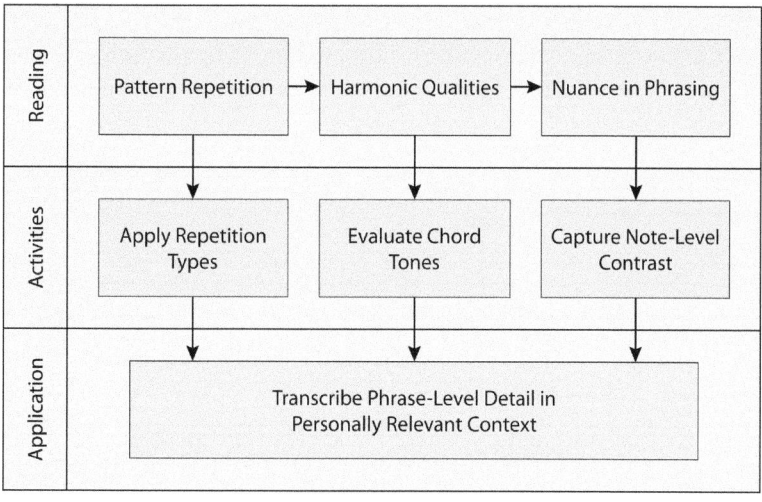

Figure 10.1 Chapter 10 map.

DOI: 10.4324/9781003511946-13

112 A Music Transcription Method

Pattern Repetition

Music with a broad appeal generally includes repetition, at both passage and phrase level. Repetition at the phrase level is based on *recurring note patterns*. For example, a melodic pattern of six notes may be played several times in a row. Similarly, a 2-measure accompaniment pattern may be repeated several times without any variations. These cases describe an exact repetition of the initial pattern. In contrast, a 1-measure drum groove may be played for eight measures, but introduce slight variations over that time span. Contemporary music notation offers symbols to capture both, pattern repetition *with* and *without variation* (Feist, 2017). The transcriptionist's objective is to determine which type of repetition should be notated.

Groove and Time

In genres with broad appeal, *pattern repetition with variations* is associated most frequently with *rhythm sections* playing a groove. Chapter 7 covered the steps to transcribe rhythm charts, including groove information. Whenever a new or substantially different groove is introduced to a section, its core is typically notated in detail over the first one or two measures. Thereafter, slash notation indicates that the musicians should play time (Houghton et al., 1994). *Groove* and *time notation* are especially common with drum parts, but are also found in other rhythm section parts. Transcriptionists can capture repetition by determining the groove's core attributes and degree of variation over time.

To determine the *groove's core attributes*, the transcriptionist should listen to several phrases of the section in question. The goal is to get an overview of recurring patterns of *one or two measures* in length. As for drums and unpitched percussion, these patterns should include the timings and types of instrument hits, for example, kick, snare, and cymbals (Rock, 1993). As for basses, the patterns should imply note timings and the type of melodic progression present. Finally, patterns for polyphonic instruments should include note timings and the type of voicing structures present. The initially notated patterns should include those *notes recurring most prominently* and exclude less prominent, sporadic notes. This practice ensures the readability of groove patterns.

Measure Repeat Signs

In contrast to time notation, some patterns are repeated literally, with very *minimal variation*. There exist two common approaches to notating exact repetition. First, pattern

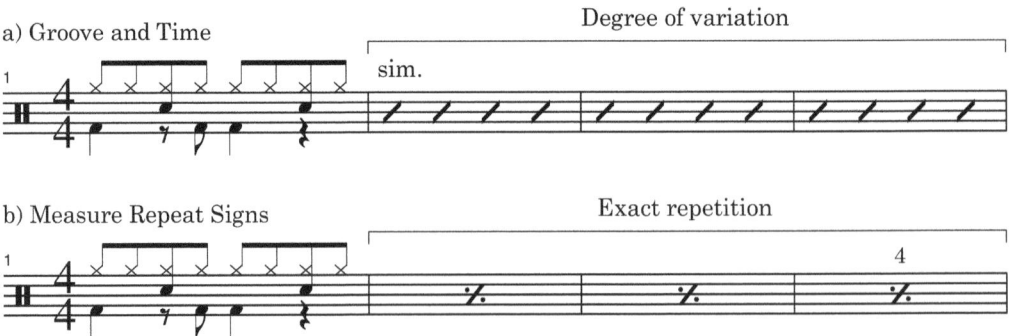

Example 10.1 Drum groove, time, and measure repeat signs.

repetitions of one or two measures' length can be summarized through *1-measure* and *2-measure repeat signs*. The initial pattern is written out note-by-note, while any repetitions are notated through the corresponding measure repeat sign (McGrain, 2002). Second, repetition can also be written out *note-by-note*. This approach is most effective with patterns whose length does not match the length of a 1-measure or 2-measure repeat sign. Repetition should also be written out note-by-note if a pattern is too long or complex to memorize.

Although no specific application rules exist, *measure repeat signs* are commonly found in rhythm section and percussion parts. These types of performers are perhaps most familiar with measure repeat signs. The use of measure repeat signs helps highlight repetition, declutter the notation, and ultimately *increase* the *sheet music's readability*. Consequently, performers may find it easier to *grasp* the present *repetition conceptually*. Measure repeat signs can also be found beyond rhythm section and percussion parts, for example in passages with ostinatos or textural effects. Note that, while 4-measure repeat signs exist, their use is discouraged (Nicholl & Grudzinski, 2007).

Decision-Making

The best approach to *notating pattern repetition* has been *subject to ongoing debate* among industry practitioners. Some prefer a more literal notation, while others prefer slashes and measure repeat signs. With the *readability implications* of both approaches in mind, transcriptionists should first decide whether the notation should capture as much detail as possible, or if it should summarize the music more conceptually. For example, if studying a recorded performance in-depth, performance details are best transcribed note-by-note (Gorow, 2002). Conversely, if the intention is to perform a recorded work by following broader guidelines, summarized notation helps establish these guidelines.

Once the *decision about notation detail* is solidified, transcriptionists may pursue the respective approach. For an in-depth transcription, pattern repetition should be written out note-by-note. If any patterns of one or two measures' length repeat exactly, they may be summarized through measure repeat signs (Gould, 2011). In contrast, for a transcription of broader performance guidelines, the transcriptionist should first identify the main groove patterns and compositional elements. Main groove patterns are typically found in the first few measures of new sections. The remaining groove measures may then be tentatively marked with slash notation and verbal performance instructions. If a groove repeats without variation for an entire section, measure repeat signs can be considered. To avoid confusion, it is recommended to use either *only slashes* or *only measure repeat signs* within the same groove.

Section Activities

Listen to the online audio examples provided:

1. Create a note-by-note transcription, but replace all exact repetitions with measure repeats.
2. Create a transcription with broader guidelines, including groove patterns, time, stop time, and cues. Notate any non-repeating phrases note-by-note.

Harmonic Qualities

Transcribing harmony *note-by-note* includes notating the *exact voicing structure*. In other words, transcribed voicings include both the exact pitches played and their vertical order. In contrast, *chord symbols* act as a framework to *summarize harmonic qualities*. Chord symbols capture a chord's bass note and corresponding harmonic intervals (Chen et al., 2020). However, chord symbols do not specify the vertical order of these harmonic intervals. When transcribing chord symbols, transcriptionists match the heard notes with the chord symbol that most closely represents these notes. Sometimes, these notes are clearly attributable to one chord symbol. In these cases, the chord symbol captures every heard note. While this case is ideal, it is not always guaranteed. The more common scenarios include voicings with fewer or more notes than common chord symbols can frame. These cases require a more detailed vertical and horizontal analysis.

Vertical Scope

As covered in Chapter 6, chords consist of *constellations of harmonic qualities*. Chord symbols capture these qualities as harmonic intervals in relation to a chord's root note. Each interval describes a part of the chord's harmonic quality. Genres with broad appeal differentiate between the following qualities:

- Foundations: Root, 3rd, 5th, 6th, and 7th.
- Extensions: 9th, 11th, and 13th.

Basic chords consist of a combination of foundational qualities and their alterations. These chords include major, minor, diminished, augmented, suspended, and those same types with the major 7th and minor 7th interval respectively. In contrast, *extensions* build on the fundament of foundational qualities (Levine, 1995). Extension qualities, also known as upper structure in Jazz theory, *add color* and *nuance* to the sound of basic chords. By definition, they only exist together with foundational qualities, but not independently. General listeners tend to be most familiar with foundational harmonic qualities.

With foundational and extension qualities in mind, it is recommended to first determine a chord's bass note, then *identify* the present *harmonic qualities ascendingly*. From a theoretical perspective, a chord symbol is complete if it captures all the *present notes*. However, two exceptions are common in practice. First, a heard chord may point toward a specific chord symbol, but may be missing one or several intervals of that chord quality (Cutler, 2019). For example, a seventh chord may include the 13th, but exclude the 9th and 11th. In this case, the transcriptionist needs to decide whether to notate a standard 13th chord symbol, or to document the absence of the other two intervals. Second, a heard chord may point toward a specific chord symbol, but may include more notes than that chord symbol frames. For example, a major chord may also include a 9th. In this case, the transcriptionist must decide whether to consider the 9th as part of the chord symbol.

Horizontal Scope

In a *simple scenario*, chord symbols are transcribed directly from *block chords*, for example, from an accompaniment part. In this scenario, it is clear which notes to factor into the chord symbols. However, *most arrangements* contain *more complex elements* than block

Example 10.2 Bass and harmonized melody, captured note-by-note, without chord symbols. Stanton (2019), Shoegazer, mm. 48–50, on *Secret Place*. Transcribed by Andreas Häberlin. Printed with permission of Justin Stanton.

chords. Therefore, chord symbols are most often derived from elements in addition to, or in place of, block chords. Examples include bass lines, broken chords, and harmonized melodies and countermelodies. These elements frequently include non-chord tones that fall between foundational harmonic qualities (Lowell & Pullig, 2003). Consequently, the decision which notes to factor into chord symbols becomes more complex.

Non-chord tones are major *distractors* during chord analyses, mainly because it is initially unclear if chord symbols should capture their presence (Solomon, 2019). To identify and bracket these non-chord tones, one must consider which notes carry the most emphasis horizontally. The first step is to determine the likely timing and length of a chord symbol, as well as its foundational harmonic qualities. Thereafter, any *notes beyond* these *basic qualities* should be examined, by prominence, for potential inclusion in the chord symbol. Prominent notes, including those played at a comparatively loud volume, placed on stressed beats, or held for a comparatively long time, tend to be more suitable as chord tones than notes played less prominently.

Decision-Making

Chord symbol complexity remains an area of debate among transcriptionists. With the vertical and horizontal scope of harmonic qualities in mind, it is very common to feel uncertain about the choice of chord symbols. In this context, it is important to understand that chord symbols have *finite potential to capture* harmonic qualities and constellations (Sikora, 2022). In genres with broad appeal, chord symbols are used to summarize key qualities and make them readable at a glance. Chord symbols that capture a high level of harmonic detail or that follow each other in close succession will decrease readability. Therefore, rather than aiming to describe every harmonic quality, transcriptionists should capture the *level of detail appropriate* for the sheet music's purpose.

Overall, deciding about chord symbol complexity follows the decision-frame covered in Chapter 8. Projects in *early production stages* or with improvisation may benefit from simplified chord symbols. In this case, chord symbols should capture *primarily foundational harmonic qualities*. This approach leaves room for musicians to experiment with extension qualities (Levine, 1995). In contrast, *polished arrangements* may benefit from chord symbols that describe harmonic qualities in *more intricate detail*. However, the transcriptionist should keep in mind musicians' stylistic backgrounds and expertise. For example, a complex jazz chord symbol may be understood by a professional jazz musician, but not by someone with an informal background in jazz. Overall, it is recommended to factor in the project stage, improvisational components, and musicians' backgrounds to determine the level of chord symbol detail. *Local chord symbol conventions* should also be factored into this decision.

Section Activities

Select and listen to a familiar music recording:

1. Determine conducive locations for chord symbols, then identify the basic and extended harmonic chord tones present.
2. Decide on the desired complexity of the chord symbols, then create the chord symbols. Explain which factors informed your decision.

Nuance in Phrasing

Foundational and dependent layers can be transcribed successively at various levels of detail. However, some notation decisions must be made at the intersection of these layers. This final section discusses several nuances at the phrase level. At this granular view, notation decisions concern *audible nuances* between notes of the same phrase. In this context, two important aspects to consider are melismas and articulation shading. When transcribing at the *phrase level*, the objective is to determine a level of notation detail that supports the sheet music purpose and musicians' backgrounds.

Melismas

Large parts of this book focus on instrumental music. One vocals-based topic that must be discussed is the melisma. Melismas are a type of vocal ornament that comprise several consecutive notes sung over the same syllable (Barker & Huesca, 2018). In the context of music transcription, two types of melismas should be mentioned. First, *composed melismas* are created by the writer or arranger and are *integral to the work*. Second, *improvised melismas* are a tool for creative expression. In contrast to composed melismas, improvised melismas are used at the *vocalist's discretion*. Their sound ranges from prominent and intentional to subtle and subconscious.

Composed melismas should always be transcribed note-by-note. In contrast, improvised melismas may be transcribed at various levels of detail. However, the most immediate objective is to *decide* if a heard melisma is likely *composed* or *improvised*. The difference between composed and improvised vocal elements is not always reliably traceable by ear (Hawkins, 2017). Therefore, the decision-making process is rather exploratory and case-by-case. As a general guideline, melismas that recur identically and *make the work*

Example 10.3 Melisma example. Hémy (1864), "Angels We Have Heard on High," mm. 9–14, in *Crown of Jesus Music* (p.162). Work in public domain.

recognizable are more likely to be *composed*. Transcriptionists should cross-reference recurring melismas for this purpose. In contrast, melismas that do not recur, or that recur with *noticeable variation*, are more likely to be *improvised*. Transcriptionists may follow the guidelines in Chapter 8 to determine an appropriate level of notation detail for improvised melismas.

Articulation Shading

Rhythmical values and section dynamics capture a general perspective of the notes played. These parameters establish rhythm and overall loudness. However, to establish *nuance between different notes*, articulations are necessary (Jacobson, 2015). As covered in Chapter 6, two articulation types are relevant in this context. First, emphasis-based articulations indicate an individual note's *attack strength* compared with its surrounding notes. Second, length-based articulations indicate a note's *duration* in relation to its note value. Both articulation types help musicians perform music with greater nuance. The following paragraphs describe how musicians of different backgrounds may interpret length and emphasis-based articulations.

The prevalent *length-based articulations* include the tenuto, staccato, and staccatissimo. A tenuto requires a note to be played for its full duration (Heussenstamm, 1987). Conversely, staccato notes are traditionally played at half their length, and staccatissimo at an even shorter length. *Classical musicians* tend to be more familiar with these *specific conventions*. In contrast, musicians of *contemporary commercial genres* tend to treat staccatos

Emphasis	Full Duration		Shortened Duration	
	With Intent	Neutral	Neutral	Pronounced
None	♩̄	♩	♩̇	♩!
Some	≥♩	>♩	>♩̇	Less Idiomatic
Ample	^♩	^♩	Less Idiomatic	Less Idiomatic

Figure 10.2 Matrix of composite articulations.

and staccatissimos as *perceived* short and very short *note values* respectively. In this scenario, quarter notes and shorter values with staccato dots are simply treated as short notes. Overall, length-based articulations can convey nuanced note lengths without the need to notate exact note values. Transcriptionists should use length-based articulations to simplify rhythmic appearance where practical, but factor in musicians' understanding of staccatos and staccatissimos.

Second, the most established *emphasis-based articulations* include the *marcato* and *accent* (Heussenstamm, 1987). Marcato describes a note with a forceful attack. Experienced sheet music readers tend to be more familiar with this articulation. In contrast, the accent describes a slightly less forceful attack. Most reading musicians are familiar with this articulation. Further distinctions exist, but their definitions tend to be less standardized. Overall, the level of *length* and *emphasis-based* articulation detail is at the *transcriptionist's discretion*. Factors to be considered include those outlined in Chapter 8.

Industry Voice: Working With Choreographers on Broadway

Andreas: How are different articulation types important for dance music arrangers?

Zane: As a dance music arranger, when I'm writing something down, it's usually in a format for a pianist to play in the rehearsal room. I'll write some kind of bass line in the left hand, and the basic harmonic material in the right hand. The melody is usually already in the chart. As for articulations, 80% of that depends on what the choreo requires. The more articulations you put in the music, the less guessing the musicians have to do. That saves a lot of time! The string players will read almost anything you put on the paper, so that's easy. But it's the horns that we, or I as a dance arranger, use the most to help the dancers.

There's a lot of material that needs to be accentuated beyond just general playing. Is the note staccato? Is it long? How does the phrasing go? That's where I'm a little more particular about the articulations. Once I finish an arrangement, we play it in the room to make sure it works for the dancers. Then we get with the orchestrator. The more information I can give the orchestrator, the more it's going to sound like what's in my head (and the choreographer's) before we get to orchestra rehearsals. So, I try to give the orchestrator as much information as possible in that regard. It's usually the horns that I'm writing out in detail, and some special string effects like tremolo or pizzicato. But my primary concern is with the horns, and I try to be as exact as possible for them.

Zane Mark – Dance Music Arranger, NYC
*Boop! The Musical, A Wonderful World:
The Louis Armstrong Musical*

Section Activities

1. Find and listen to a familiar music recording featuring vocals. Transcribe the vocals while distinguishing between improvised and composed melismas. Reflect on the contextual effectiveness of your transcription.

2. Find and listen to a familiar music recording. Decide on the desired level of articulation shading, then transcribe. Reflect on the contextual effectiveness of your transcription.

End-of-Chapter Activity

Applying everything you have learned in this chapter, find a personally significant recording of groove-based music. Transcribe the rhythm section parts with pattern repetition and chord symbol qualities in mind. Also consider nuances in phrasing as you transcribe.

Chapter Summary

This chapter covered pattern repetition, harmonic qualities, and nuances in phrasing as related to music transcription. Musicians' backgrounds, the production stage, and the sheet music purpose should all be factored in when deciding about phrase-level notation detail. Conducive notation detail at the phrase level is readable and supports creative performance decisions. The section activities provided learner opportunities to practice decision-making about foundational and dependent music information layers. Finally, the end-of-chapter activity provided an opportunity to practice decision-making on a groove-based, personally relevant work.

Learning Outcomes

The learner should now be able to:

CO 1: Evaluate contextual notation decisions about foundational and dependent layers.
CO 2: Integrate procedural transcription skills with contextual decision-making.

Up Next

Chapter 11 covers the interpretation of orchestration components in context of music transcription.

References

Barker, P., & Huesca, M. (2018). *Composing for voice: Exploring voice, language and music* (2nd ed.). Routledge. https://doi.org/10.4324/9781315277172
Chen, T.-P., Fukayama, S., Goto, M., & Su, L. (2020). Chord jazzification: Learning Jazz interpretations of chord symbols. *Proceedings of the 21st International Society for Music Information Retrieval Conference* (pp. 360–367). https://doi.org/10.5281/zenodo.4245444
Cutler, T. (2019). *Bending the rules of music theory: Lessons from great composers.* Routledge. https://doi.org/10.4324/9781351069168
Feist, J. (2017). *Berklee contemporary music notation.* Berklee Press. ISBN: 978-0-876-39178-5
Gorow, R. (2002). *Hearing and writing music: Professional training for today's musician* (2nd ed.). September Publishing. ISBN: 978-0-962-94967-8
Gould, E. (2011). *Behind bars: The definitive guide to music notation.* Faber Music. ISBN: 978-0-571-51456-4
Hawkins, S. (2017). *Pop music and easy listening.* Routledge. https://doi.org/10.4324/9781315089669
Hémy, H. F. (1864). Angels we have heard on high [Sheet music]. In *Crown of Jesus music* (p. 162, mm. 9–14). Thomas Richardson & Sons. https://play.google.com/books/reader?id=7C0xaM4Zp9cC&pg=GBS.PA162&hl=en

Heussenstamm, G. (1987). *The Norton manual of music notation*. W. W. Norton. ISBN: 978-0-393-95526-2

Houghton, S., Ranier, T., Viapiano, P., & Warrington, T. (1994). *The complete rhythm section*. Warner Bros. Publications. ISBN: 978-1-576-23990-2

Jacobson, J. M. (2015). *Professional piano teaching: A comprehensive piano pedagogy textbook. Volume 2: intermediate-advanced levels*, ed. E. L. Lancaster, & A. Mendoza. Alfred Music. ISBN: 978-0-7390-8169-3

Levine, M. (1995). *The Jazz theory book*. Sher Music. ISBN: 978-1-883-21704-4

Lowell, D., & Pullig, K. (2003). *Arranging for large jazz ensemble*. Berklee Press. ISBN: 978-0-634-03656-9

McGrain, M. (2002). *Music notation: Theory and technique for music notation*. Berklee Press. ISBN: 978-0-793-50847-1

Nicholl, M., & Grudzinski, R. (2007). *Music notation: Preparing scores and parts*. Berklee Press. ISBN: 978-0-876-39074-0

Rock, B. (1993). *The encyclopedia of groove*. Alfred Music. ISBN: 978-0-769-23367-3

Sikora, F. (2022). *Jazz harmony: Think – Listen – Play – A practical approach*. Schott Music. ISBN: 978-3-795-74930-9

Solomon, J. W. (2019). *Music theory essentials: A streamlined approach to fundamentals, tonal harmony, and post-tonal materials*. Routledge. https://doi.org/10.4324/9781315167749

Stanton, J. M. (2019). Shoegazer [Instrumental]. On *Secret place*. J Stant Music. https://open.spotify.com/track/0pBnjHRndKPSLBiQV0j36C

11 Orchestration

Chapter Overview

This chapter covers the transcription of sound sources and dynamics in an orchestration context. The first section covers the identification of individual sound sources through their sonic profiles, playing techniques, and secondary information. The second section then covers the identification of heterogeneous and homogeneous sound sources in stacked composite sounds. Finally, the third section explains the transcription of timbre-based dynamics to reconstruct the original performance dynamics. The chapter activities help learners practice the attribution of timbre to individual sound sources, stacked sound sources, and dynamics. In summary, this chapter offers strategies to transcribe notation detail with increased attention to orchestration.

Learning Outcomes

After reading this chapter, the learner will be able to:

CO 1: Analyze the sonic characteristics of individual and composite sound sources.
CO 2: Reconstruct recorded dynamics with consideration for timbral characteristics.

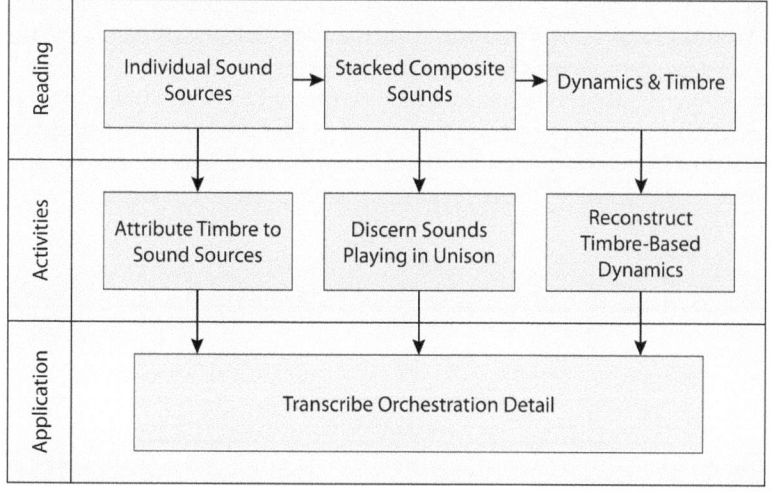

Figure 11.1 Chapter 11 map.

DOI: 10.4324/9781003511946-14

122 A Music Transcription Method

Individual Sound Sources

There exists a vast range of *musical instruments*, all with their unique sonic characteristics. Sooner or later on their journey, transcriptionists will unavoidably encounter unfamiliar sound sources. For example, someone unfamiliar with the sound of a bass clarinet may register the sound but fail to identify its source. Similarly, a transcriptionist may find it difficult to distinguish between two homogeneous-sounding sources. For example, a transcriptionist unfamiliar with brass instruments may be unsure if a segment is played by a trombone or French horn. The *unique sonic qualities* of musical instruments fall under the larger umbrella of *orchestration* (Dolan & Rehding, 2018). To help pinpoint an unidentified sound source, the transcriptionist may evaluate the source's sonic profile, playing techniques, and broader context.

Sonic Profiles

Although a sound source may be initially unknown, its sonic characteristics can help identify it. The covered approach starts with a *process of elimination*. First, the transcriptionist should assess the source's *played range*. The upper and lower limits of the range can be defined by each note's pitch and octave register. A common labeling system in music with broader appeal is the scientific pitch notation (de Clercq, 2024). To instantiate this step, the standard range of a concert flute is C4–C7, whereas C4 marks the lowest, and C7 the highest playable note (Nestico, 2014). If the heard range includes notes outside the flute's standard register, the flute can be ruled out as a candidate. For example, an upper range limit of concert G7 will rule out the flute, even if the source sounds flute-like. Note that the process of elimination is similar, but less precise, for *unpitched percussion sounds*: Those sources can be attributed to general *high, mid, and low registers*. For example, a drum-like sound in the low register rules out higher drum sounds like high and mid toms.

After ruling out the obvious candidates, a *process of disambiguation* begins. Each instrument consists of one or more playable registers, and each register has its own *timbral characteristics* (Rimsky-Korsakov, 1964). For example, a clarinet's lowest register sounds dark and sonorous, while its highest register sounds bright and piercing. In comparison, a flute's lowest register sounds dull and whistling, while its highest register sounds clear and whistling. Orchestration books cover these and further examples with increased timbral granularity. With the played range in mind, the transcriptionist should analyze the heard timbre and name its source (Cutting & Rosner, 1974; Grey, 1977). Note that learning to recognize sound sources by their timbre is a *gradual growth process*. It is recommended to start familiarizing with the most relevant sound sources in one's environment, then gradually *expand one's horizon* to cover further sources and their timbral characteristics.

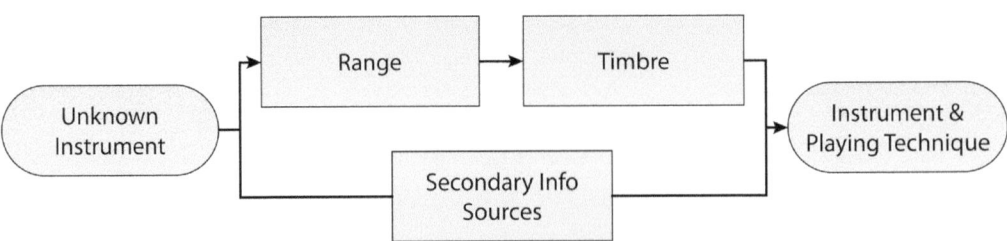

Figure 11.2 Pinpointing sound sources.

Playing Techniques

Timbre is strongly affected by playing techniques specific to certain instruments or instrument types (Sevsay, 2013). These techniques describe the way that a *tone is generated or manipulated* over time. Among the vast range of playing techniques, one of the most common techniques is the use of *muted sounds*. In context of *brass* and *orchestral strings*, mutes are attachable objects that change the instrument's timbre (Miller, 2014). The resulting sounds are especially pronounced and timbrally diverse on brass instruments. On string instruments, a mute creates a mellower sound. In the context of guitars, basses, and similar stringed instruments, mute effects are commonly achieved by dampening the strings with the palm or fingers (Houghton et al., 1994). The resulting sounds are shorter and of muffled quality. Many further examples exist beyond these popular muting techniques.

The *tools for sound production* also affect the timbre significantly (Sevsay, 2013). For example, the use of arco bows or finger pizzicati with orchestral string instruments creates contrasting sounds. Similarly, felt and wood *beaters* hitting a mallet instrument also create distinct sounds. The same concept holds true for *fingers* or *plectrums* hitting the strings of a guitar, bass, or similar instrument. Yet another example is the use of *brushes* or *sticks* on a snare drum. The list of tools for sound production is virtually endless. All things considered, both mute techniques and tools for sound production shape an instrument's timbre significantly. These playing techniques and others help illustrate sound sources in greater detail and, therefore, *should be notated* as part of the transcription.

Industry Voice: Takedown as a Creative and Methodical Craft

Andreas: What are your expectations for someone who does takedown for you?

Claire: In situations when there's a tight deadline, which is fairly common, there's limited opportunity to talk to my takedown person about specific moments. So the best situation for them is to have an idea of what's happening in the scene, provided it's a ballet or film project, and then they'll usually see the notes, and the pictures or markers that I created in my DAW to describe the action. These notes can have an important bearing on how they notate the music texturally. However, I think ultimately, it's about building a relationship with the person who's doing your takedown. It's good for them to get to know your style, seeing several projects through completion, knowing what edits I requested after a takedown, and what things I perhaps didn't expect them to know. That sparks conversations and learning that ultimately help the next project. So I think the personal relationship helps in the end. One interesting finding is that we name instruments differently between different countries. There are even different names and notation references between the United States, New Zealand, and Australia. Local differences in labeling can have quite big consequences if they slip through the editing phase and end up being in the score.

Andreas: What advice would you have for musicians who are just starting out?

Claire: Check your work carefully. Especially if you're taking down music for somebody else. If you're taking down for yourself, you're going to be fairly accurate, but if you're taking down for anybody else, that level of accuracy is really what's going to continue getting you work. Takedown is an

> important part of learning how to be a composer. It's like looking at the back end of the painting or music piece and discovering, through repeated listening, how things are constructed. And these tools help you achieve similar things in your own music.
>
> Claire Cowan – Composer & Orchestrator, New Zealand
> *Cinderella* and *Hansel & Gretel*, with Royal New Zealand Ballet

Synthesizers and Samplers

Beyond acoustic and amplified instruments, there exist two instrument types that, by design, *imitate the sonic properties* of sound events. Synthesizers and samplers are electronic instruments with a number of *controllable parameters*. These controls help shape a sound's sonic characteristics at a granular level. The most essential controls include:

- Source type: Oscillator or sampled sources with a given timbre.
- Amplitude envelope: A note's volume over time.
- Filter envelope: A note's timbral representation over time, for example brightness.

Most synthesizers and samplers allow storing the control values of a sound as presets. Countless further controls exist to shape the sound of synthesizers and samplers. The availability and complexity of these controls has developed significantly since the early days of synthesizers (Wilson, 2020).

Synthesizer sounds follow the same notation guidelines for foundational layers as other sound sources. However, given their extensive scope of sonic profiles, synthesizer sources require *additional descriptors* detailing the heard sound. Essential descriptors include the source's role, timbre, and audible effects. The following list offers a few examples:

- Role: Lead, pad, bass, FX, riser, downer.
- Timbre: Mellow, bright, metallic, airy.
- Effects: Chorus, delay, vibrato, distortion.

In addition, some synthesizer models are recognized across the music industry for their unique sonic characteristics. The most known models include the Roland TR-808 Drum Machine and the Yamaha DX7 Electric Piano (Russ, 2008). If recognized during transcription, it is recommended to *include model information* in the sound source description.

Secondary Information Sources

Further to analyzing the sonic characteristics of sound sources, transcriptionists may also determine line-up information by examining the work's *surrounding context*. For published music, a simple first step is to research the list of performers involved in the recording, also known as *recording credits* (Nathan & Morgan, 2008). These may be found in the credit sections of digital streaming platforms, on the liner notes of physical releases, or in online databases. Although credits may not identify the exact instruments featured, they may help *narrow the scope*.

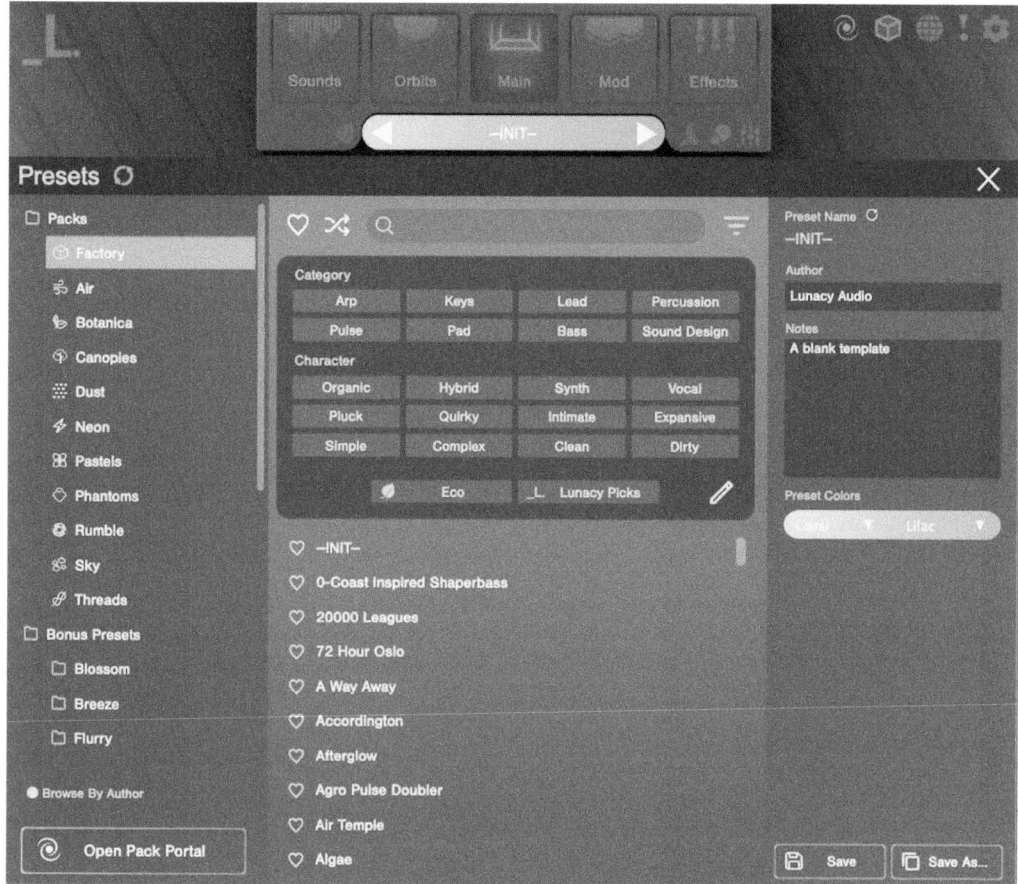

Figure 11.3 Preset categories in creative software sampler CUBE (2023). Printed with permission of Lunacy Inc.

A second step is to examine the audible line-up in context of the *music style*. After naming the familiar instruments, one may search for *streamlined similar line-ups* in that music style. For music of established artists and performers, hints about line-ups may also be found in music videos, documentaries, interviews, blogs, articles, fan communities, and similar media. Finally, it is always worth discussing a work's line-up with an *expert of that music style*. While informal, these research avenues can help solve, or at least approximate, the puzzle of an unknown instrumental line-up.

Section Activities

Listen to the online audio examples provided:

1. Without naming the sound sources, describe their individual sonic profiles.
2. Name each sound source and playing technique. Articulate a plan to identify the remaining unknown sound sources.

Example 11.1 Synthesizer descriptors in bass part and lower staff of keys part. Maher (2016), Replica, mm. 21–22, on *Idealist*. Transcribed by Andreas Häberlin. Printed with permission of Michael T Maher.

Stacked Composite Sounds

It is very common for two or more sound sources to play the same part concurrently, note-by-note. The result is a stacked composite sound, also called *doubling* (Rimsky-Korsakov, 1964). Stacked composite sounds may occur as instrument doublings for a few notes or a passage. They may also occur for an entire work, for example, as an orchestral double bass part. As a general rule for music with broad appeal, the larger the instrumentation is, the more sources tend to play the same part concurrently. With each additional instrument doubling the same part, it becomes more difficult to differentiate between these instruments. Composite sources can be broadly categorized into *heterogeneous* profiles, *homogeneous* profiles, and *sections* of the same instrument. Note that there are no specific increments between contrasting and similar profiles.

Heterogeneous Doublings

When two sound sources with heterogeneous sonic profiles play in unison, they create an *audible contrast* (McAdams et al., 2022). As a result, the two sound sources are *clearly distinguishable* by ear. Within stacked composite sounds, contrasting sound sources are the easiest to identify. It is simply recommended to familiarize with the sound of the sources relevant to the music style in question. The following examples pair sound sources with contrasting sonic profiles playing the concert middle C:

- Violin and oboe.
- Piano and baritone saxophone.
- Harp and marimbaphone with wooden mallets.
- Clarinet in B♭ and trumpet with harmon mute.

Homogeneous Doublings

When two sound sources with homogeneous sonic profiles play in unison, their sounds *blend together*. Consequently, it becomes more *difficult to differentiate* between these two sound sources (McAdams et al., 2022). Homogenous composite sounds require more aural training to identify. Transcriptionists should primarily study the sonic profiles of individual sound

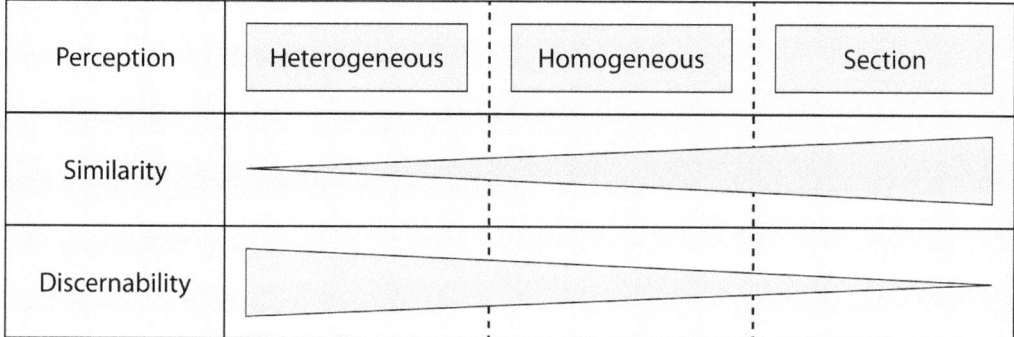

Figure 11.4 Timbral contrast in composite sound sources.

sources and their homogeneous doublings. An alternative strategy includes panoramic listening as discussed in Chapter 2. Homogeneous doublings tend to be panned across the listening panorama, and can sometimes be dissected based on this panning. The following examples pair homogenous sound sources playing the concert middle C, at an *mf* dynamic:

- Violin and viola.
- French horn and clarinet in B♭.
- Flute and violin.
- Bassoon and violoncello.

Sections in Unison

In some cases, *several instruments of the same* type will double a segment in unison. The resulting sound is somewhat analogous to several paintbrush strokes of the same color, made at the same location on the painting. With each stroke, the color becomes increasingly present and prominent. In analogy, unison sections in music emanate a *richer, fuller sound* than single sound sources. This is common with orchestral instruments, and particularly with members of the orchestral strings family (Berlioz, 2010; Kennan & Grantham, 2024). With unison sections, the main question is how many players are doubling the selected part. The difference between one and several instruments performing the same part is *audible with some practice.*

However, it is more difficult to discern between *two* and *several instruments* doubling the same part. This situation is common with string orchestra sections. As the number of doubling instruments grows, it becomes more practical to capture the *section's ballpark size*. For example, the heard sound might resemble a small, medium, or large first violin section. Note that instrument sections vary in numbers by music style and era (Chon et al., 2018). In orchestral contexts, the transcriptionist may familiarize with the sound of section sizes by *studying scores and recordings* of the relevant industry field or era.

Section Activities

Listen to the online audio examples of stacked composite sounds provided:

1. Without naming the sound source pairs involved, describe the level of timbral contrast in each pair.
2. Name each source involved in the stacked composite sound. Articulate a plan to identify the remaining unknown sound sources.

128 A Music Transcription Method

Dynamics and Timbre

A critical but little discussed orchestration topic is the intersection of dynamics and timbre. The central idea is that an instrument's *timbre changes* when played at *different dynamic levels* (McAdams, 2019; Siedenburg & McAdams, 2017). For example, a note played quietly on a trumpet will have a mellow tone. In contrast, the same note played loudly will not only sound louder, but also have a brighter tone. Each sound source has its own dynamic-based scope of timbral characteristics. Transcriptionists who *familiarize with the intersection* of dynamics and timbre can determine dynamic markings with greater granularity. This framework is particularly helpful in reconstructing an instrument's performance dynamics at the time of recording.

Conceptual Intersection

Dynamics and timbre behave similarly in acoustic and amplified instruments. Each instrument type has a *unique dynamic scope* that frames the quietest and loudest performance dynamics possible. Different instrument types have different dynamic ranges (Meyer, 2015). For example, a bassoon can play quieter than a tuba at its lowest dynamic, but not as loud as the tuba at its highest dynamic. The dynamic scope further *differs between* an instrument type's *registers*. For example, a soft dynamic is easy to achieve in an oboe's mid register, but difficult in its lowest register. Similarly, a loud dynamic is easier to achieve on a piano's lowest register than on its highest register. Finally, each register's dynamic scope is *accompanied by a timbral scope* (Reymore et al., 2023). A specific note played on a specific instrument, at a specific dynamic level, will have a unique timbre.

In contrast, dynamics operate more independently from timbre in *electronic instruments* (Russ, 2008). Synthesizers and samplers may offer *independent control* over timbre and dynamics, for example, through MIDI velocity, aftertouch, or continuous controllers. In this example, a note played at a louder dynamic retains the same timbre. Conversely, timbre controllers tend to introduce dynamic changes: A brighter timbre is often accompanied by a louder dynamic, while a darker timbre tends to be accompanied by a softer dynamic. *Dynamics* and *timbre* controllers can be linked to amplify the intersection of both parameters. Common ways to link these parameters include keyboard tracking, macro knobs within the synthesizer, or hardware MIDI controllers.

Volume Balance in Mixed Music

After music has been recorded, it is typically mixed, a process that includes *adjustments to the loudness* of individual sound sources and the recording as a whole (Gibson, 2018).

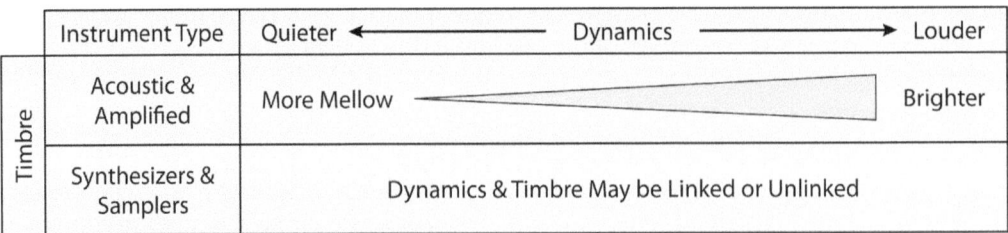

Figure 11.5 Dynamic and timbre interaction.

For example, a single instrument's loudness may be increased by several decibels to make it stand out. As another example, a mix engineer may reduce a recorded instrument's dynamic scope, so the volume difference between its loudest and quietest notes is smaller. Mix engineers make dynamic tweaks for both *artistic reasons* and to ensure that the mix meets *quality standards* for publication. As a result, some sources may sound more prominent on a recording than during a live performance, and some will sound less prominent.

From an orchestration perspective, mixing can *alter the natural relation* of dynamics and timbre in a performance (Hepworth-Sawyer & Hodgson, 2016). For example, backing vocals recorded at *ff* may have been lowered in volume to leave space for the lead vocals. The *ff* timbre persists, but the backing vocals sound much quieter on the mixed recording than during the recording session. As another example, an upright bass recorded at *f* may be raised in volume to make it match the volume of a large pop ensemble. The *f* timbre persists, and the upright bass will be more audible in the mix than its natural volume would allow. In summary, mixing can elevate or lower the *prominence* of sound sources in a mix, while preserving each source's *timbre*.

Contextual Framework

With the intersection of dynamics and timbre in mind, *transcribing dynamics can feel counterintuitive*. In case of acoustic and amplified sources, a source may sound quiet in the mix, despite its obvious *ff* timbre. Similarly, a source may predominate a mix, but emanate a *p* timbre. As for synthesizer presets, the relations between dynamics and timbre are even less clear. That is because each synthesizer preset is crafted with its own sonic properties and requires a case-by-case evaluation of how dynamics and timbre intersect (Pejrolo & Metcalfe, 2017). Many transcriptionists feel unclear whether to transcribe dynamics based on a source's prominence in the mix, its timbre, or a combination of both. Transcribing *prominence captures the volume* balance in the mix, while transcribing *timbre captures the dynamics* of individual sound sources.

The *choice of approach* depends on the larger picture: In some cases, transcriptionists may want to *preserve the volume balance* between melodies, chords, basslines, and further arrangement elements. This scenario is common with musicians who plan to further arrange and refine the transcription, but maintain the volume balance as heard on the recording. In other cases, transcriptionists may focus on *preserving the timbre* of individual sound sources. This scenario is more common with musicians looking to approximate the timbre of sound sources through orchestration. A *combination of both approaches* occurs if the mix preserves the natural relation of dynamics and timbre in a performance.

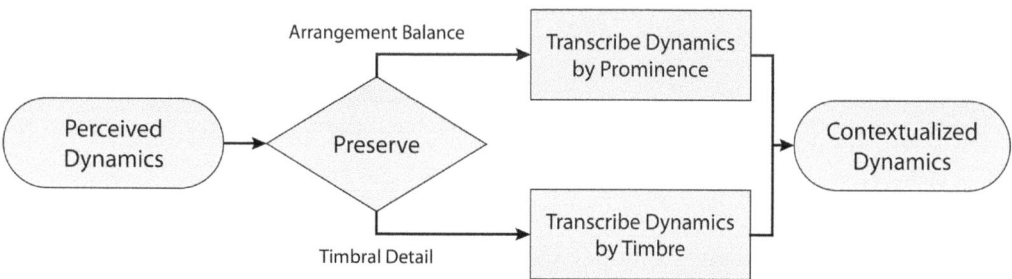

Figure 11.6 A framework for transcribing dynamics and timbre.

Section Activities

Listen to the online audio examples provided:

1. From what you know about each sound source, describe the dynamics based on the heard timbre.
2. Next, identify those sound sources that you were less familiar with. Articulate a plan to learn about these sources' dynamic and timbral intersection.

End-of-Chapter Activity

Applying everything you have learned in this chapter, find a personally relevant, published music recording that includes a larger line-up. Select a brief passage and transcribe all heard parts. Also identify all heard single and composite sources in the process. Next, add dynamic markings with consideration for the timbral characteristics of sound sources. Reflect on any challenges encountered during the process.

Chapter Summary

This chapter covered the identification of individual sources, stacked composite sources, and the intersection between dynamics and timbre as part of music transcription. Overall, individual and heterogeneous composite sound sources are easier to identify than stacked, homogeneous composite sound sources. Dynamics can be transcribed by prioritizing a sound source's prominence or timbre. The section activities provided learner opportunities to explore aspects of orchestration and articulate learning strategies to expand one's understanding of orchestration. Finally, the end-of-chapter activity provided an opportunity to apply the discussed orchestration aspects to a personally relevant project.

Learning Outcomes

The learner should now be able to:

CO 1: Analyze the sonic characteristics of individual and composite sound sources.
CO 2: Reconstruct recorded dynamics with consideration for timbral characteristics.

Up Next

Chapter 12 covers several industry opportunities for music transcriptionists.

References

Berlioz, H. (2010). *A treatise upon modern instrumentation and orchestration* (M. C. Clarke, Trans.). Cambridge University Press. (Original work published 1858). https://doi.org/10.1017/CBO9780511694936

Chon, S. H., Huron, D., & DeVlieger, D. (2018). An exploratory study of western orchestration: Patterns through history. *Empirical Musicology Review*, 12(3–4), 116–159. https://doi.org/10.18061/emr.v12i3-4.5773

CUBE (Version 1.5.0) [Computer software]. (2023). Lunacy Inc. https://lunacy.audio/products/cube/

Cutting, J. E., & Rosner, B. S. (1974). Categories and boundaries in speech and music. *Perception & Psychophysics*, 16, 564–570. https://doi.org/10.3758/BF03198588

de Clercq, T. (2024). *The practice of popular music: Understanding harmony, rhythm, melody, and form in commercial songwriting*. Routledge. https://doi.org/10.4324/9781003331155

Dolan, E. I., & Rehding, A. (Eds.). (2018). *The Oxford handbook of timbre*. Oxford University Press. https://doi.org/10.1093/oxfordhb/9780190637224.001.0001

Gibson, D. (2018). *The art of mixing: A visual guide to recording, engineering, and production*. Routledge. https://doi.org/10.4324/9781351252225

Grey, J. M. (1977). Multidimensional perceptual scaling of musical timbres. *The Journal of the Acoustical Society of America*, 61(5), 1270–1277. https://doi.org/10.1121/1.381428

Hepworth-Sawyer, R., & Hodgson, J. (Eds.). (2016). *Mixing music*. Routledge. https://doi.org/10.4324/9781315646602

Houghton, S., Ranier, T., Viapiano, P., & Warrington, T. (1994). *The complete rhythm section*. Warner Bros. Publications. ISBN: 978-1-576-23990-2

Kennan, K., & Grantham, D. (2024). *The technique of orchestration* (7th ed.). Routledge. https://doi.org/10.4324/9781003130680

Maher, M. T. (2016). Replica [Instrumental]. On *Idealist*. Mazarito Music. https://open.spotify.com/track/29XYgm5IoKIa60mix3lW0F

McAdams, S. (2019). Timbre as a structuring force in music. In K. Siedenburg, C. Saitis, S. McAdams, A. N. Popper, & R. R. Fay (Eds.), *Timbre: Acoustics, perception, and cognition* (pp. 211–243). https://doi.org/10.1007/978-3-030-14832-4_8

McAdams, S., Goodchild, M., & Soden, K. (2022). A taxonomy of orchestral grouping effects derived from principles of auditory perception. *Society for Music Theory*, 28(3). https://doi.org/10.30535/mto.28.3.6

Meyer, J. (2015). *Akustik und musikalische Aufführungspraxis* (6th ed.). Erwin Bochinsky. ISBN: 978-3-932-27595-1

Miller, R. J. (2014). *Contemporary orchestration: A practical guide to instruments, ensembles, and musicians*. Routledge. https://doi.org/10.4324/9781315815008

Nathan, R. J., & Morgan, B. (2008). *But where do I sign? A guide to understanding the music industry and its contracts, copyrights, and licenses*. Music Law Press. ISBN: 978-0-982-13960-8

Nestico, S. (2014). *The complete arranger* (Rev. ed.). Fenwood Music Co. ISBN: 978-1-502-74511-8

Pejrolo, A., & Metcalfe, S. B. (2017). *Creating sounds from scratch: A practical guide to music synthesis for producers and composers*. Oxford University Press. ISBN: 978-0-199-92189-8

Reymore, L., Noble, J., Saitis, C., Traube, C., & Wallmark, Z. (2023). Timbre semantic associations vary both between and within instruments: An empirical study incorporating register and pitch height. *Music Perception*, 40(3), 253–274. https://doi.org/10.1525/mp.2023.40.3.253

Rimsky-Korsakov, N. (1964). *Principles of orchestration: With musical examples drawn from his own works in two volumes bound as one* (Rev. ed.). Dover Publications. ISBN: 978-0-486-21266-1

Russ, M. (2008). *Sound synthesis and sampling* (3rd ed.). Routledge. https://doi.org/10.4324/9780080926957

Sevsay, E. (2013). *The Cambridge guide to orchestration*. Cambridge University Press. ISBN: 978-1-107-02516-5

Siedenburg, K., & McAdams, S. (2017). Four distinctions for the auditory "wastebasket" of timbre. *Frontiers in Psychology*, 8, Article 1747. https://doi.org/10.3389/fpsyg.2017.01747

Wilson, N. (2020). Introduction. In N. Wilson (Ed.), *Interpreting the synthesizer: Meaning through sonics* (pp. xv–xix). Cambridge University Press. ISBN: 978-1-527-55002-5

Part IV

Resources

Part Overview

Chapters 12, 13, and 14 cover several guidelines toward applying music transcription with music industry projects. Chapter 12 covers three common career profiles and strategies to find work. Chapter 13 shares several concepts and strategies for project management. Chapter 14 discusses foundational workflow principles for music transcription projects. In summary, Part IV guides learners through applying their skills in a music industry context.

Learning Outcomes

After reading Part IV, the learner will be able to:

BO 4: Build industry leverage through music transcription.

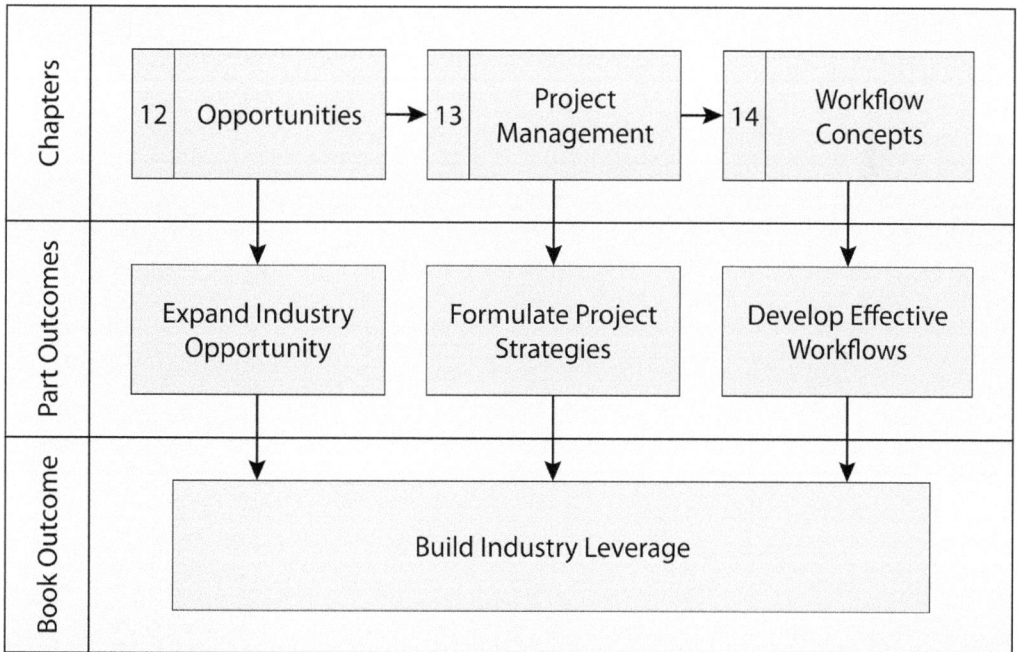

Figure 0.4 Part IV map.

DOI: 10.4324/9781003511946-15

12 Opportunities

Chapter Overview

This chapter covers several strategies and considerations for finding industry opportunities for music transcription. The first section illuminates the role of music transcription with the three common career profiles of arrangers, orchestrators, and music copyists. The second section then covers several aspects of connecting with the music industry through collaborative opportunities, industry networking, and offering music transcription services online. Finally, the third section covers strategies for industry visibility and best practices to sustain a music career. The section activities help learners take actionable steps to grow transcription opportunities in a field of interest. In summary, this chapter illuminates common practices to secure and maintain industry opportunities.

Learning Outcomes

After reading this chapter, the learner will be able to:

CO 1: Explore the integration of music transcription with related disciplines.
CO 2: Employ strategies to create industry opportunity.

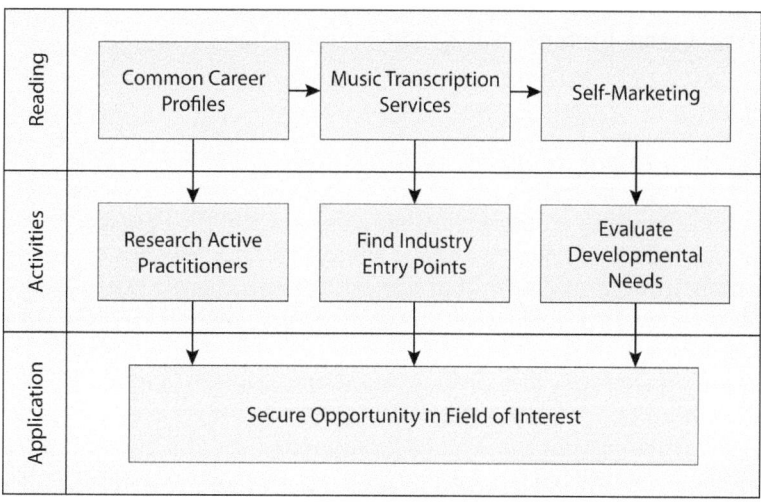

Figure 12.1 Chapter 12 map.

DOI: 10.4324/9781003511946-16

Common Career Profiles

Relatively few professionals specialize entirely in *music transcription as a service*. That is because, in the music industry, music transcription is a tool in the process of creating polished sheet music (Maz, 2023). Most opportunities entail turning given source materials into print-ready or printed sheet music for a specific instrumentation and purpose. Like in other industries, clients hire professionals to *take care of the process* that separates source materials from a finished product. In this sense, music transcription is an unknown variable that clients may not even be aware of, but are willing to pay for as part of a project.

Music transcription covers the notation of sheet music from audio and MIDI sources. As highlighted in previous chapters, this process differs significantly from simply engraving existing sheet music. Many transcriptionists offer their services as part of music *arranging*, *orchestration*, or *copyist* work. Together, these three career profiles frame the majority of opportunities that include creating sheet music. Of course, collaborative and assistant roles may include any combination of these profiles and, therefore, music transcription.

Arrangers

These practitioners *customize a musical work* for a specific style, instrumentation, and sometimes a specific occasion or artist (Nestico, 2014). Source materials for arranging include anything from rough sketches to published works. For example, a client may request horn and string arrangements for a work in progress. In this case, the arranger enriches the existing sketch with further arrangement elements. As another example, a client may request a marching band arrangement of a top 40 song for a halftime show. In this case, the song's core elements are preserved while the song is adapted *to fit the context*.

A common client request is the arrangement of an *existing work* based on audio or audiovisual sources, for example, from Spotify or YouTube. Before any arranging can take place, the arranger must secure an arrangement license (Greenburg, 2020). Subsequently, the recording may be transcribed for arrangement purposes. Transcriptions for arrangements include any *combination* of melodies, chord patterns, bass, percussion, and further groove-based elements. The transcription process covers those *elements deemed most central* to the planned arrangement. In other words, transcription serves as a tool to retrieve a work's central elements for further processing.

Orchestrators

These specialized practitioners make an existing work fit to a *specific instrumentation*. Orchestrators have a deep understanding of musical instrument characteristics, timbral features, and each instrument's scope of playability (Suskin, 2009). They also have an advanced understanding of orchestral textures and the volume balance between different instruments. Clients hire orchestrators to ensure that a musical work *sounds effective* given the target instrumentation. Based on the differences between source materials and target instrumentation, the orchestrator makes *subtle enhancements* or more *pronounced interventions*.

Orchestration projects may also include music transcription (Sapiro, 2016). Film scoring is among the most prominent examples: Today's industry convention is to *sketch music cues* in a DAW, with virtual instruments. For each film music cue, the music department creates and delivers a mockup to the film director for review. Once a cue is approved, and provided there is a recording budget, the mockup is then *transcribed to sheet music*, orchestrated on paper, and recorded by real musicians. Orchestrators typically receive stem sessions with

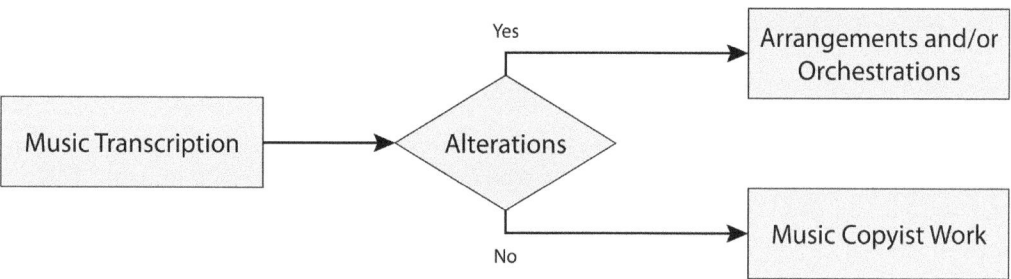

Figure 12.2 Types of opportunities.

audio and MIDI files, which they then transcribe and orchestrate. The objective is to create *idiomatic instrumental parts* that sound effective during the recording session.

Music Copyists

This profile broadly frames the responsibilities of notating, editing, proofreading, formatting, printing, and binding *sheet music for projects* (Maz, 2023). Music copyists offer *package solutions* for clients' sheet music needs. Projects may include any combination of the preceding skills. For example, a client may need proofreading and formatting services for an upcoming work premiere. As another example, a client may need a formatted, printed, and bound score and parts for a finished band composition. Some music copyists specialize in select skills, while others offer a broader scope of services. *Two major music copyist camps* consist of those who offer in-house printing and those who do not.

Music transcription is a highly *in demand skill* for music copyists. Many clients need music notated from a variety of audio and MIDI sources. However, clients often lack the time, music dictation skills, or operational proficiency to transcribe music on their own. Instead, these clients pay professionals to turn any source files into polished, ready-to-use sheet music. Clients include composers, but also arrangers and orchestrators who choose to outsource music copyist work. Music copyists who transcribe can *find opportunities* including album recording projects, tours and other live performances, and official artist sheet music.

Section Activities

1. Reflect on the career profiles of arrangers, orchestrators, and music copyists. Which one resonates most with you, and why?
2. Google several active practitioners in your field of interest. What types of projects have these practitioners worked on?

Music Transcription Services

It is an exciting time to join the music industry. Technological innovation has lowered the entry hurdles of music-making significantly (Brown, 2014). *Technology empowers* both older and younger generations to express themselves through music. A prominent example, music production software allows writers with minimal music theory or notation knowledge to *create original music*. However, many writers reach a point when sheet music becomes more central to their endeavors. For example, writers may want to *record or perform* their works with larger ensembles, or they may want to release official sheet music of their works. This market creates ample *opportunity for support roles* including arrangers, orchestrators, and music copyists.

Apart from music education, the vast majority of music industry opportunities are *freelance work*. This holds true for music performers, writers, producers, and other music practitioners at all levels (Klein, 2013). The few full-time opportunities in the industry are equally prestigious and competitive. In other words, the chances of making a music career based on freelance work are significantly higher than the chances of securing a full-time music performance, writing, or production position. Therefore, this chapter focuses on *freelance music transcription opportunities*.

Collaborative Freelancing

The music industry is a *people's business*. Musicians collaborate with other musicians constantly to bring their projects to fruition. For example, a singer-songwriter may hire a producer to help create commercial-quality song recordings. In turn, the producer may hire an arranger to provide a strings arrangement for one of the songs, and session musicians to record the strings arrangement. Each collaborator contributes their *specific expertise* toward the project's success. The number of industry examples is endless. In summary, when musicians require help with a project, they tend to hire their *favorite collaborators*.

Musicians also like to keep their schedules filled with recurring and rewarding opportunities. Creating a *busy schedule* requires booking projects constantly and with a *chance of overbooking*. Consequently, sometimes there is not enough time to complete all booked projects alone. When this situation occurs, musicians tend to *delegate* excess work to *trusted colleagues* with similar expertise. For example, a music copyist may prioritize a high-stakes project and delegate an incoming smaller project to a trusted colleague. This approach applies to roles across the music industry. With few exceptions, musicians who delegate projects handle client conversations to retain present and future projects with that client.

Meeting Musicians

With a basic understanding of the freelance industry, the importance of growing one's *professional network* becomes apparent (Beeching, 2020). Thankfully, the information age is making it easier than ever before to meet fellow industry practitioners. Subject to their homebase, musicians can join industry events and communities locally, online, or travel to larger events and conventions. The music industry offers an overwhelming number of *networking opportunities*. To identify the most suitable options, musicians should evaluate which industry events and communities are immediately *relevant to their craft* and within range of their available resources.

Professional organizations are a great starting point for early career musicians. These organizations often provide workshops, mentor programs, contact directories, and networking events. Musicians at all career stages join professional organizations to *stay current* on industry matters, and to *stay connected* with each other. Example organizations include musicians' unions, performing rights societies, as well as craft-focused societies. Within the United States, arrangers and orchestrators may consider joining the American

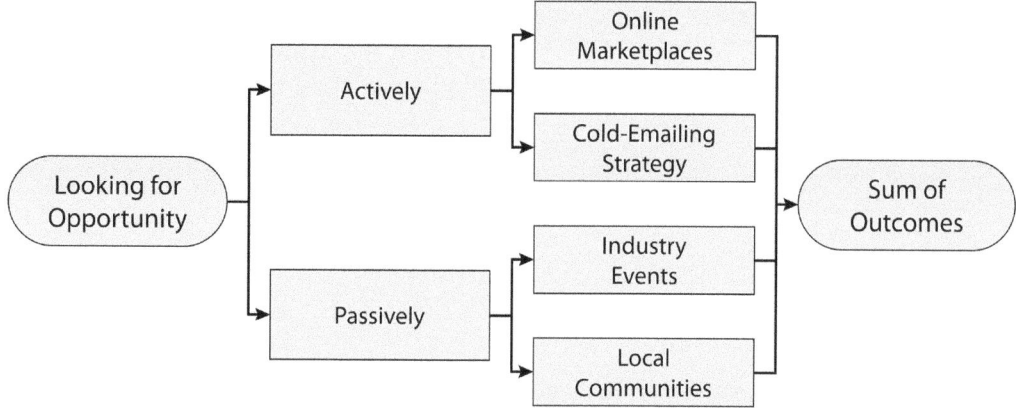

Figure 12.3 Finding industry opportunities.

Society of Music Arrangers and Composers. Similarly, music copyists can find invaluable resources and guidance from the American Federation of Musicians. Finally, graduates of music degree programs may also consider connecting with their university's local alumni chapters.

Selling Online

A more direct path to finding opportunity is to offer *music services online*. The online music services market has grown significantly since the beginning of the 21st century. Music professionals may choose to offer their services online through marketplaces, independently, or a mix of both. Online service platforms expand on the concept of *hiring collaborators* with unique expertise. Clients visit these platforms to find quick solutions for their problems. For music transcriptionists, the online marketplaces Fiverr, Upwork, and PeoplePerHour are worth exploring. Additionally, several dedicated music transcription companies, including My Sheet Music Transcriptions, Tunescribers, and Tune Transcriber, are also worth exploring. Overall, online service platforms may serve as an entry point for *practitioners* to gain experience and learn how to monetize music transcription.

A second avenue is to offer online music transcription services independently. This avenue involves more proactive and directed communication (Farquharson, 2007). Some practitioners find the thought of cold-emailing prospective clients daunting. However, against certain traditional beliefs, many modern music services, including *music transcription*, can be and are fulfilled entirely *through email correspondence*. Film scoring orchestrators and non-printing music copyists are prime career examples with online potential. Although some situations still require phone calls and in-person meetings, email correspondence is a natural part of industry collaborations and selling to prospectives. Email correspondence has several advantages:

- Collaborators must articulate key points concisely.
- Emails can be checked and replied to asynchronously.
- Emails help document project terms.

Countless music practitioners work online for *convenience and flexibility*. Ultimately, the worst outcome of cold-emailing prospectives is a negative response or non-response.

Section Activities

1. Based on your career profile of interest, research where fellow professionals meet. Which industry events are in your immediate range?
2. Given your current tools, skills, and communication preferences, research potential clients and marketplaces. What opportunities appear in your immediate range?

Self-Marketing

Music professionals, particularly freelance musicians, all have their own *schedules and timelines*. It is common to work a mix of seasonal opportunities, steady gigs, one-time sideman projects, and personal projects. Understandably, musicians' schedules are complex and constantly evolving. Additionally, musicians' *collaborative needs change* based on their timelines and responsibilities. For example, an early stage singer-songwriter may supplement income with seasonal teaching artist opportunities, then focus on artistic projects and touring during off-seasons. In this case, the artist may have an increased need for collaborators during their off-season. As another example, film scoring professionals often experience *peak and low seasons*. Peak seasons cause an influx of work and may create a temporary need for collaborators, for example, orchestrators and music copyists. In contrast, film scoring professionals may complete projects alone during low seasons.

It is important to keep in mind the big picture of musicians' backgrounds and timelines when meeting new music industry professionals. Not every industry professional has, or will have, work to offer. However, musicians do take note of fellow professionals, especially if these professionals *demonstrate relevant expertise*. When the time comes, these musicians will look for collaborators (Feist, 2013). In this regard, every *gathering of musicians*, formal or informal, is an opportunity to network. Those musicians who have work to offer

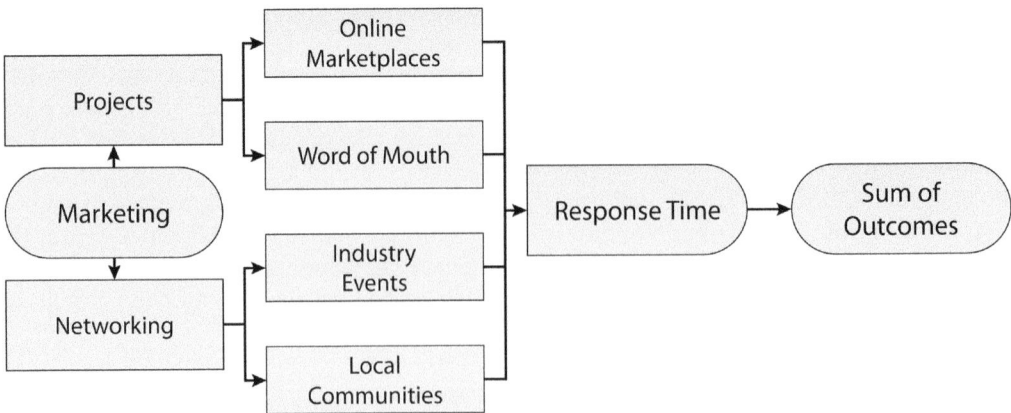

Figure 12.4 An opportunity mindset.

may reach out unpredictably at any time in the close or distant future. It is entirely possible to receive a work call on the day of making a new connection, and it is just as possible to receive that call several years later. In summary, spending time with musicians frequently increases the *likelihood of finding opportunities*.

Showcasing Expertise

Musicians take note of others' expertise in several ways. Perhaps the most competitive way to showcase expertise is the ability to *deliver quality work quickly* and with minimal friction, especially when time is of the essence. This holds true for projects of any scale, but especially for *high stakes projects*. There is hardly anything more impressive than a friendly professional who completes a sophisticated job at an expedited timeframe and with quality results. Note that it is possible to showcase these problem-solving skills in both local and online settings.

For all but the oldest generations of established musicians, it is also critical to have an *online portfolio* that showcases past project involvement relevant to their line of work. The portfolio serves as an extended business card that showcases a professional's *type and quality of work* (Beeching, 2020). Because the music industry is diverse in terms of styles, skills, and culture of practices, portfolios should articulate *styles-based expertise* and involvement. A strong portfolio features a musician's highest quality work in the part of the industry they intend to pursue. With growing experience, the inclusion of industry credits also becomes increasingly important.

Industry Voice: A Tool of the Trade

Andreas: How are the timelines in your parts of the industry?

Yaron: I just got a call recently from David Lai, a theatrical music contractor/producer on Broadway. He was in the final stages of rehearsals for *A Wonderful World: The Louis Armstrong Musical*. He asked me to record some music, and so I needed to do some transcription and record a dance section for the song "When You're Smiling." David said: "This is not a terrible rush, but can you have it done for tomorrow?" Timelines can be your enemy many times, but you have to deal with them.

Andreas: How is transcription relevant to you at this time and going forward?

Yaron: I believe that every professional musician, at every stage in their musical career, uses what we call: "A bag of tricks." In this "bag," they have all kind of "tricks" that they call upon in time of need. I think that the ability to transcribe in a relatively easy way depends on the music, and the music can vary in its degree of difficulty. Your transcribing ability is a very important component of your "bag of tricks." I always regard it as a very helpful tool, a tool that you might need to use quite often.

Yaron Gershovsky – Pianist, Composer, Arranger & Music Director, NYC
The Manhattan Transfer

Word-of-Mouth

As a people's business, the music industry allocates many opportunities based on word-of-mouth (Baskerville et al., 2022). If a musician cannot find a suitable collaborator on their own, they will likely ask their *trusted circle* to recommend someone. The higher the project stakes, the likelier the opportunity will be offered to someone through a word-of-mouth *recommendation*. Some of the highest profile music teams in the world hire almost exclusively based on recommendations. This practice maximizes the *likelihood that collaborators deliver* to expectations in high-stakes environments, where failure would be costly to all involved parties. Examples include the music teams of David Foster, Michael Bearden, and the Grammy Awards.

Several best practices increase the *likelihood of being recommended* by word-of-mouth. In brief terms, a musician should demonstrate relevant expertise, be pleasant to work with under pressure, and deliver the expected quality within the agreed timeframe. Although these three practices are not always communicated, musicians pay close attention if fellow professionals *fulfill* these *unwritten expectations*. Members of the music teams listed earlier all show extraordinary expertise, remain calm and results-focused almost anytime, and deliver their absolute best work within the available timeframe. Overall, demonstrating expertise, being pleasant, and delivering quality on time are great values that support a lasting music career.

Section Activities

1. Google several active professionals in your field of interest. What components do their online portfolios include?
2. Analyze which areas of visibility and best practices might be most immediate for you to develop further.

End-of-Chapter Activity

Applying everything you have learned in this chapter, devise a three-month plan with the goal of landing one or more projects in your field of interest. For example, this could include arrangements, orchestrations, or music copyist work with a music transcription component.

Chapter Summary

This chapter covered common career profiles, music transcription as a service, and self-marketing as related to music transcription opportunities. Networking and visibility are key to finding opportunities in career-relevant industry parts. Opportunities are often offered through word-of-mouth and tend to reach those who showcase expertise, are pleasant to work with, and deliver quality on time. The section activities provided learner opportunities to research active practitioners, find industry entry points, and evaluate developmental needs. Finally, the end-of-chapter activity provided an opportunity to devise a strategy to generate project leads in a field of interest.

Learning Outcomes

The learner should now be able to:

CO 1: Explore the integration of music transcription with related disciplines.
CO 2: Employ strategies to create industry opportunity.

Up Next

Chapter 13 covers several project management concepts.

References

Baskerville, D., Baskerville, T., & Elton, S. (2022). *Music business handbook and career guide* (13th ed.). Sage Publications. ISBN: 978-1-071-85424-2

Beeching, A. M. (2020). *Beyond talent: Creating a successful career in music* (3rd ed.). Oxford University Press. ISBN: 978-0-190-67058-0

Brown, A. R. (2014). *Music technology and education: Amplifying musicality* (2nd ed.). Routledge. https://doi.org/10.4324/9781315857862

Farquharson, M. (2007). *Writer. Producer. Engineer. A handbook for creating contemporary commercial music*. Berklee Press. ISBN: 978-0-876-39053-5

Feist, J. (2013). *Project management for musicians: Recordings, concerts, tours, studios, and more*. Berklee Press. ISBN: 978-0-876-39135-8

Greenburg, J.-M. (2020). Custom arrangements: Print licensing for the digital age. In S. M. O'Connor (Ed.), *The Oxford handbook of music law and policy*. https://doi.org/10.1093/oxfordhb/9780190872243.013.6

Klein, J. (2013). *Welcome to the jungle: A success manual for music and audio freelancers*. Hal Leonard Books. ISBN: 978-1-458-47449-0

Maz, A. (2023). *Music technology essentials: A home studio guide*. Focal Press. https://doi.org/10.4324/9781003345138

Nestico, S. (2014). *The complete arranger* (Rev. ed.). Fenwood Music. ISBN: 978-1-502-74511-8

Sapiro, I. (2016). *Scoring the score: The role of the orchestrator in the contemporary film industry*. Routledge. https://doi.org/10.4324/9781315857824

Suskin, S. (2009). *The sound of Broadway music: A book of orchestrators and orchestrations*. Oxford University Press. https://doi.org/10.1093/oso/9780195309478.001.0001

13 Project Management

Chapter Overview

This chapter covers general guidelines, as well as guidelines for the planning and execution phases of music transcription projects. The first section provides guidelines for client communication, project scope and timeline, and terms and conditions. The second section then covers several aspects of project planning through initial assessments, establishing terms with clients, and project setup. Finally, the third section discusses project execution including task prioritization, delivery, and revisions. The section activities help learners identify areas of development and frame projects with an emphasis on clarity and communication. In summary, this chapter shares key considerations for the effective management of transcription projects.

Learning Outcomes

After reading this chapter, the learner will be able to:

CO 1: Manage a transcription project full cycle.
CO 2: Utilize high-level supportive project management concepts.

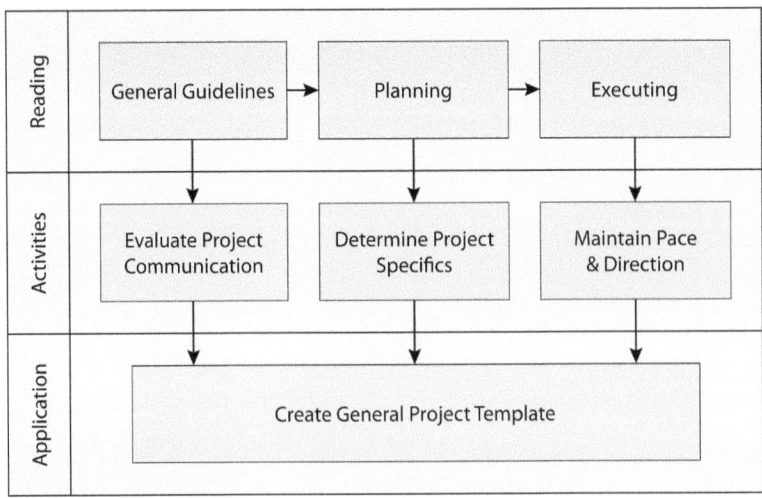

Figure 13.1 Chapter 13 map.

DOI: 10.4324/9781003511946-17

General Guidelines

Music transcription is a *client-centric service*. Transcriptionists are hired to complete tasks that exceed the client's ability or timeframe. In essence, transcriptionists build and walk the often-dreaded bridge between recordings and sheet music. While projects with arranging and orchestration duties may include creative components, music transcription by itself is mostly a systematic task (Klapuri & Davy, 2006). When clients hire transcriptionists, they are generally looking for a *smooth and timely* service experience. Beyond these general expectations, every client has a unique set of collaborative *expectations and preferences*.

Client Communication

Clients do not always articulate their *project expectations* in sufficient detail. Therefore, it is the transcriptionist's responsibility to learn about the client's project needs. A great habit to cultivate is to be receptive by mirroring the client's *communication preferences* and pace. Some clients prefer to write emails, while others use text messages. Again others will call or use a mix of communication channels. Briefly speaking, each music industry practitioner has their own communication preferences, and much can be learned from a client by mirroring their preferences (Hovinga, 2023). Communication also extends to *digital collaborations*. Some clients prefer to exchange files through shared cloud storage or file transfer services. Again others prefer email attachments. Of course, the modalities also depend on the file dimensions.

As discussed throughout the book, music transcription requires ample attention to detail. Naturally, this requirement extends to *client correspondence*. An effective communication style should be clear, articulate, directed, and concise. The goal for all involved parties is to move forward constructively, with *mutual confidence* and respect for each other's time. Because transcriptionists frequently work with creatives, communication should also convey *respect for others' creative work* at all times. Artists are emotionally invested in their art, and it is critical for collaborators to be respectful whenever discussing an artist's work (Frascogna & Hetherington, 2004).

Scope and Timeline

At the beginning of one's transcription journey, projects take longer to complete, and the completion timelines are often unclear. Naturally, it takes time to acquire the aural skills,

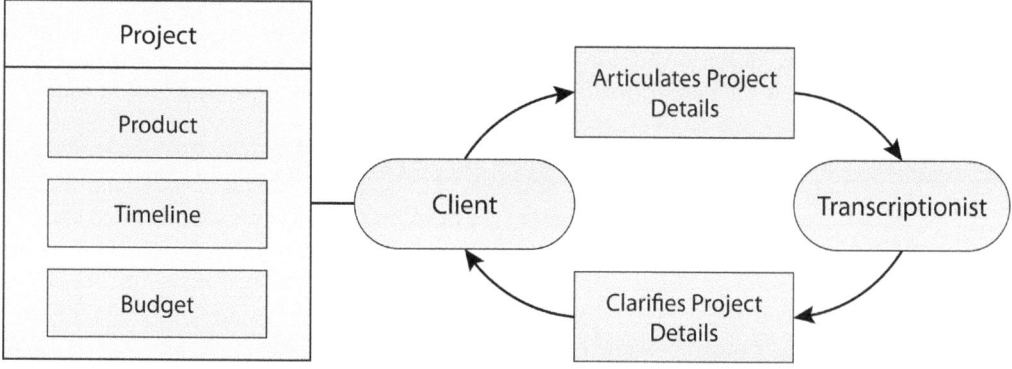

Figure 13.2 Client ecosystem.

decision-frames, and digital literacy to advance in the craft. The transcription speed and timeline predictability increase gradually with experience. Similar to starting out in any part of the music industry, it is recommended to *find smaller projects* with low stakes and relaxed timelines (Hovinga, 2023). For example, instead of accepting a last-minute transcription project for a scheduled orchestral recording session, it would be safer to help a client with a lead sheet for a casual performance that is at least a week away. The second scenario offers ample opportunity to *gather initial experience* and, more importantly, *make forgivable mistakes*.

Together with delivery quality, delivery timelines are perhaps the most important metric for clients. With *higher project stakes*, mistakes and delays become *less forgivable*. For example, film scoring orchestrators often have a brief time window to prepare sheet music for a scheduled scoring session (Sapiro, 2016). Any delivery flaws or delays will jeopardize the session and may result in lost session fees. Additionally, session re-scheduling will set back the overall production timeline. Similarly, sheet music-based performances require sheet music *delivery in time* for rehearsals. Any delays may impact the production quality.

Even with growing experience, it is always important to *establish responsible timeframes* and arrange for trusted collaborators to help as necessary. Additional *buffer time* should be factored in for new clients and unfamiliar project types. All things considered, if the timeline of a high-stakes project appears unrealistic, it is recommended to decline the responsibility and protect one's professional reputation. The music industry takes close note of collaborators who deliver performance and those who do not (Popyk, 2003). A declined high-stakes project is generally better for one's reputation than a missed deadline for a high-stakes project.

Industry Voice: Process and Collaboration in Film Scoring

Andreas: What's your takedown process from DAW to sheet music?

Vanessa: On complex projects with multiple cues per film or series, I usually split up the orchestration process on the team as follows:

1. MIDI cleanup in the DAW, exported later on as MIDI file. This includes quantizing attacks and ensuring note durations are correct. For example, pedaling notes would have their correct length, percussion would go into its "single note" reference, etc.
2. After that, the MIDI export gets moved to a second "cleanup" process, done in the notation software (Sibelius in our case). Each instrument's articulations end up on a single staff for optimization, to make the notation as clear as possible.
3. The next step is to move the cleaned up version into the sheet music template. During this process, we include articulations, dynamics, instrumental balance, any extra doublings if necessary, and chord symbols if needed, if other polyphonic instruments are involved.
4. The above process is taken care of by the orchestration team. As the composer, I then do final revisions and checkups on details.
5. The lead orchestrator does the final checkup.
6. We then export the score and individual parts.

> In the end, we usually split the process between three people.
>
> - MIDI cleanup and parts export (1, 2, 6)
> - Lead orchestrator (3, 5)
> - Myself as the composer (4)
>
> In terms of timelines, I usually start sending cues to the orchestrator upon a cue's approval, so we don't wait until the end to start the orchestration process. It usually takes around two to three weeks' time to orchestrate a whole project.
>
> I'd also add the importance of having good ear training and a transcription method when doing recording sessions, in order to respond to or fix things as we go. It's important to be efficient and quick to address possible errors.
>
> Vanessa Garde – Film Composer, Madrid, Spain
> *Kepler Sexto B*, *Rosa's Wedding*, *The Fury of a Patient Man*

Terms and Conditions

Prior to accepting a transcription project, it is important to establish the delivery specifications and modalities, timelines, and project budget. Preliminary terms help *clarify the expectations* of the involved parties (Farquharson, 2007). With new clients, it is best practice to document terms and conditions in a location that is accessible to all parties. *Documentation* practices vary widely: Some teams sign formalized agreements, while others establish terms directly through email or text correspondence. Again others establish terms in-person or during a phone call. In any case, it is recommended to write a *summary of terms* that the involved parties can access at any time.

Further terms to consider include *project data management*. At a basic level, projects include project information, source materials, file templates, revision log, and deliverables. As projects grow in scope, project data management becomes more critical to a project's success. *Access and structure* are among the most important requirements. Given the larger music industry's digital shift, many clients expect to collaborate through shared project folders on cloud storage platforms (Shelvock, 2020). In other words, clients will see all, or at least part of the transcriptionist's project folder. To help the client navigate the project folder, it is critical to maintain a consistent folder structure, file labeling system, and file version history. Transcriptionists should inquire about potential *client preferences* for project data management as early as possible.

Section Activities

Reflect on a recent collaborative experience:

1. What were the other party's communication preferences? How concisely did they articulate their project needs?
2. What personal areas of development can you find concerning the discussion of project scope and timeline?

Planning

To create a *sense of accountability* between the involved parties, project terms should be mutually accepted before any work commences. Like in related music industry parts, transcriptionists should evaluate the project's initial situation, desired outcomes, timeline, and resources necessary to complete the project. This initial planning phase helps clarify the *requirements and expectations* of the involved parties. Once the project terms have been established and accepted, the transcriptionist can start setting up the project. Note that, from time to time, transcriptionists may be required to sign a non-disclosure agreement before receiving any project details or materials.

Initial Assessment

The transcriptionist should always get a *preliminary idea* of the project and scope. This initial assessment should cover the source materials, target format, and delivery timeline. With these parameters in mind, it is crucial to listen to, at least, a representative sample of the source materials to *assess the transcription effort*. As discussed in Chapter 3, source materials could be of any quality, high or low. This quality must be factored into the project's scope and effort required. At this preliminary stage, the transcriptionist should answer the following questions:

- What is the target sheet music format?
- What are the due dates of the deliverables?
- How many minutes of music require transcription?
- When will the complete source materials be available?
- Will this project also require arranging, orchestration, or copyist work?

Note that the final question inquires beyond transcription work. Arranging, orchestration, and copyist work are specific responsibilities that take *extra effort* and, therefore, should be quoted accordingly in the project terms. Clients will not always differentiate between transcription and *additional responsibilities*. This may be in part because arranging, orchestration, copyist, and transcription work are defined inconsistently (Sapiro, 2016). If a client does not articulate the exact expectations, it is up to the transcriptionist to *confirm* the client's *desired outcomes* and determine the best path toward these outcomes. It is acceptable to quote a simplified package fee for clients unfamiliar with the responsibilities of arrangers, orchestrators, and copyists.

Establish Terms

Following the initial assessment, it is recommended to *estimate* the *time necessary* to complete the project. It should be noted that different transcriptionists work at vastly different paces. The only semi-reliable estimate can be drawn by comparing the present project to a similar project completed in the past. To develop a better sense of one's *personal pace*, transcriptionists should always *track* their *time when transcribing*. Also, if the delivery timeline requires hiring collaborators, it is recommended to get a sense of their work pace over time too.

With the estimated effort in mind, transcriptionists may continue to outline project terms. While projects can, and sometimes will, start without establishing terms first, it is recommended to *clarify expectations beforehand*. This holds especially true when working with a new client. The following terms are helpful to discuss:

- A short summary of the questions answered during the initial assessment.
- The proposed project fee structure.
- Payment terms, including when payments will be made.
- The number of revisions included at no additional cost.
- If it is acceptable to hire contractors.

Note that some clients have reservations against further contractors joining the project. To move forward with mutual confidence, it is important to discuss this possibility ahead of time. As for *returning clients*, it is tempting to assume project terms based on previous experience. However, the transcriptionist should still clarify expectations, even if just through *casual verbal checks*.

Fee structures vary widely across industries and individuals. Some professionals charge by the page transcribed or hours worked. Others charge a flat rate per transcription, or even a project flat rate. In the United States, union-regulated arranging, orchestration, and music copyist work stipulates certain fee structures. Outside of union-regulated work, there exist no fixed rules. Clients may also have preferences for fee structures, and it is recommended to find an approach that makes all involved parties feel confident in the project. Many client relations start with a *small test project* to explore how the collaborations feels (Feist, 2013). Test projects help the involved parties decide if they want to pursue a more involved collaboration.

Project Setup

Once project terms are solidified, it is time to *initialize the project*. It can feel tempting to start transcribing without any further planning. However, real-world projects require looking beyond the processes discussed in Parts II and III of the book. At this stage, transcriptionists should address the following aspects:

- Managing project files, including folder structures, file versions, and labeling practices.
- Scheduling automated data backups.
- Logging questions and revisions.
- Creating a notation file template.
- Hiring collaborators.

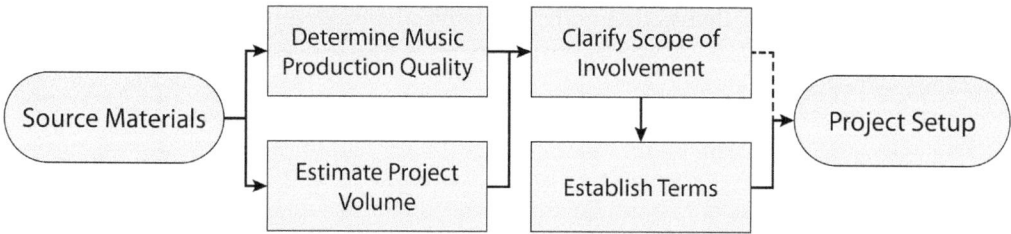

Figure 13.3 From project assessment to setup.

Consistent file management and data backups are paramount in the music industry, particularly with larger collaborative projects (Zager, 2021). It is very easy to lose track of unstructured files, and very difficult and time-consuming to re-establish that structure once it is lost. One effective way to *structure projects* of any scale is *by project phase*. For example, all source materials and project info can be grouped in a first folder. Next, all music notation files are grouped in a second folder. Finally, all deliverables can be grouped in a third folder. Folders should be *numbered consecutively* by project phase. Furthermore, each folder may contain sub-folders to keep track of file version histories and structure larger numbers of files.

Similarly, it is important to keep track of any *questions and revisions* that arise while working on the project. Perhaps the most structured approach to document these items is to use a *collaborative spreadsheet* such as Google Sheets. Spreadsheets are especially effective with large projects that require streamlined workflows. Alternatively, certain notation software applications also allow users to enter sticky comments at specific locations. Some clients prefer the workflow of writing comments within notation files.

Section Activities

Review the project examples provided, then:

1. Outline any important terms and compile a list of preliminary questions for the client.
2. Set up a project folder, scheduled data backups, revision logs, and a sheet music template.

Executing

Once a project is set up, it is time to start transcribing. The process is the same as described in Parts II and III of this book. However, in contrast to self-directed transcription, applied industry projects require a more strategic approach. The *client's needs* are at the *center of any decision-making*. Clients outsource music transcription to receive quality results while saving time, money, or both. Although exceptions exist, most projects are time-sensitive. Therefore, it is key to approach the transcription process in a way to create quality results quickly and with consistency.

Prioritize

With project timelines in mind, it is the transcriptionist's responsibility to *structure the delivery* so that both the project and its individual parts reach the client in the agreed timeframe. Some projects have one deadline for all deliverables, while other projects are split into parts with individual deadlines. In general, it is a good idea to create a *task list with priorities*. The deliverables due the soonest should be completed first, regardless of their complexity. If the delivery timeframe is short, it is also worth *outsourcing overflow tasks* to trusted collaborators (Feist, 2013). Note that outsourcing, especially at short notice, often introduces a delay based on the other transcriptionist's schedule. Therefore, whenever possible, the main transcriptionist should complete the most urgent tasks, while delegating less urgent tasks to collaborators. It is recommended to assign collaborators only a few tasks at a time, with the incentive to receive more tasks upon quick delivery. Overall, these strategies place the main transcriptionist in control and *minimize teamwork-based delays*.

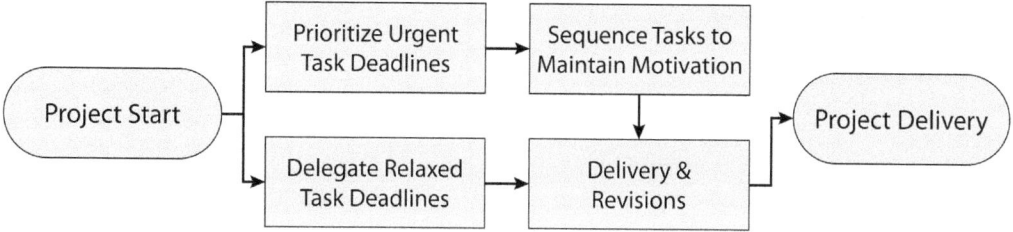

Figure 13.4 Transcription phase.

Personal motivation should also be factored into the workflow. At any time during one's transcription journey, but especially during the earlier years, motivation can slow down projects. For example, a passage or work may feel complex and challenging to transcribe. Naturally, a smooth workflow requires mileage applying the decision-frames covered in Parts II and III. Whenever the transcriptionist encounters an *unfamiliar situation*, the workflow is interrupted while they explore new notation decisions. Another common motivational challenge is a project's *large scope*. It is common to feel overwhelmed with project scopes that exceed one's previous experience. To *maintain motivation* in both cases, it is worth breaking down each transcription into simpler and more complex tasks, then *complete tasks in order of complexity*, starting with the simplest. The roadmap section in Chapter 5 (pp. 56–58) provides a point of reference.

Delivery and Revisions

Across the music industry, it is common for clients to *request adjustments* to the initial delivery (Karlin & Wright, 2004; Sweet, 2014). Transcriptionists can expect to learn about a client's notation preferences gradually, while working on a project. For projects with relaxed deadlines and lower stakes, it is acceptable to deliver a presentable draft, then finalize the sheet music after revisions. Conversely, high-stakes projects should be polished before delivery to minimize revisions. Although occasionally painful, revisions are an *integral part* of the *client experience*. It is good practice to address all client revisions that, in the transcriptionist's judgment, will *improve the project quality*. However, if a revision request will likely compromise the project quality or workflow, it is worth recommending alternatives to the client.

Overall, the best moment to *ask transcription-specific questions* is at the time of the first delivery. At this time, the client can *relate* any raised questions directly *to the sheet music*. An ideal delivery should include the sheet music, questions specific to transcription segments, and any general comments or questions. The client's answers can then be addressed during a *streamlined revision*. For larger projects, and if pre-agreed, this initial delivery is also a good time to ask for part of the project fee.

Section Activities

Review the project examples provided:

1. In which order will you transcribe the works and their parts to meet the delivery timeframe?
2. Transcribe a brief segment, then list any questions in your revision log.

End-of-Chapter Activity

Applying everything you have learned in this chapter, create a general project template for a recurring client or line of work. Consider project terms, file management, collaborators, priority lists, revision logs, and sheet music templates. Streamline your process as much as possible, while keeping the client experience simple and straightforward.

Chapter Summary

This chapter covered general guidelines, project planning, and project execution as related to managing client-centered music transcription projects. Given the vast scope of project types, clients, and project variables, moving forward with mutual confidence is key for every step. A streamlined yet flexible project management approach is critical to delivering quality with consistency. The section activities provided learner opportunities to relate to various aspects of project management. Finally, the end-of-chapter activity provided an opportunity to create a project template in a personally significant area.

Learning Outcomes

The learner should now be able to:

CO 1: Manage a transcription project full cycle.
CO 2: Utilize high-level supportive project management concepts.

Up Next

Chapter 14 covers several workflow concepts.

References

Farquharson, M. (2007). *Writer. Producer. Engineer. A handbook for creating contemporary commercial music.* Berklee Press. ISBN: 978-0-876-39053-5
Feist, J. (2013). *Project management for musicians: Recordings, concerts, tours, studios, and more.* Berklee Press. ISBN: 978-0-876-39135-8
Frascogna, X. M. Jr., & Hetherington, H. L. (2004). *This business of artist management: The standard reference to all phases of managing a musician's career from both the artist's and manager's point of view* (4th ed.). Billboard Books. ISBN: 978-0-823-07688-8
Hovinga, A. (2023). *How to build relationships in the music industry: A guide for musicians.* Rowman & Littlefield. ISBN: 978-1-538-18409-7
Karlin, F., & Wright, R. (2004). *On the track: A guide to contemporary film scoring* (2nd ed.). Routledge. https://doi.org/10.4324/9780203643907
Klapuri, A., & Davy, M. (Eds.). (2006). *Signal processing methods for music transcription.* Springer New York. https://doi.org/10.1007/0-387-32845-9
Popyk, B. (2003). *The business of getting more gigs as a professional musician.* Hal Leonard. ISBN: 978-0-634-05842-4
Sapiro, I. (2016). *Scoring the score: The role of the orchestrator in the contemporary film industry.* Routledge. https://doi.org/10.4324/9781315857824
Shelvock, M. T. (2020). *Cloud-based music production: Sampling, synthesis, and hip-hop.* Focal Press. https://doi.org/10.4324/9781351137102
Sweet, M. (2014). *Writing interactive music for video games.* Addison-Wesley. ISBN: 978-0-133-56351-1
Zager, M. (2021). *Music production: A manual for producers, composers, arrangers, and students* (3rd ed.). Rowman & Littlefield. ISBN: 978-1-538-12851-0

14 Workflow Concepts

Chapter Overview

This chapter covers the areas of procedural considerations, systems thinking, and digital literacy as they apply to music transcription. The first section discusses procedural guidelines to achieve a results-oriented workflow. The second section then discusses a systematic approach to music information retrieval for transcribing sheet music with a degree of control and consistency. Finally, the third section illuminates the field of digital literacy and its impact on music transcription workflows. The section activities help learners self-evaluate their setup, process, and pertinent skills to identify areas of development. In summary, this chapter offers several strategies to establish an effective transcription workflow that prioritizes quality and consistency.

Learning Outcomes

After reading this chapter, the learner will be able to:

CO 1: Evaluate contextual music transcription workflows.
CO 2: Optimize personal music transcription workflows.

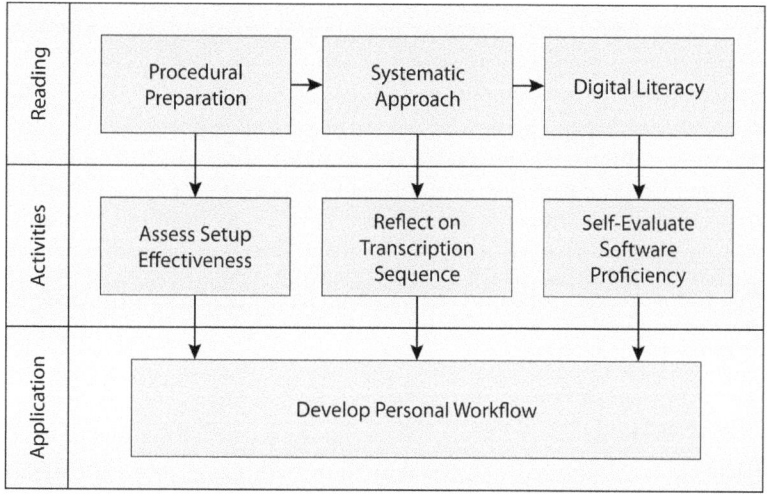

Figure 14.1 Chapter 14 map.

DOI: 10.4324/9781003511946-18

154 A Music Transcription Method

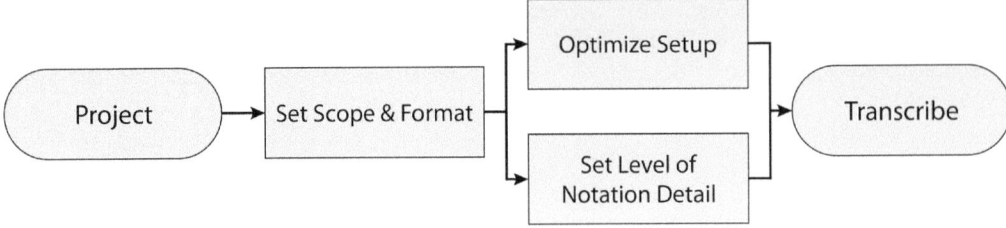

Figure 14.2 Procedural preparation.

Procedural Preparation

When planning a transcription project, it is good practice to *envision the final product* ahead of time. With an idea of the final product, one may work backwards to determine the setup and transcription guidelines necessary to create that product. Once the outcome, setup, and guidelines are established, the transcriptionist can *focus on the process*. Conversely, without adequate preparation, it may be unclear what music information layers to transcribe and for which sheet music format. It may also be unclear which tools and strategies to use, and how to interpret the heard music information. Overall, an absence of procedural preparation tends to lead to a less targeted outcome. Given the many complex decisions to be made throughout the transcription process, adequate *preparation is paramount*.

Optimize Setup

Music transcription requires ample aural and analytical skills. However, these skills can only be applied effectively with the *proper transcription tools* available. For example, there is no value in listening to bass frequencies on a listening device incapable of playing these frequencies. Similarly, the absence of slower playback speed options will make it difficult to discern quiet tones in a chord. As another example, it would be difficult and time-consuming to transcribe an expansive orchestral recording in detail with pencil and paper. Many more examples exist for each tool type, as well as for the listening environment. Overall, a thoughtful and intentional transcription setup is *critical to an effective workflow*.

With the exception of playback devices, the same tools generally work well in all transcription scenarios. It is recommended to follow the Chapter 3 guidelines to build a *personalized transcription setup*. This setup is an *investment point* similar to other music activities, including composing and performing. While the setup may be more affordable than a professional-grade music instrument, it is key to invest in tools that offer the *specific functionality* necessary for music transcription. Further to building the setup, transcriptionists should also ensure that all tools are connected and in immediate reach to operate. A common pitfall is a pitch reference tool, for example, a piano, located at the other end of the room. In this scenario, the transcriptionist would need to walk across the room to play the piano for every pitch reference.

Plan with Outcome in Mind

As discussed throughout the book, *goal-setting* in music transcription is critical to *establishing a roadmap*. Countless sequential decisions must be made throughout the transcription stages, from project planning to finalizing. Each decision made builds on previous decisions and impacts subsequent decisions. Without a specific outcome in mind, it will be difficult to make *targeted decisions*. In analogy, a mountaineer who attempts the first ascent of a mountain will make many impactful sequential decisions through all phases of the undertaking. Although the path may be initially unclear, each decision is made in support of reaching the mountain summit. The same journey applies to music transcription. Every transcribed work represents a personal first ascent. Therefore, every decision should help the transcriptionist reach the self-defined outcome. Overall, outcome-based planning relates to the research field of *path dependence* (David, 1985; Garud & Karnoe, 2001).

Adhering to the *outline process* discussed in Chapter 4, transcriptionists should determine the transcription scope and target sheet music format at the very beginning of the process. These decisions *establish the framework* of the blank canvas. Two more outcomes to be factored in concern the *notation decisions* discussed in Part III. Transcriptionists should determine a level of notation detail that is appropriate for the sheet music purpose. Finally, determining musicians' backgrounds and notation preferences will guide any notation choices. With the transcription scope, target format, notation detail, and musicians' preferences in mind, the transcriptionist can start populating the blank canvas. While these initial decisions may appear time-consuming, they ensure that any notation decisions *support the project outcomes*.

Section Activities

1. Assess the readiness of your current transcription setup. Which parts of your setup cause the most bottleneck areas in your transcription process?
2. Next, reflect on your planning for a recent transcription project. How did your identified target outcome impact your process timeline and clarity?

Systematic Approach

Musicians pursue a vast range of *workflow approaches*, from creative and spontaneous to systematic and predictable. Music creators in particular follow their own, unique workflows to create new music. The craft of music writers revolves around creating meaningful and impactful music. Structural planning may or may not be a conscious part of a music creator's workflow. In contrast to music creation, *music transcription* captures existing

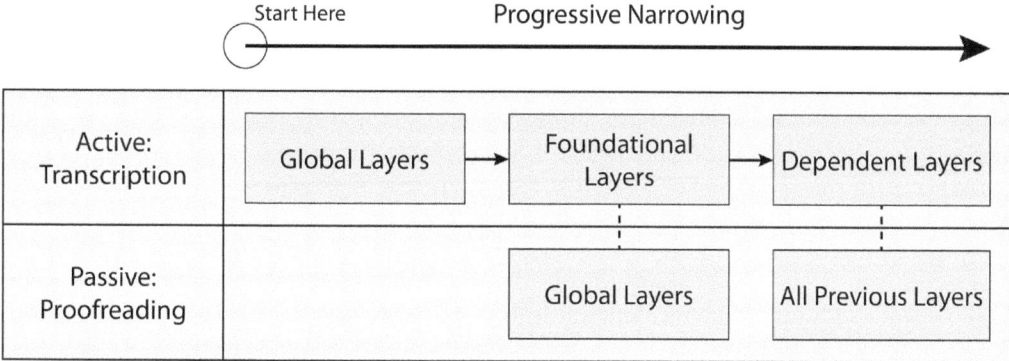

Figure 14.3 Controlled progression.

music rather than creating new music. Although music transcription may include creative notation decisions, it is primarily a *systematic information retrieval process* (Bhattarai & Lee, 2023). The objective is to capture existing music in as much detail and with as much accuracy as practical.

Progressive Narrowing

A central strategy in this book is the progression from a broad perspective to a more granular perspective. To ensure accuracy and consistency, the transcriptionist progresses from global to dependent layers in *controlled stages*. The transcription starts with a broad perspective on global music parameters and gradually works toward the more granular perspective of coloration and dynamics. This *systematic approach* helps group transcription decision-making by music information layer. For example, any questions encountered while transcribing rhythm can be addressed with an *increased overview* while transcribing foundational layers. After answering all rhythm questions, the transcriptionist may then shift their attention to the next group of layers and answer any arising questions pertaining to those layers. Overall, this process shows similarities to a progressive narrowing approach in qualitative research (Elsherif, 2024).

Progressive narrowing is also critical to *reversing* any *transcription errors* discovered later during the process. The analogy of a pioneering cave explorer helps explain this approach: Cave explorers typically use a guide rope during cave explorations. The guide rope helps the explorer backtrace the path traveled up to this point. If encountering a dead end, the explorer can return to the most recent junction and try a different path. Overall, this approach helps explore the cave systematically. The same principle holds true for progressive narrowing in music transcription: Global, foundational, and dependent layers represent the explored path. As long as the transcriptionist progresses from initial outline to granular details sequentially, with a *guide rope*, it always remains clear which decisions were made at what stage, and based on what information. Even if errors are discovered later in the process, it will be easy to *backtrace and correct* the decisions leading up to those errors. Conversely, if a transcriptionist skips any phase, for example, the outline, and starts transcribing details without a clear roadmap, any errors will be considerably more difficult to recognize and more laborious to correct.

Proofreading with Every Layer

Some musicians may find it difficult or uninspiring to progress through a transcription in controlled stages. This holds especially true for *music creators* who may use transcription as an outlet to articulate their stream of musical ideas (Collins, 2012). As part of this approach, music creators may transcribe music information layers in any order that comes to mind, but not necessarily in a systematic order. While a *creative approach* to transcription can be valuable in the music writing process, it comes at the risk of *decreased transcription consistency* and accuracy. Consequently, proofreading creatively oriented transcriptions will take additional time.

In contrast, a *systematic transcription approach* allows for ample attention to detail and embedded proofreading throughout the transcription process. The systematic approach serves as a *sequential checklist* of music information layers to be transcribed, starting with global layers and ending with dependent layers. Pursuing this approach, each layer receives undivided attention at least once during the process. Proofreading layer by layer is an established practice with music engravers (Fetherolf, 2019). Furthermore, transcribing one layer at a time allows for *passive proofreading* of already notated layers. For example, if a mix of four foundational and dependent layers are transcribed sequentially, the transcriptionist has three opportunities to spot an error made in the first layer while transcribing subsequent layers.

Section Activities

1. Reflect on a recent transcription project: Did you progress through global, foundational, and dependent layers more sequentially or concurrently? What implications might your choices have?
2. Reflecting on your general process, how many corrections do you find yourself making during the transcription process versus at the end of the process?

Digital Literacy

Operational proficiency with technology is frequently among the most overlooked skills in music transcription. There is a common belief that strong aural skills automatically translate to fast music transcription. However, this belief ignores the role of digital literacy in the transcription process. Digital literacy in music describes the skills related to the proficient and responsible use of digital technology in a specific music discipline (Randles & Burnard, 2022; Wissner, 2023). In the context of music transcription, digital literacy describes the skills necessary to operate *playback and notation software* with fluency and proficiency. Two operational aspects of digital literacy are the ability to leverage the software's functionality and to customize workflows to suit personal needs and preferences.

Software Functionality

Commercial software applications are designed to help users complete tasks. Software developers anticipate common user tasks and create *software solutions* for these tasks (Dhillon, 2022). For example, the arrival of music notation software has turned sheet music engraving into an increasingly digital discipline. The advantages of using software include faster task turnarounds with higher quality results. Effective applications *automate laborious tasks*

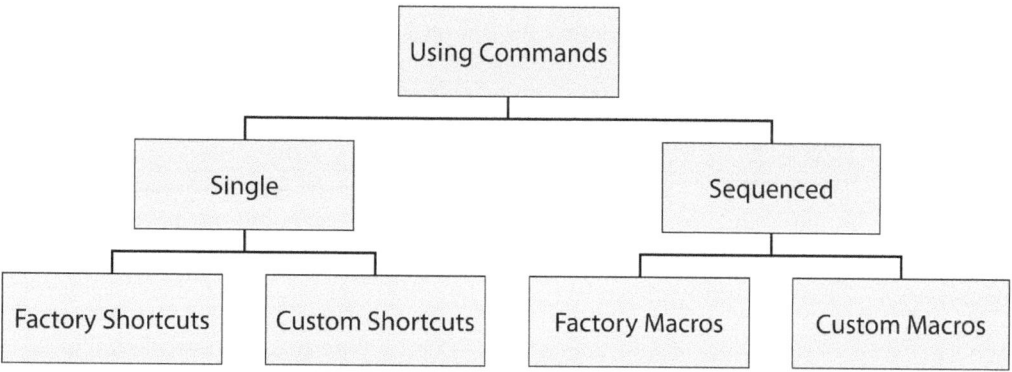

Figure 14.4 Software workflow and digital literacy.

and produce *quality results* with less effort. In many fields, users have a choice between competing software applications capable of completing the same tasks. Although different applications may produce varying output quality, extant commercial software generally meets industry quality standards. However, workflows can vary significantly between software applications, and particularly between music notation applications (Nowakowski & Hadjakos, 2023a).

The main application types in music transcription are playback and notation software. It is recommended to familiarize, at a deeper level, with the *functionality used most frequently* during transcription. For *playback software*, this functionality includes beat mapping, playback navigation, and playback effects. Much of the time transcribing is spent listening to audio snippets in a stop-and-go fashion. To work effectively, transcriptionists must be able to operate playback software seamlessly. For *notation software*, key functionality includes note entry, note editing, arranging, and entering dependent layers. Naturally, most time is spent entering and editing music information layers (George, 2004). Both playback and notation software tend to offer several avenues to trigger the same functionality. Transcriptionists should study these avenues carefully and explore which ones work best for them.

Industry Voice: The Road Toward Process Improvements

Andreas: How do you navigate the technology side of music transcription?

Oriol: Workflow wise, I think it's important to have the audio source float on top of the screen, so it stays in place. Being able to switch quickly between listening and notating is key. Maybe use an app like Transcribe! or a DAW to make playback more effective. There are many tools to process the audio and listen to it in a more favorable way for transcription. For example, it's quite useful to adjust an audio source's tuning when it is not in 440 Hz. It's also important to master the art of shortcuts and using the mouse as little as possible. For example, we use MIDI keyboards to input repetitive patterns. It's so much easier to use shortcuts to write note values and add intervals on top of other notes. Another consideration is to add a second computer screen with additional panels and tools. If you want to take shortcuts yet a step further, you could even purchase an Elgato Stream Deck. It's a little screen that lets you bind commands from the notation software to physical buttons. And of course, a decent pair of headphones is key. Headphones are good for audio quality and accuracy, but they can be more intense and demanding on your ears when compared to speakers. Personally, I'm also a fan of noise canceling headphones, to ensure I'm not listening at an unhealthy volume. Bottom-line, I think it's important to spend enough time making sure that the configuration and settings are right for you. Don't postpone your workflow improvements. Make sure everything is as smooth and optimized as possible. It takes a while, but once everything is in place, you just become exponentially faster over the years and fully enjoy the transcription work from start to finish.

Oriol López Calle – Music Entrepreneur, Barcelona, Spain
CEO of My Sheet Music Transcriptions

Customized Workflows

Commercial playback and notation software comes with a selection of *factory keyboard shortcuts*. These shortcuts allow fast-tracking otherwise time-consuming manual tasks through key commands. Any shortcuts pertaining to transcription functionality should be *memorized and practiced* while familiarizing with the software. However, sooner or later on their journey, transcriptionists will encounter repetitive tasks that take ample time to complete, that interrupt the transcription flow, and for which there exist no factory shortcuts (Nowakowski & Hadjakos, 2023a, 2023b). As a common example, it may be necessary to select and edit several notation objects with matching criteria. If performed manually, this process includes treating notation objects more individually. A faster workflow could include *batch-treating* these notation objects. Transcriptionists tend to identify these bottleneck areas with growing software proficiency. Those who reach this point can explore *customized workflows* to streamline and automate recurring laborious tasks.

One way to establish custom workflows is to create *customized shortcuts*. Software developers increasingly recognize that users have different workflow preferences. That is why many commercial software applications allow users to assign their favorite commands to customized shortcuts. Music transcriptionists can leverage this functionality to assign their *most used commands* to customized keyboard shortcuts. These shortcuts help enhance a user's personal transcription workflow further. Finally, a more advanced way to customize workflows is to trigger several commands sequentially through a single shortcut. This type of shortcut is referred to as a *macro*. In music transcription, macros can help *automate multi-step music notation tasks*. The plugin collections of Sibelius and Finale provide a helpful collection of macros. Users without coding knowledge may use these factory plugin collections. Conversely, users with coding expertise may use Sibelius' *ManuScript* or Finale's *FinaleScript* programming language to create their own plugins.

Section Activities

Reflect on your current music transcription software setup:

1. How effective is your playback navigation? Which note entry mode do you prefer and why?
2. Identify several avenues to optimize your transcription pace. Consider the possibilities of customizing workflows and exploring different built-in workflows in your software applications of choice.

End-of-Chapter Activity

Applying everything you have learned in this chapter, perform a comprehensive personal workflow evaluation. Factor in your current setup, planning, transcription sequence, and software proficiency. Identify several areas of development and devise a plan to address any necessary improvements in these areas.

Chapter Summary

This chapter covered procedural preparation, a systematic approach, and digital literacy skills as related to music transcription workflows. In contrast to more creative music activities, music transcription is primarily a systematic music information retrieval process.

Beyond strong aural skills, it is critical to understand that an effective workflow requires thoughtful planning, discipline throughout the process, and the ability to operate relevant music software with proficiency. The section activities provided learner opportunities to evaluate personal workflows and pinpoint areas of improvement. Finally, the end-of-chapter activity provided a learner opportunity to evaluate the personal music transcription setup and articulate a plan for workflow improvements.

Learning Outcomes

The learner should now be able to:

CO 1: Evaluate contextual music transcription workflows.
CO 2: Optimize personal music transcription workflows.

References

Bhattarai, B., & Lee, J. (2023). A comprehensive review on music transcription. *Applied Sciences, 13*(21), Article 11882. https://doi.org/10.3390/app132111882

Collins, D. (Ed.). (2012). *The act of musical composition: Studies in the creative process*. Routledge. https://doi.org/10.4324/9781315612256

David, P. A. (1985). Clio and the economics of QWERTY. *The American Economic Review, 75*(2), 332–337. https://www.jstor.org/stable/1805621

Dhillon, B. S. (2022). *Applied reliability, usability, and quality for engineers*. CRC Press. https://doi.org/10.1201/9781003298571

Elsherif, H. M. (Ed.). (2024). *Foundational theories and practical applications of qualitative research methodology*. IGI Global. https://doi.org/10.4018/979-8-3693-2414-1

Fetherolf, D. (2019). *The G Schirmer manual of style and usage* (4th ed.). G. Schirmer. https://www.classicalondemand.com/products/manual-of-style

Garud, R., & Karnoe, P. (Eds.). (2001). *Path dependence and creation*. Psychology Press. https://doi.org/10.4324/9781410600370

George, S. E. (2004). *Visual perception of music notation: On-line and off-line recognition*. IRM Press. https://doi.org/10.4018/978-1-59140-298-5

Nowakowski, M., & Hadjakos, A. (2023a). Estimating interaction time in music notation editors. *Proceedings of the 16th International Symposium on CMMR, Tokyo, Japan* (pp. 335–346). https://doi.org/10.5281/zenodo.10113069

Nowakowski, M., & Hadjakos, A. (2023b). Online survey on usability and user experience of music notation editors. *TENOR: 8th International Conference on Technologies for Music Notation & Representation, Boston, USA* (pp. 6–15). https://doi.org/10.17760/D20511476

Randles, C., & Burnard, P. (2022). *The Routledge companion to creativities in music education*. Routledge. https://doi.org/10.4324/9781003248194

Wissner, R. A. (2023). Using public musicology to teach digital literacy in music history. In L. Hays & J. Kammer (Eds.), *Integrating digital literacy in the disciplines*. https://doi.org/10.4324/9781003445326-11

Index

Note: Pages in *italics* refer to figures, and pages in **bold** refer to tables.

accompaniment, 92
anacrusis. *See* pickup measure
arrangement, *41*, 43, 58, 118, 136;
  complexity, 36–37
articulacy, 89–90
articulation, *63*, *117*, 118. *See also under* note
artificial intelligence. *See* music: information retrieval
audiation, 18–19
audio-to-MIDI. *See* takedown

bar. *See* measure
beat: mapping (*see* meter); markers, 27; stressed, 88, 102, 115
bpm (beats per minute): 44, 47. *See also* tempo
Brock, Zach (violinist, composer), *104*
Burch, Emily Williams (music educator), 6–7

career: profiles 13, 136; stages, 58, 138, 141
chord symbols, 67, 70, 114–115. *See also* voicings
classical, 4, 117
click track, 100. *See also* meter
client, 137, 145, 147, 151
coda. *See* navigation signs
collaborators 138, 140, 142, 148–50
comping. *See* accompaniment
Cooper, Boh (keyboardist, music director), 45–46
Cowan, Claire (composer, orchestrator), 123–24
cue notes, 79, 82
Curwen hand signs. *See* solfège

dal segno. *See* navigation signs
DAW (Digital Audio Workstation), 23, 73, *75*
demo recording, 7, 23, 37
dependent layers (music information), 14, 16, 68; categories, *63*, **64**
dictation. *See* music: dictation
doubling (orchestration technique), 126

downbeat, 45, 106–107
dynamics, 66–67, 117, 128–29

ear training (aural skills): 5, 145
feel, 105
fermata, 107–108. *See also* tempo
film scoring, 76, 139, 140
fixed and movable do. *See* solfège
form (structure), 13, 90, 99–100
foundational layers (music information), 14, 51, 156
frameworks: auditory, *16*, *18*, *127*; career, 8, *137*, *139*, *140*; music analysis, 44, 51, 68, *122*, *128*, *129*; procedural workflow, 4, *57*, *69*, *74*, *155*; project planning, 36, 94, *145*, *149*, *151*, *154*; setup, 24, 26, 30, *157*

Garde, Vanessa (film composer), 146–47
Gershovsky, Yaron (pianist, arranger, composer), 141
global layers (music information), 14, 43, 74, 156
groove: -based music, 4; degree of variation, 112–113

Häberlin, Andreas (music excerpts), *41*, *42*, *51*, *66*, *89*, *105*
harmonic: intervals, 56, 67; progression (pace) 82; qualities, 68, 114, 116
headphones, 26, 158

improvisation, *91*, 94, 96
inner hearing. *See* audiation
instrumentation, 9, 95. *See also* orchestration

Jamrok, Gregory, (Fine Line Music Service), 65–66
jazz, 9, 114

key signature, 47. *See also* tonal center
Kodály Method. *See* rhythm: syllables; solfège

Lanzetti, Bob (guitarist, composer), *103*
lead sheet, 38, *40*
learning outcomes: I. preparation, 3, 12, 22; II. process, 35, 50, 61, 72; III. interpretation, 87, 98, 111, 121; IV. resources, 135, 144, 153; book-level, *xi*; part-level, *1*, *33*, *85*, *133*
listening: analytical, 19, 37; dimensions, 14–16
literacy: digital 157, technology, 5
looping (playback), 24–25
López Calle, Oriol (My Sheet Music Transcriptions), 158
lyric sheet, 38, *39*
lyrics, 38, 64, 69–70

Maher, Mike "Maz" (vocalist, composer), *126*
Mark, Zane (dance music arranger), 118
masking, 17, 58. *See also* mix
master rhythm chart, 39, *81*
measure, 102, 106; repeat signs, 112–113
melisma, 116–17. *See also* lyrics
melody, *15*, 54–55, 79
meter (metering), 44, 103, *104*
metric grid, 88, 92
metronome: mark, 46, 105
McQueen, Chris (guitarist, composer), 27–28
MIDI: data, 77; keyboard, 29–30, 158
mix (audio), 14, 76, 128
multi-file, 73–74. *See also* stems
music: dictation. 6, 51; engraving, 28, 88; information retrieval, 8
music notation: detail, 91, 93–96, 113, 155; prescriptive, 7–8, 88
music notation software, 28, 47–48; Dorico, *29*; Finale, Sibelius, 159
music transcription; as a service, 139, 145; scope, 36, 114; setup, 5, 149
musical instrument. *See* sound sources

navigation signs, 99–100
note: emphasis, 62, *117*; length, 51, 54, 62, 117

orchestration, 76, 136. *See also* timbre: and dynamics
ornamentation, 63–64

Parrilla-Koester, Dylan (band director), 95
particell, *42*, 43
phrase (musical), 62, 69, 116
pickup measure, 102
playback: device, 5, 24. *See also* DAW
Pliska, Gregory (composer, orchestrator), 13–14
proofreading: 137, 156–57

quantization (MIDI), 78

readability, 88–89
reduction, 43, 79, *80*
reference tools (music transcription), 26, 47, 55
rehearsal marks, 99
Reifler, Erin J. (theater musician), 54–55
repetition. *See* navigation signs; measure: repeat signs
rhythm: chart 79 (*see also* master rhythm chart); section, 82, 93; syllables, 51–52
Romberg, Martin (classical composer), 101–102
rubato, 105, 107. *See also* tempo

score reduction. *See* particell; reduction
score study, 90, 127
sheet music format, 38, 154. *See also* target format
sheet music preparation, 9, 65, 146
shortcuts, 158–59
sightreading, 96
slash notation, 56, 91–93
solfège, 52, 55
sound sources, 18, 122, 126
Stanton, Justin (keyboardist, trumpeter, composer), *115*
stems (audio/MIDI), 23, 75, 77–78
sub-beats, 51, 101, 103
swing, 45, 105

Takadimi. *See* rhythm: syllables
takedown (audio/MIDI), 75, 123, 146
target format (sheet music), 73, 78, 148, 155. *See also* sheet music format
tempo, 104, 106
texture, 65, 136
timbre, 17, 90, 127; and dynamics, 128–29; instrument recognition, 18, 122–24
time and stop-time, 56, 79, 112. *See also* slash notation
time signature, 46, 101, *104*
timeline (project), 76, 141, 145, 147, 150
tonal center, 47, 90
Transcribe! (software), *25*, 30, 158
tuning, 25, 158
Turnbull, Tracie (composer, orchestrator), 76
Turner, Elizabeth Allen (singer, musical theater writer), *15*, *39*, *40*, *53*, *81*, *108*

virtual instruments: sampler, 65, 124, *125*; synthesizer, 124, *126*, 129
voicings, 56, 114; dense, 17, 57

work environment, 25–26
workflow, 69, 151; dictation, 52–53; setup, 29, 150, 154, 158
Willis, Michelle (singer, songwriter), *80*